Out of the
TRANSYLVANIA NIGHT

Aura Imbarus

Aura's courage shows the degree to which we are all
willing to live lives centered
and an authentic sense of s

What People •

Unforgettable! This book gives the pioneer spirit courage and the brave heart bravado.

—Adrian Maher, filmmaker, Discovery Channel

If you grew up hearing names like Tito, Mao, and Ceaușescu but really didn't understand their significance, read this book!

—Mark Skidmore, Paramount Pictures

A remarkable account erasing a past, but not an identity. Thought-provoking, inspirational—and comforting.

—Todd Greenfield, 20th Century Fox Studios

This book is sure to find its place in memorial literature of the world.

—Beatrice Ungar, editor-in-chief, *Hermannstädter Zeitung*

Out of the Transylvania Night is a compelling and spell-binding story of a fiercely independent young woman growing up at the height of worldwide Communist power and then the rapid fall of the Iron Curtain. We must never forget what her story ultimately teaches . . .

—Sharrie Williams, author,
The Maybelline Story—and the Spirited Family Dynasty behind It

Under Communism, Aura's family lost its fortune but kept their jewels. Under capitalism, she made a fortune and lost the jewels. And then lost the fortune as well. Such is the paradox found within the pages of this amazing and unforgettable story.

—Lindy Hudis, producer, IMPACT Motion Pictures

We all have much to learn about freedom; certainly anyone born without it will search until they find it. This is an incredible story about pain, strength, courage, defiance, and healing.

—David Haspel, producer

Out of the Transylvania Night presents an emotional journey through both free and closed societies, revealing how freedom is also found in the self and not only the destination.

—Ilie T. Ardelean, founding chairman and president, Romanian-
American Professional Network (RAPN)

Out of the Transylvania Night is an exciting and truly memorable search for personal freedom.

—Alexander R. Marmureanu, MD, president and CEO, California
Heart and Lung Surgery Center, UCLA Medical Center

To remember is a tedious, hurtful process, especially if you lived what us Romanians did. Many of us prefer to forget and to erase, once for all, those humiliating memories. But, can you really annul your childhood? Aura's capacity to remember and to dream makes this a book for all who, at one point or another, need to restart or reboot their lives—and in her case, to find a new country to call "home."

—Daniela Crasnaru, famous Romanian poet

There are many beautiful places in the world, and I'm sure this book will put Romania on your list of "must see" countries. Aura's story is an eye-opener about the beauty and richness of the culture and people of Romania, and I applaud her for sharing these experiences with us.

—Mike Costache, president, Miss Universe Romania Organization

Out of the Transylvania Night reveals, beyond all doubt, the power and range of an individual's voice to be heard above the noise of dissent and the struggle to reign over oppression.

—Prof. Rajen Vurdien, PhD, Saddleback College,
and former diplomat, United Nations Development
Program language coordinator in China

Out of the Transylvania Night is a testament to the majesty of the human spirit to see how far we will go to triumph over oppression and adversity. We are better for the journey through this book.

—Catalina Popescu, Romanian celebrity,
founder of the famous Catalina Bar and Grill Jazz Club

Out of the
TRANSYLVANIA NIGHT

Aura Imbarus, PhD

BETTIE YOUNGS BOOKS

About the Cover:

The heavy-lidded, lens-shaped skylights known as "the eyes of Sibiu," dating back to the 14th century, are a familiar sight in Transylvania. Once used to allow fresh air into attics where food was stored, under Ceaușescu's regime the "eyes" were used to watch and spy on Romanians.

The "eyes" tower over the famous landmark, Liar's Bridge (built in 1859), the first iron-cast bridge in Romania, built to connect the upper town to the lower town. Legend has it that if you told a lie while standing on the bridge, it would collapse.

The emblem is Sibiu's coat of arms, displaying the two swords used by the founders of the city to mark the place where the city was built some eight centuries ago.

Disclaimer: This is a true story and the characters are real, as are the events. However, in some cases, names, descriptions, and locations have been changed. Some incidents have been altered and or combined for storytelling purposes. In some cases, time has been condensed for narrative purposes, but the overall chronology is an accurate depiction of the author's experience.

Cover design by Tatomir A. Pitariu and Jane Hagaman
Cover photo by Emily M. Yeo
Photograph of author by Martin Mann Photography

BETTIE YOUNGS BOOKS PUBLISHING COMPANY
www.BettieYoungsBooks.com

If you are unable to order this book from your local bookseller, you may order directly from the publisher.

Library of Congress Control Number: 2010905292

ISBN 978-0-98430-812-5
10 9 8 7 6 5 4 3 2 1
Printed on acid-free paper

Contents

PART III: DAWN

Acknowledgements

First and foremost, to my Rica, my amazing mother; you have always loved me to the core, even from the beyond in which we are promised, "I will send an angel to guard you along the way." I am eternally grateful for being loved by you. Dad, you are my rock and my safety net! Michael, you are my soul mate!

To Buni, Grandpa, and Aunt Bettie for holding my hands and heart throughout my childhood! And to the entire Imbarus family who instilled within me a warrior spirit! To Nelu Gandila and my Chiorean family—you have been supportive of me, and I thank you for it. Emily, my sweet, bright goddaughter, you are a shining light.

When friends go the distance for you, they are called extended family: Monika Szekely, Adriana Constantin, Mark and Diana Skidmore—you are this to me, and more.

To the love and friendship of Fashi and Yafa Lavi; Sam and Leslee Mayo; Robert Razvan Redford, Carmen Carrillo, Corina and Adrian Tatomir Pitariu, Ingrid Bedrosian, Voicu and Ina Cerghizan: your kindness buoys me, and I am grateful you are in my life. Dumitru Ciocoi-Pop and family—my admiration for you is a wonderful contribution to my life. From those early days of growing up with family who taught me that to be educated is a way to know freedom, the pursuit of education has always been profoundly important to me. So thank you to Dr. John Schmitt for your vote of confidence in my becoming an educator.

Not many times in life do we meet someone who teaches us to dream bolder and paint in colors more fascinating than we might otherwise do for ourselves. In meeting Bettie Youngs, all have been true for me. Thank you, Bettie, for believing in me and for helping me to give life to the potent memories that lay dormant so deep within my heart, ones whose power in me and over me, I thought I'd surely have to deny in this lifetime. To have lived both in a country at war under a brutal Communist regime and in the "City of Angels"—where individual liberty glitters as bright as the lights of Hollywood —is, for me, a great paradox. Writing about these dichotomies has been both difficult, and freeing.

To Tatomir Pitariu for the gorgeous and meaning-filled cover on this book, and to editor Peggy Lang for setting my words to music, an indebted and heartfelt thank you! And, to the creative genius of the production staff: Jane Hagaman, Tania Seymour, and Cynthia Mitchell.

A special thanks to the incomparable team at Levine Communications, especially Michael Levine and Liam Collopy—you are excellence personified.

To West High School and Lucian Blaga University—you are my second nature, and my home.

And last—but not least—to my readers; may this book find a home in your heart.

Foreword

by Dumitru Ciocoi-Pop, PhD

The alluring appeal of examining one's past resides precisely in its temporal and spatial distance, and choosing to re-evaluate, re-live, and sometimes even to reconstruct it can be a two-edged sword. Is self-awareness worth the struggle for existence in the spiritual purgatory of revisiting the past? It certainly is, if we are to trust Aura Imbarus, for whom not only a life's journey, but also a heart's quest ends in the timeless realization that "truth is all things; and of all things, self is the truth of each" (The Upanishads, 2.1.20). In sum, not only time's perception, but also one's freedom, springs from the self, not merely as a mental construct or illusion meant to alleviate the daily struggle, but as a proof that the only type of reality we can objectively analyze is that of our consciousness.

In our time of blogs, chats, forums, and personal web pages, of talk shows, call in shows, and reality shows, one might be tempted to think that a literary genre such as the memoir would no longer do justice to the voyeurism of the average consumer of entertainment. Our homes and minds are constantly flooded with bits and pieces of other people's existence, the result being a disturbing ménage a l'infini where everything is displayed and ridiculed. Who, we may wonder, would be still willing to read a memoir with everyone from Hollywood top-rankers to New Jersey young folks putting their trivial daily routine on display? Why bother to read books when there is MySpace, Jerry Springer, and Oprah to do away with our hankering after *panem et circenses*? The only answer I can give is: for the necessity of genuine sharing. What many of us can witness is the seemingly endless playacting, deceiving, and faking that pervade our daily existence. We are so obsessed with being natural that we become increasingly artificial. It seems that the more we try to get rid of our masks, the more they become part of us until we cannot tell what is true self and what is artificial construct. In Aura Imbarus's literary confession the genuine represents the perspective forming experience of the entire story, which unfolds naturally and convincingly, offering insight not only into social and political realities unfamiliar to the average American reader, but also into the mysteries and strivings of the female heart. Out of the Transylvania Night can be read and enjoyed by women as well as by men, by teenagers and by adults, because it deals with the eternal and essential strivings of the human heart, "in conflict with itself," as William Faulkner would say. Millions of people have directly experienced Communist realities, but there has been only one Solzhenitsyn. Millions have pursued the American Dream, but fewer have grasped its essence. And even more people have tried to make other people relate to their experience, but only very few have actually managed to make the string of collective human spirituality vibrate by means of an individual account of vast suffering.

This is undoubtedly the fundamental merit of Aura Imbarus's literary journey into the past. Highly personalized and touching upon issues unfamiliar to many of its potential readers, this engrossing book deals with experiences, conflicts, thoughts, longings, strivings, disappointment and rebirth that are part of the collective human heritage. The longing for freedom is not necessarily more acute in a communist country than in any other country. Because real freedom, the one the author attains, comes with self-awareness and is not time- or space-dependent. At the end of the book, Aura Imbarus reaches the awareness that, just like happiness, fulfillment, hope, or emotional balance, freedom, too, is a spiritual construct which breaks away from external circumstances, or the "objective reality." We cannot but agree with the author that such an individualized form of collective freedom is the crowning of all eternal human strivings for liberty. And although sometimes fate may brutally decide that some of us be born in prisons, we can choose to be reborn free, through the far-reaching love of freedom which can make us endure and prevail.

Out of the Transylvania Night offers you a rewarding opportunity to look for better self-awareness in other people's otherness.

Note: Romanian personality Dumitru Ciocoi-Pop, PhD, is former president of Lucian Blaga University, Sibiu, Transylvania, and Professor of American and British Studies at the same institution. A beloved international advisor and popular activist for human rights, Dr. Dumitru Ciocoi-Pop was imprisoned for two years for speaking out against the Communist regime.

Part I
The Transylvania Night

"Then you shall live up there where
the stench shall not reach you."

—*Prince Vlad II Draculea, to a servant made ill*
by the stench of thousands of impaled men, women,
and children (the servant was subsequently impaled)

The Eyes of Sibiu

THE TREES ON MY STREET HAD GROWN MICROPHONES, AMONG THE ten million microphones that bloomed in the whole of Romania—one for every two and a third people. The sense of constant scrutiny pervaded us like a ghost of old Vlad Draculea, Vlad the Impaler, whose castle still stood on the other side of the Carpathian Mountains from my town of Sibiu.

Perhaps that was why, on the gray morning of December 21, 1989, I had no sense that everything, literally everything, was about to change. The fortunes of my family had gone through considerable changes in the past, especially after the Communists took over, but in my eighteen years of life, *change* had come to mean little more than the plunge from one Five Year Plan to the next. Other kinds of change were not encouraged, at least not by the government. Other kinds of change were what the microphones were listening for.

As for me, on that morning, all I wanted to do was eke out a little Christmas—a holiday that had officially ceased to exist over forty years before. My parents and I were getting ready to go shopping in the Piata Mare and Piata Mica—plazas great and small—and Balcescu Street. The word "shopping" meant both more and less than it says. It did not mean "go out and buy what you want." It did not even mean "go out and buy what you can afford." But it did mean "go out and get in line early, or get nothing." As a result, my mom had taken a day off from her job as a lab technician in a sweets factory, and Dad would be leaving afterward for his job as an electronics technician at the Sibiu Airport. I was going because this was my first day of winter break from school, and I wanted to find a pretty new dress to cheer my *buni,* my father's mother, on the coming illicit holiday. I also wanted to look nice myself that day, because an interesting "someone" might be out shopping, and I hoped to draw an admiring gaze.

But should I risk wearing my red faux Coco Chanel jacket? I admired the garment made of material smuggled in from our German relatives. Perhaps it would be wiser to play it safe with the black sweater Buni had knitted for me. She and I had worked out the design together, and she'd managed to turn the yarn into something fashionable. Romanian co-op fabrics tended to be gray, gray-and-brown plaid, black, dull checks or stripes, or, occasionally, a few somber shades of blue and green—never any colors that were warm or bright—all sharing a drab ugliness, as if grayness had spread like toxic mold, entering houses, covering our bodies, taking over our lives and dulling our minds.

"Come on, Aura, hurry up for goodness' sake!" my dad called from the front door. "What's taking you so long?"

"Coming," I answered.

Mom walked into my room to help me out with my crucial decision.

Even under a Communist regime that frowned upon anything that made an individual stand out, including personal appearance, I was picky about my clothes and had been creating my own wardrobe since I was fourteen. I loathed the clothing from the trade co-ops, the *cooperativa mestesugaresca,* with their dusty shelves and rusty metal hangers offering garments that looked more like uniforms for prisoners or orphanage donations. Mismatched suits were either too short or too long and required an expert tailor's skill to redesign them into anything presentable. On the black market—another special meaning of the word "shopping"—I constantly sought out fabrics, accessories, zippers, buckles, thread, buttons, and lining, purchasing these treasures with money I'd earned tutoring during the last four years of high school. I copied designs from catalogs sent by my relatives in Germany and smuggled into the country. I also created dresses for Mom and for Buni, who rewarded me with money for every "A" on my report card. Because I was a straight-A student, my little "stipend" allowed for a few nice things—if we could find them.

"Aura, sweetheart . . . just pick something, and let's go." My mother was soft and round and her eyes always reminded me of Sophia Loren's, dark and sparkling, beautifully outlined by her long, curled eyelashes and perfectly shaped eyebrows. "Come on!"

"Maybe I'll just wear my black sweater with my green wool pants. I don't think it's so chilly outside."

This minor decision might have saved my life.

The ice crunched beneath my boots as I trudged with my parents across the slick walkways. Our house grew smaller behind us, and the bare chestnut trees, childhood friends that harbored my shoes among their green branches in summer, blurred the house further, as if erasing our safe haven. We turned right onto Rusciorului Street and walked past Suru, the corner tavern named after a mountain peak. Through the familiar streets we plodded, past houses with faded and flaking paint, their dingy bricks chipped. Ghostly slanted chimneys loomed, as if ready to collapse on our heads. Even at 6:30 AM people hung around outside, dressed in their dreary, unwashed clothing, throwing away their meager salaries on alcohol, the only pleasure that could soften the grueling boredom of working long repetitive hours, six days a week, in local factories. The reek of sweat, government vodka, and homemade moonshine made my nostrils sting. If my fellow citizens looked at me at all, their expressions were sulky. Most averted their eyes. Dad nudged my elbow to hurry me along.

As we passed the railroad station, I heard a train approaching, coming from Copsa Mica. Emissions from a nearby factory that produced carbon black for dyes had earned this station the distinction of being one of the most polluted in Europe. The factory's steady belch coated homes, trees, and even animals with soot. A smelter in the area emitted noxious vapors that caused lung disease, impotence, and a life expectancy nine years below Romania's average.

The uneven pavement and potholes made the streets a dangerous place to walk. The houses became increasingly decayed; carbon dust and the sickly green of moss and mold rendered a uniform drabness that extended to the discolored window curtains hanging in tatters inside dirty, cracked windows.

Dad said, "It's going to snow again." He nodded toward the low gray clouds that were moving along the vast white Carpathians just south of Sibiu. "Maybe a blizzard."

Yesterday and all last week, the weather had been mild, the cold sun shining in vibrant blue skies, glaring off the snow on the steep tiled roofs, melting and freezing into silvery icicles, brightening the sidewalks along the dirty streets. This city could be a truly enchanting place if its old world charm were restored. Now, the leaden sky dampened my holiday mood.

I shivered. The red jacket would have kept me warmer. I tugged my black knit angora beret—which I thought looked quite flirtatious against my auburn hair—down over my ears and pulled on black leather gloves, gifts from my parents after careful saving. Despite the deprivation in our lives, I considered myself, at age eighteen, quite fashionable. By Western standards, my clothing might not have been special, but in my city of Sibiu in Transylvania, I stood out—which wasn't exactly a good thing.

As if reading my thoughts, my father glanced at my neck and recoiled. "Aura! Dear God!" He turned to my mother. "Do you see what she's wearing?" Then, to me in a lower voice, "Are you *crazy?*" He looked around. For the moment the streets around us were not crowded, but there were always the microphones, and the people peering out of their dingy windows.

I felt the blood rush into my cheeks as if they'd been pinched. I'd hoped that for once I could wear my jeweled Byzantine cross set with diamonds, a cross no longer than the end of my thumb. I'd received it from Buni when I passed my entrance exam to Octavian Goga High School. It was a family heirloom, passed down in secrecy through generations to avoid having it confiscated by the many oppressive governments that had held power over the years. I was so proud to have received it, and I knew better than to show it off, but it was almost Christmas, and what good was having something sitting in a box, never being able to publicly enjoy it?

"Cover it up. Now!" Dad said. "You already draw too much attention. Do you really want to get us all in trouble because of your vanity?"

My mother jumped in to save me, calling my father by his pet name. "Fanel, don't make such a fuss for nothing. There is nobody around us anyway."

"Nobody *you* see," Dad said. "That doesn't mean they aren't here, watching, listening, following our moves. We must always be in control. Use your mind before you act, Aura!"

"OK. I will. I promise." I tucked in my white gold cross, so cold, a virgin to strangers' eyes, so beautiful.

Just then, two neighbor ladies crossed our path, but we didn't exchange a Christmas greeting. We nodded, and they sort of twitched. One of the women in a threadbare gray coat eyed my beret and green pants and murmured something to her companion, most likely criticizing my attire, which defied the government-mandated drabness. Clothing that exhibited any semblance of individuality was forbidden because individuality threatened the Communist agenda. I suspected I was already on a blacklist somewhere, and the whispers of the women sent a chill up my spine. Dad was right. Spies were always listening, watching, checking every piece of mail. Every other neighbor became a secret agent and informant for the *securitate*.

As long your face registered all the pessimism, sadness, and pain you felt, nobody thought anything of it, but if you squinted in defiance or spilled over with excitement or laughed in merriment, someone would notice you and wonder why. He or she would start watching you. The homeland that had produced Vlad Draculea— Dracula's prototype—had somehow infected the soul of our President and General Secretary of the Communist Party of Romania, Tovarasul Nicolae Ceauşescu. *Tovarasul* meant "comrade of comrades," the one most equal among equals—in other words, dictator.

No hint of morning sun penetrated the heavy cloud cover, and the mountain's icy breath left my woolen clothes feeling like skimpy summer-weight cotton. On the walkway ahead of us, a child coughed, and Mom started coughing as well. I had heard other people wheezing and hacking up phlegm behind the closed doors we passed. During winter the temperature in all public places couldn't exceed 16° Celsius (61° Fahrenheit). The government rationed gas and allowed each family a mere twenty kilowatts of electricity per month. The temperature in our homes during our long winters never reached anything close to comfortable. Mom and I both suffered from bronchitis and asthma due to the cold temperature at home, at school, and at work.

As we neared the town squares, the number of people on the street steadily increased, building to numbers greater than usual— the only clue that revealed any holiday expectations. An outside observer would have assumed we were on a grim march of some kind. There were no decorations, no carols playing from speakers, no gypsy music, no color anywhere. Throughout the year, no one exhibited purpose, no hope for the future, no desire. Yet at Christmas, so many seemed to reach deep down in their souls to rekindle a reason to live. In their homes they sang covertly and danced around small fir trees, snitched from forests guarded by government rangers. For the miners who toiled in dank, black holes in the earth to the plant workers who labored long hours for subsistence wages to the peasants who scraped away at their dry plots of land, the Christmas season offered the only flicker of gaiety.

I searched the faces of young men for the one I most wanted to see, but I saw no one I knew that day, though I glimpsed wary animation, an occasional expression that could turn into a smile. Certainly, no one suspected that the Christmas season of 1989 would be any different from those of the last five years, or the five years before that.

We turned left onto Karl Marx Street with its state-run markets. We always hit them early, before everything was gone. The basic staples of survival—bread, milk, sugar, butter, potatoes, and meat—had become increasingly scarce during the current Five Year Plan, and lines stretched ever longer. Only last week, my parents had awakened at 3:00 AM to stand in line until 6:00 AM to get milk. My mother had saved eggs to bake a pie that would last the family two weeks. Luckily, we still owned a refrigerator with a freezer that worked, though both were often empty. Each month, the state allowed each individual to buy no more than ten eggs, 500 grams (just over one pound) of meat, one liter of cooking oil, and half a kilo of sugar. Provided they were available at all.

Mom dragged me into a government grocery store while Dad waited outside. I stared at the gray, dusty shelves offering mustard, more mustard, and even more mustard. Jars of pickles filled other shelves, but our lives were already sour, so who needed pickles? We passed right by the dark, unrefined soy oil for cooking and the bottles of horrible-tasting cola-colored juice made from prunes. Mom beelined over to the produce section, only to find a display of nearly rotten apples. Though Ceaușescu had outlawed Christmas, its celebration was tolerated to some extent, so one time per year, grocery shops received oranges and bananas, wondrous flavors we would savor and remember throughout the whole year. On Christmas Day last year, a working day, my parents had rushed out early in the morning to queue up to buy one kilogram of each of the fruit delicacies—which, in English, I used to mistakenly call *delicatessens*. But on this gray morning of the twenty-first, no part of the exotic fruit shipment had arrived.

Next we tried the refrigerated section. There, a few small bricks of cheeses that were mixed with starch or flour lay beside *bucuresti salami,* consisting of soy, bone meal, and pork lard, and, the pièce de résistance, *tacâmuri de pui,* chicken wings, gizzards, and claws.

"Pfhh!" Mom snorted.

Of course, she didn't really expect much better. Our renowned Sibiu and "Victory" salamis, along with high- and mid-grade meats, were strictly for export. Goods of any quality went out into the world, a world that was supposedly starving, so we were told, although my uncles in Germany had a different story.

Mom and I stopped to gawk at one display of endless bottles of cheap champagne called *vin spumos.* We thought of it as fizzled wine. Why would anyone need sour champagne? What government mockery was this? What did they imagine worthy of celebrating? Another year lived near starvation? A moment to toast the idea that under Communism, equal rights meant equal misery?

We couldn't even whisper these thoughts to each other in public, but Mom gave me a look that told me she was thinking the same thing.

Dad stepped inside and subtly tapped his watch. Since the checkout queue stretched for what looked like a half-hour wait, we left with nothing. Time to move to the other shopping area, the one no one spoke about but everyone depended on. There we would meet one of Mom's underground connections, made through somebody who knew somebody who had a supply of things the stores didn't sell. At Christmas, people tried to buy almost anything not made in Romania, like women's clothing and blue jeans. Any American brand cost the equivalent of between $100 and $300 for a new pair of jeans. French and German cosmetics sold well also, along with electronics from Western Europe or Japan, and chocolates from Switzerland, Germany, France, or Belgium. Currency, gold, and other jewelry were traded only on the black market, so authorities couldn't track them. Everyone was supposed to declare the jewelry among his or her possessions. The diamonds on the beautiful cross I wore exceeded the limit allowed as a personal possession. Dad was right. I was an idiot to wear it.

We trekked on toward the imposing Piata Mare, where the

famous "eyes" of the buildings looked down on all who entered. Originally a grain market in the early 1400s, later the site of beheadings, hangings, and cages for "crazy people," the square gave rise to a unique architecture. Its buildings featured attic windows that peeped out of the smooth rise in the roof—instead of a gable—forming an uncanny "eyelid" that hung over dark, recessed panes. It looked as if black, unblinking human eyes, sometimes five of them to a single stretch of tiled roof, were always watching you. With Ceaușescu in power, it was especially disturbing and eerie. You had no idea what or who was hiding behind those windows.

Closer to the piata, Mom kept looking around, subtly shifting, so she could scan for our black market man without drawing attention. She most wanted to buy items that served as a second currency in Romania: Kent, Marlboro, and Camel cigarettes, Johnny Walker and Teacher's Scotch whiskey, or Ballantine's Scotch—the "currency" that would purchase what you really wanted. To get medical care, you had to bribe nurses, doctors, dentists, even hospital security guards. To get a raise or secure a job, you bribed your boss. Bribing the City Hall administration was the only way to acquire a permit or approval, or to avoid fines. You bribed the *militia* (police) to get out of trouble—real, pending, or imaginary. You bribed your auto shop to get your car fixed, if you were lucky enough to have a car. You bribed the manager at your grocery store to share the good news when they were "getting something," like fresh meat, sugar, oil, or any other "delicatessens." Even if you shopped in approved department stores, you had to bribe managers to buy the occasional imported appliance, clothing, or other goods. Romanians were forbidden to possess foreign currency, particularly US dollars and German deutsche marks. People went to jail for transactions of merely forty US dollars.

We were looking for a "Gigi Kent," part of the underground world. His real name might be George, but he'd go by his nickname, Gigi. His specialty was his surname, as in Kent cigarettes. One Gigi Kent was a doorman at the Continental Hotel and wore a uniform. He sold chocolate, soap, peanuts, and cigarettes. He was a god to anyone in a hurry for American cigarettes.

There was another possible side to this sort of god, however. Like policemen, postmen, security officers—anyone likely to encounter many people in the course of a day's work—black market operators were potentially valuable to the machinery of state operations. So while Gigis could be true underground traders, they could also be strands of the authority's web. Anyone who tried to buy, say, $500 worth of cigarettes from Gigi Kent risked getting into instant, big trouble. He or she could be arrested and held by the police or securitate and intimidated during the night. By the next morning that "customer" would very likely agree to become an informant. If the police determined that the new informant was well connected or had a sizable social network, he would be "invited" back to the securitate, and there, in some petty bureaucrat's office, would "negotiate" his future "support" for the principles of Communism. His future and that of his family would depend on whether or not "they" decided that he might prove valuable to them in the future.

Despite all this, we kept moving toward the square to connect with our new Gigi Kent. I was eager to see if this particular contact carried chocolate—which I craved like an addict—but I was also nervous. We carried no bundles or shopping bags of groceries as camouflage. I feared the consequences of the wrong attitude, the wrong comment being overheard, the wrong black market vendor turning our names over to the securitate. If we were caught, they'd discover my cross. I must have looked frightened because Mom gave my hand a little squeeze.

Just inside the Piata Mare, we turned toward Perla, a bakery. No one who could be a Gigi Kent stood there smoking, though we were exactly on time.

"He's not coming," I said, pouting a bit. "Ohh, I could almost taste the chocolate."

"Let's go to the Piata Mica," Mom said. "You can get your fabric for Buni."

We started walking again. I kept thinking about the Gigi Kent's failure to appear. Selling things was his job, even if illicit. Why didn't he come? Did he know something we did not? Or was I just tense in general? I wanted an ordinary shopping day. Soon enough I'd be applying to college and taking exams; the coming year would be very hard. *An Armageddon year,* I told myself.

I pulled my sweater tighter around myself.

As we neared the smaller square, two men dressed in black rushed past us, speaking a foreign language. The securitate usually wore black, as if on endless funeral duty, but we rarely heard foreign languages in the street.

"Aura!" Mom said. "What were they saying?"

I had taken foreign languages since the age of four and was familiar with English, French, and German. "Something in a Slavic language. I really didn't get it."

"Slavic? Interesting," Dad said. "Wonder who they were. . ."

We were approaching the entrance to the Piata Mica, where a thirteenth century Council Tower separated the large square from this smaller one. I looked up at one of the slanted roofs and its "eye." Snow covered the lid, and icicles hung from it like hoary, defeated eyelashes. It seemed to me that "Old Frosty Man," an imagined gift-giving figure enthroned in the Communist coup against Saint Nicholas, must have had such an eye.

Snow began to fall, melting into my hair at the back of my neck and dampening my face. A cold white shawl settled on the shoulders of my sweater. The snowflakes danced in lazy flurries, reminding me not of a Christmas carol but of the delicately insinuating opening adagio of Ravel's *Bolero.* A fragile moment of beauty and simple perfection . . .

A series of loud pops erupted, then intensified into volleys of gunfire. Echoes rebounded, the bullets seeming to come from everywhere at once. People screamed and scattered, the peace of the previous moment turning to helter-skelter, pandemonium. Bullets zinged past my ears. Children clung to their parents, who hustled them away or crouched to shelter them.

I stared into the square, where dark figures lay in white snow stained scarlet. A woman stood stiff with shock, looking at the sky. It seemed to me that the shooting came from the rooftop eyes. . . .

My father's arm crashed against my back and drove me onto the ice and cobblestones in the street.

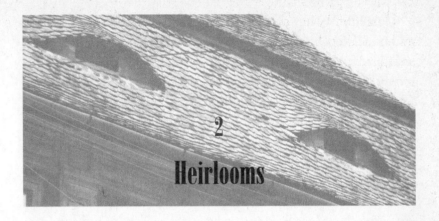

2

Heirlooms

STEADY RIFLE VOLLEYS AND RANDOM GUNFIRE SENT BULLETS WHISTLING above me. Ricochets shrilled off the light posts and the bare tree trunks. I tried to flatten myself against the snow and ice, the rough cobbles of the street gouging into my face. I breathed in snow, freezing my nose and lips. For a moment, time froze the hourglass, each grain as slow-moving as a glacier.

I didn't dare raise my head, even to see if the snipers were advancing. All along Piata Mica, adults and children screamed, shrieked, shouted out prayers, swore, wailed.

"God save us!"

"Where are these bastards?"

"EVA! Eva? EVA? Oh, my God!"

Boots pounded the snow. My heart thundered so fiercely, I thought it would bang its way out of my chest. I was numb, panting, hysterical. My breath escaped in white puffs, revealing my position. The snowfall intensified, powdering me as if I were slowly fading away into the whiteness.

Something cold clamped my gloved right hand. I raised my head just enough to look in that direction. My mother's hand had found mine, though her face was still buried in snow.

Gunshots still crackled in the air. Sirens blared in the distance, and frenzied people rushed away from the Piata Mare. I heard the shuffling footsteps of the elderly, the quick *moosh-moosh-moosh-moosh* of young people running in a tumultuous, screaming panic. I wanted to join them, but an iron vise gripped my left arm, dragging me through the snow, my elbows digging a path. My father said, "Crawl, Aura!" He spoke my name through clenched teeth. "Rica, hurry!"

Mom and I obeyed instantly. Shards of ice and grit covered by the snow ground into my knees and elbows as we scuttled along. Creeping along the sidewalk, pressing against the walls of houses, I fixated on every attic window. The "eyes" of Sibiu harbored murderers.

Who were these snipers? Where did they come from? What did they want from us? Why were they hiding themselves in the attics? Why were they firing at us?

That was when I realized that if I'd worn my red jacket, I would have been an ideal target and drawn fire to my family.

Still crawling, we reached the part of the street that ran underneath the old Liars' Bridge—the first cast-iron bridge in Romania—which connected the upper town to the lower. A popular legend claimed that if a person told a lie while standing on it, the quaint old structure would collapse with the liar's weight. It clearly wasn't true. Communist officials crossed it all the time, and the bridge continued to support them.

On the other side of the bridge, the street seemed wider than ever. There were no people there, not even a stray dog. We crawled like frantic reptiles to the bottom of Karl Marx Street.

"Okay, run for it!" Dad said.

As I stood, I half-turned my face in the direction of the still relentless gunfire. An explosion shook the earth, and then another.

Some survival instinct took over in me, and I ran with a hell fury inside, trampling anything in my path, flying over the ice patches, leaping in great strides over banked snow.

I must escape . . . find safety . . . must not slow down . . . God, I don't want to die, I don't want to die, I don't want to die!

I gasped frigid air into my lungs and felt like I was a fugitive not only from that moment, but from my whole life. I was aware of myself as a Romanian with so little to run to. I had a sense of losing my identity and vanishing into a white abyss. Yet I wanted to live. I raged against "them" for stealing my country and wanting to take my life and my family's lives. I ran. With every stride, I felt a conviction that beat within my pounding heart, knowing my anger was greater than my fear. I gritted my teeth with the rebellion that teemed in my soul that morning as I ran.

I ran.

Rusciorului Street! We flew around the corner onto the street that I walked every day to go to high school. It never felt so long, never so ominously empty. At this time of day, I would normally be about to salute the tri-color flag that stood alongside Nicolae Ceauşescu's portrait, which hung in every classroom, before singing the Romanian anthem, "Trei Culori Cunosc Pe Lume" ("The Three Colors I Know in This World"). But now . . . would there be any more school? Would I live to graduate?

A few drunks stood around Suru's tavern, bleary-eyed, too drunk to comprehend the popping noises and the blasts. One watched us with a puzzled expression, mouth open.

My mother wheezed, barely able to catch her breath. Further down the block, I glimpsed an old man inside one of the houses, one of many people whose silhouettes I saw on my way to school. In that split-second as I ran by, I read pain on the man's face. I had seen this expression before. It was as if his eyes were begging for forgiveness for a world he hadn't created but hadn't been able to prevent.

The old man had probably fought in the great world wars, and maybe those other wars had begun for him in just this way, with sniper fire, explosions, and neighbors running in terror. Our history bore many boot prints, hordes fighting for a homeland in Romania. Early Romans conquered and mixed with Dacians, whose descendants battled and assimilated Slavs, Greeks, Hungarians, and Saxon Germans. Our ancestors were warriors.

Was that what was happening? The start of World War III?

As soon as I glimpsed our bare chestnut trees, I rasped, "Our house!"

We rushed past the trees and scrambled inside, slamming and bolting the door behind us. My mother and I flopped onto kitchen chairs, trying to catch our breaths. I could still hear the distant gunfire.

"What is happening?" Buni asked. "I've been at the window since I first heard explosions! Is it tanks?"

"I don't know," my father answered and hurriedly related the story of Christmas shoppers being gunned down, our long crawl through a war zone, our dash home.

My stoic, levelheaded grandmother had survived both world wars. Eighty-four years old with white curly hair, she was as tall as an Amazon and acted like a woman half her age.

"Quick!" she commanded. "We'll barricade ourselves inside."

All I wanted was to sit down and warm myself, but like a trained battalion, we dispersed in all directions, each with a mission. Dad closed the front shutters outside and locked all the doors. Then he and Buni climbed the attic stairs, past the sausages we'd hung to dry in the cold air at the top of the stairs, and brought down wooden planks. Dad, Mom, and I angled irregular boards to fit into the wooden window frames that sat recessed in our eighteen-inch thick brick walls. Driving in long nails, we secured the two dining room windows and my two bedroom windows, which all faced the street, and other windows at the sides and back. Buni prepared sandwiches and hot tea. Mom rounded up warm clothing, and I made myself helpful with whatever anyone needed me to do. We turned on one single light bulb in the kitchen and gathered around it, suddenly quiet, not really knowing what to say or how to face this new reality. I was too upset to eat my sandwich. I just sat there holding my lovely cup of hot tea, sent by our German relatives, smelling its fragrance, the steam warming my face.

More gunfire. It was still at a distance, from a different part of town.

Who were these aggressors and upon whom were they firing?

We began calling all our friends and relatives. Snipers were firing throughout the city. Heavy gunfire was also raining down from the Continental Hotel and the municipal hospital. A few people reported having seen hulking strangers around the city last night, believed to be foreign soldiers. I told Buni about the men dressed in black speaking a foreign language.

"Damned bloody Cossacks!" Buni made a spitting sound. "Wonder how many girls have been raped. . . ."

"You know what Diana said a few days ago?" I asked.

"Your friend from school?" Mom asked.

"Yes. Her father's in the Romanian army. He said that four MiG-29s arrived in Romania." I knew from the times Dad took me to work with him in the control tower at Romanian Airlines that the Soviet Union had built these planes to counter the American F-15 and F-16 fighter jets.

We stared at each other a moment, and then Dad turned on the television, which Uncle Nelu—on a visit from Germany—had bought from the duty-free boutique, called "The Shop," using a year's worth of Buni's savings. We could not go inside The Shop, for everything was sold in foreign currency. We watched the television only rarely, fearing it might break easily, but that day we tuned in without hesitation. Instead of seeing a controlled close-up of our "beloved" president on the screen—as we expected—a live camera feed panned Romanian masses protesting in the main square of Bucharest and booing Ceaușescu as he stepped onto a balcony and tried to deliver another of his wooden speeches, one already heard many times. He seemed totally baffled and shocked by everything going on around him.

We watched as the securitate—the presidential watchdogs—singled out people in the crowd. They tried to arrest them in the manner they were used to, but the masses wove left and right, distracting their attention. Ceaușescu withdrew and later gave a televised speech from the studio inside the central committee building declaring "martial law" due to events at Timisoara, claiming there was an ongoing "interference of foreign forces in Romania's internal affairs" by "Hungarian fascists" and an "external aggression on Romania's sovereignty." Whatever that meant.

TVR, our only Romanian TV station, rehashed Ceaușescu's words and further suggested Arabs as possible aggressors. Dad turned it off.

"Events at Timisoara?" I asked him, astounded. "What was he talking about?"

"I heard a little about this," Dad explained. "There was a revolt in Timisoara five days ago. I heard it on Voice of America and Radio Free Europe, but the details were sketchy."

My mother sighed, clearing away the plates and napkins. My uneaten sandwich would be saved for another time. "Uprisings come and go. Conspirators are punished. Life goes on."

"And how many people will be taken away after this and disappear forever?" Dad asked.

Anger came through in his words. My parents' political thinking frequently diverged. My mom was a diligent worker and preferred to be compliant rather than risk the official harassment meted out to those who resisted or defied authority the way my father did. She had agreed to be the official Communist Party Secretary where she worked; she had actually been the person who had welcomed Ceaușescu to Sibiu during one of his visits.

Dad banged his teacup down on the saucer. "Rica, even if you serve this bastard, his words have never blinded you. How can you be so immune to what's happening now?"

She carried the plates to the sink. "I'm afraid. You're already blacklisted, Fanel. Aura too, probably. I don't want anything to happen to you two and Buni. I don't want to make waves."

"And so you close your eyes?"

"No, I do not. I just do whatever is in my power to keep this family safe."

"Safety means getting rid of the regime." Dad's voice was insistent. "There is no other way!"

Fresh gunfire volleyed, sounding perhaps three blocks away.

Dad cocked his head toward the sound. "I think Colonel

Dragomirescu is behind the snipers here in Sibiu. It's his way of telling us not to get any ideas like they did in Timisoara."

We all looked at each other, suspecting Dad's theory was correct—but if so, it was a threat that didn't stop me from wanting to support any rebellion against the securitate.

"Since Nicu Ceauşescu isn't a bastard like his father," Dad said of the president's son, "he makes Dragomirescu nervous."

Dragomirescu was Elena Ceauşescu's right hand, her "eyes and ears," charged with constantly monitoring Nicu, who had been appointed by his parents to rule Sibiu, a post similar to being a governor. Nicu, however, had dismissed all the special agents who were supposed to supervise and report his daily routines to his mother. The son was known for his non-allegiance to his family and their politics, so this might have made Dragomirescu think that any citizens of Sibiu who liked Nicu must be discouraged from getting any crazy ideas. But I did anyway.

"Dragomirescu has brought the damned bloody Cossacks down on us!" Buni made her spitting sound again. Then she went a little pale. "We must hide the china and jewelry!"

Mom agreed. "Fanel, give me the key. Aura, come help us."

From its hiding place in a drawer, Dad retrieved the long iron key to the cedar chest that held the remaining evidence of what the Imbarus clan had been before "those bastards took all of our land and wealth," as Buni often repeated about the Communist takeover.

In the dining room, she threw a ragged old quilt over the polished splendor of the two hundred-year-old dining table made from the gnarled wood of nut tree roots, and spread on it the family's heirlooms. The array was worthy of a Sotheby's estate sale, but it was more than just jewelry: it represented the success, prestige, and position the Imbarus family had held before the Communist takeover. This treasure had inspired my childhood fantasies. Looking backward in time, I had pictured my blonde, blue-eyed great-aunt Maria wearing the three strings of pearls with her beautiful silk dresses as she rode off in a carriage. I had imagined the amber necklace with beads ranging from light cream to dark brown hanging around the neck of the tall, proud Ana Imbarus. And there were gold pinky rings with stones of onyx and emeralds, no doubt worn by my great-great uncles, Iosif, Valentin, and others. Gazing forward in time, I had imagined myself wearing the ring with the flower petals of rubies and the leaves of emeralds . . . one day, after a higher justice restored my family's properties.

"Hurry!" Buni said. "We're going to bury these in the cellar."

"Not in the *dirt?*" I cried.

"Yes, underneath the potatoes."

Dad went down to dig proper holes.

Buni handed me soft torn cloth, and Mom brought in a stack of old newspapers. I set about wrapping necklaces, bracelets, brooches, clasps, coronets, girdles, earrings, and strands of gold beads, then knotting the bundle into a little bag and wrapping it in the paper. As a child, I had learned the names of gemstones by asking questions about this jewelry. Amber, jasper, lapis lazuli, and my favorites, amethysts; the clear, bright beryls and their impurities that created color: emeralds, aquamarine, yellows called heliodor that came from Russia, and pink beryls as well.

I dawdled over a ruby and sapphire necklace with matching gold hoop earrings.

"Quickly!" Mom said.

The air had turned so cold I could see my breath, but we didn't dare stop to light a fire. I wrapped the velvet-lined cases containing a tiny sack of loose diamonds, a necklace with square-cut stones of aquamarine, a chunky ring with three champagne diamonds, a turquoise cross with matching drop earrings, and a necklace with dark hematite beads, shiny as silver, teamed with tiger's-eye stones. Mom wrapped the box of old gold coins, while Buni took extra care with an antique Russian enamel cloisonné egg.

I picked up a Greek cross with an aquamarine in the center and four matching diamonds on each of its lengths, but Buni snatched it from me. "This piece belonged to Aurelia Imbarus, your great-great-grandmother."

"My namesake."

"Yes. She and her husband built the Stefan cel Mare church." She lifted the cross and kissed it. "With its unseen power, it has always kept us safe." Tears sparkled in her eyes like the little diamonds I'd just wrapped. "Put your own cross with it, Aura," she said gently.

I hesitated.

"Do it!"

I brought my cross out from under my sweater, and the whole endeavor became personal. For the first time, I had the feeling that I was about to bury a loved one.

Dad came in to collect the loose jewels and coins. These would be buried the deepest.

As he headed to the cellar, three loud explosions sounded to the west. Buni, Mom, and I sat and looked at each other, listening. Intense bursts of gunfire followed, then nothing.

We went to work frantically wrapping three sets of porcelain china, silverware and a few platters, vases and ashtrays plated with silver or hammered gold. But I balked at wrapping my silver saucer. "Can I at least keep this out for my marmalade and five o'clock cookies?"

"No, Aura, you cannot!" The gun blasts had obviously made Mom's patience run low. "We must hide everything. *Everything.* We cannot leave a trace of what *Imbarus* used to mean. Nothing that will remind them of who your father's people were."

"But, Mom, it's just one saucer. . ."

"One saucer can stir the mind of a looter. 'If this is what is displayed, then what is hidden?' That's what these dogs will think."

"By God," Buni said, "they will *not* take these from me. They took everything else, including my brothers and sisters, the servants we used to have, the carriages, even your dad's nanny. And all our property. . . . So. They will not have these last remains. Ever! As long as I live!"

Gunfire peppered away somewhere to our south. We finished wrapping, and I helped Dad take all the packages into the cold dankness of the cellar, where the war noise sounded no louder than woodpeckers tapping trees. Shaking a little with the cold, I handed Dad the wrapped items as he buried them on top of the jewelry. He carefully returned the soil, and piled potatoes on top. We nestled other items behind the array of preserved pickles in great jars, and behind canned vegetables, and among all that visibly remained of the wondrous colors of our jewels, the ruby and amber marmalades Buni made from summer fruit.

Back in the kitchen, I took the cup of hot tea with both hands that Buni had waiting for me. Still, I couldn't make the shaking stop.

"Let's eat something," Mom said. "Who knows if we'll be able to eat all that pork from the Saint Ignatius pig? Who knows what will happen tomorrow?"

She was referring to the raw pork that filled our refrigerator, its blood pooling on the shelves and trickling out at the bottom of the door. This particular bonanza had arrived the previous day, the result of the old Saint Ignatius Day custom of sacrificing a pig. We'd bought a share of my uncle's hog, though my mother's brother didn't go in for the barbarous tradition of slaughtering the pig in his backyard, as others still did.

Grafted onto a Christian saint day, the custom had originated in pagan times and included drinking a round of *tuica*—plum brandy—to the soul of the pig, an entity that would then gratefully bless the celebrants not only with the nourishment from its body, but also by putting in a good word in heaven for its slaughterers. I guess it seemed logical back then. In good years, we also loved the rich traditional *turta* cake made with butter, walnuts, and honey and rolled into thin layers to represent the swaddling clothes of the Christ Child. I think I was twelve the last time I ate a slice of turta.

"We don't dare use three hours of gas to roast that meat," Dad said. "Find something else."

With the pork and the contents of the freezer, which we had stockpiled throughout the year, we could last the winter if necessary—provided we could figure out a reasonable way to cook the food. This had often been a problem even without gunfire and explosions outside. Sometimes we couldn't pay our electric bills and lost our power, and all the carefully saved meat would spoil.

A simple supper of potatoes, toast, and polenta with farmer cheese and sour cream would make a meal that used less energy. I drank reconstituted powdered milk, acquired thanks to Mom's "borrowing" abilities. She had smuggled the milk powder from the Victory lab where she worked, putting it in a little bag she carried under her hat. She also sometimes smuggled powdered eggs, but each time she "borrowed" something, she had to pass an inspection from a security guard and a doorman. You'd think being a Party secretary would bring perks the way higher positions did, but she was as frightened of being caught and turned over to the Communists as any of her fellow workers. She took great risks during the leanest times when there was little food to live on, but also sometimes when she just wanted to see the smile on my face when Buni turned ordinary ingredients into special desserts.

As we tried to cook and eat our meal, Dad monitored the gas and electricity meter.

"Do you think they'll be totally shut off during the attacks?" I asked.

"There's no way to know," Dad said.

We had gas stoves in every room in the house, but they were all shut off except for the one in the kitchen. Even here, we often used butane canisters, charcoal, or the logs stolen from neighboring forests, or from Paltinis, a ski resort where the only people given access were the "elite" tovarasi—high-ranking comrades of the Communist Party. Stealing logs from the resort was terribly risky, for if you were caught, you would end up in jail.

The phone kept ringing with reports from friends and neighbors, describing new damage from the violence in the streets. Everyone speculated about what was going on. The gunfire would be intense one minute, and then everything would be eerily quiet, then sporadic pops and blasts could be heard.

The kitchen stove went cold, and Dad shut off the gas. Then our one light bulb died. As it turned out, all gas and electricity supplies had been shut down for the rest of the day and night. We couldn't even look outside to see if it was still snowing because of the boards on the windows, and I imagined great drifts piling up. The cold set in quickly. Dad used a *butelli* container to provide another hour of minimal warmth, and by candlelight, we turned on our radio, praying we had enough batteries to see us through however long the violence would last.

The BBC reported widespread fighting and explosions throughout the whole country.

"This is no ordinary uprising," Dad said. "People all over are fighting. This could be civil war."

He sounded both tense and excited. Buni, Mom, and I stared at him, wanting him to soften the words, saying he didn't think it would last long, or that this time maybe there would be positive reforms afterward. But we knew about the Soviet tanks that had rolled through the streets of Prague before, and the harshness of the suppression of any dissent in any of the Communist satellite countries. As grim as our lives were, we might be facing even more austerity if we survived the immediate conflict.

I dressed as if I were going outside for a walk, pulling a wool cap, long stockings and gloves on over my pajamas to keep from freezing while I slept. Mom crawled in bed with me for reassurance and warmth, an effort to keep our mutual asthma in check. I thought of the eye-shaped windows up in our attic. Attic windows were where most of the sniper fire had come from. We hadn't boarded ours up, and someone with a pick and rope could climb in that way. . . .

We lay there silently, neither of us breathing the slow deep breaths of sleep. Even during normal times, street lighting was minimal, and break-ins happened often. They would almost certainly increase during the fighting. What if the securitate decided this was the time to teach blacklisted people like my father a lesson and break in to drag him away? Or what about foreign thugs with looting on their minds? Or rape?

Every time I shivered, Mom snuggled a bit closer, and I tried not to think about my fears. At least there was no wind howling. I imagined snowflakes floating rather than falling in flurries out in the blackness of the night.

After I had lain awake for what seemed like hours, the sky must have cleared because I could see the silhouettes of our great chestnut trees through the six-inch gap in the boarded windows that aligned with the crack between the shutters outside. I could tell by the glow that the new snow was reflecting moonlight, illuminating the grace of the bare branches, as if the horror of human power struggles did not exist, and nature's stark beauty was all that mattered.

"God help us!" people had screamed in the streets.

God help us. Please! I prayed. Help my mom, my dad, and my buni!

My head became heavy and a familiar heat lulled me. In that half-awake state, before sleep claimed me fully, one of my recurring visions began playing in my mind. A crowd of people screamed and cursed, and then a ray of light covered their anger, dissolving it. An ambulance passed by like a shadow. I stepped back so it wouldn't run me over, but when I looked around again, it was gone. I was alone . . . and afraid. Then the ambulance passed me again . . . and stopped in the middle of the street. The back door opened and three bodies, beaten and trampled to death, were kicked out into the snow. Bruised, contorted, bloody, their faces were frozen in fearful grimaces. Though dead, one opened an eye and stared at me. "We did not do it . . ." he said in a slow voice. "We didn't kill anybody." Then, in a spasm, his head dropped to one side. I had this vision often. Somehow, it was important that I understand it. . . .

The vision woke me, heart pounding, lungs straining to get enough air. I opened my eyes and saw Mom sleeping beside me. Mom always liked to help me interpret dreams. She had decoded my dreams of fire, water, and of flying in a way that rang true. I wanted to ask her what this vision or dream meant, but since she seemed to be sleeping lightly, I decided not to wake her.

But I couldn't get the vision out of my head. Dead bodies in the snow . . . but not the bodies I had already seen in previous visions. This had been very different. Was it related to the fighting somehow? My eyes welled up as I stared at the fragile purity of the snow reflected in the light outside.

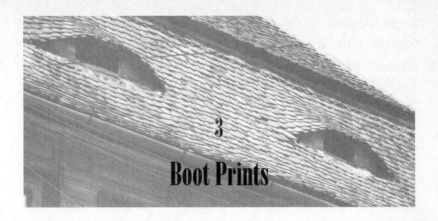

3
Boot Prints

I MUST HAVE SLEPT FOR A LITTLE, BECAUSE A NOISE WOKE ME. ANOTHER distant explosion? Were Russian tanks rolling in? Or was it something much closer? Someone climbing into the attic? Mom was gone from my bed. I was alone. Maybe the securitate had arrived to take my father away. Were they out there, pounding on our boarded windows? Was that what I had heard?

Even in ordinary times, the state was highly suspicious of my father. Opinionated, dependable, and hard-working, he could always think of a better way to do things at work and had created numerous electronic inventions, two of which served in the control tower of the Sibiu airport. He exercised every morning from 6:00 to 7:30 AM. He never called in sick or arrived late to his job. But to the regime, not only were these qualities the very ones that could have made him a dangerous opponent, they were overshadowed by the fact that he had family ties in Germany . . . and that he refused to become a tovaras, a member of the Communist Party—a comrade.

I remembered how, several years prior, a high-ranking Party official from Bucharest had come to Dad's work to inquire about the people whose names and photos were displayed on the airport's *Panoul de Onoare,* the honor employees' board. He expressed shock: This Imbarus person is *not* a Party member? The airport's director summoned my father to persuade him to join the Party. His response was again negative. They told him that his picture couldn't be on the honor board as long as he was not a Communist, so to spare his boss from the endless heat from Bucharest, my dad asked for his photo to be removed. Years later, I still treasure this picture, a proud testimony of Dad's character.

But there are many kinds of courage and many prices to pay. My father was also in trouble because of the freedom sought by two of his cousins.

Late in September of 1974—I was too young to really understand what was happening that night—I remember Dad storming back from his aunt's house down the street. He said that Petre and Nelu had been caught by the Communists while trying to float across the Black Sea to Turkey on a raft rigged from tractor and car tires. When I asked why Uncle Petre and Uncle Nelu had left us, Dad said they were sick and tired of "the idiot shoemaker"—a reference to the President's career prior to his rise to power.

An ethnic cleansing of sorts had begun. Petre, an artist and educator who was more qualified than anyone to fill a certain position at the acclaimed Brukenthal Museum in Sibiu, was not even interviewed for the job because of his German ancestry. Instead, the job was given to a Romanian Communist with little education and no art degree. Petre was infuriated, and decided it was time to try to get to Germany, to some of Tante Tilli's people. As for Nelu, he usually went along with his older brother.

They didn't bother trying to obtain permission to leave the country. That process was lengthy, expensive, and exhausting— and, worse, while waiting for potential papers to be cleared, a prospective emigrant would likely be demoted or fired from his or her job, and then imprisoned for "parasitism." Family friends who had tried to emigrate had been denied medical care and other social benefits, evicted from their homes, and publicly castigated, their children not permitted to enroll in schools. Some had been thrown in jail; others had their phones bugged and their mail service interrupted or terminated. Several lived under constant surveillance and virtual house arrest.

So my uncles sought another way out. But a Romanian patrol boat had picked them up as they dared the crossing in the Black Sea. Mom sobbed in the kitchen on Buni's shoulders. Everyone thought it meant my uncles would never be seen again.

Later, I learned that the securitate had almost beaten them to death, and then sent them to Gherla, the notorious high-security penitentiary. It was said that once you entered Gherla there was no way out except "with your legs in front," meaning *dead*. My uncles were labeled "political detainees," the most dangerous sort of people. Nelu was eventually sent to toil in the locks on the Mures River, working long hours standing in frigid water. But Petre, because of his "arrogance" and lack of cooperation with the guards, was chained and sent to an underground cell beyond the reach of natural light. The low ceiling had made it impossible to stand, and he wasn't given any bedding. His days passed in abject darkness, the only sound being that of the rats and mice swarming around his shriveled body. The thread of his life grew thinner every day.

And then, after almost two years, the authorities reviewed the cases of the Imbarus brothers and released them.

When I next saw them, they frightened me. Petre's weight had dropped from a hundred ninety-eight pounds to ninety-six. Nelu looked as ghostly as Petre, both so skinny their eyes bulged and their teeth protruded. Their heads had been shaved. They'd endured starvation, beatings, brainwashing. That was when I first heard the term *racoare* (literally "the cold") a term akin to "the slammer." The word still sends chills down my spine.

But soon Petre began painting in the garden behind their home, and when he invited me to join him, I was happy to do so. My uncles began to look like their former selves again. They were happy to be home. Still, their hatred of the Communist regime intensified beyond their power to endure it. They found a way to network their way to link up with foreign correspondents from the BBC and Radio Free Europe. They spoke out against the Ceauşescu regime, and soon people all over the world knew about them. Petre met and spoke with writer and dissident Herta Müller, who would go on to win the Nobel Prize in Literature in 2009 for writing about dictators and the people they dispossessed.

Ironically, this extraordinarily high profile provided my uncles a degree of personal security; the rest of our family was blacklisted, our phones tapped, our mail checked. To make matters worse, Petre was soon caught trying to escape the country again—and was again turned in to the securitate. They released him in September of 1977, and this time deported him from Romania and banned him from ever returning. He settled in Germany. Six months later, his brother Nelu also tried to escape. He, too, was caught, and on March 3, 1978, he received permission to leave the country for "family reunification." In time their sister, Maria, also left the country.

What a dream. Now and then one or the other of my uncles would return to Romania, but no matter how low-key they tried to be, the occasion would be marked by another late-night visit to our home by men in black, another trip downtown for my father in a black car, another sleepless night for the rest of us. Still, the courage and persistence of Petre and Nelu inspired me. So on that night of gunshots and explosions in December of 1989, I studied their photos in hopes of meeting them again someday—a day when I, too, would be free of this hellacious country.

With that thought, I fell back to sleep.

I woke to a silence as intense as the light that shone through the gaps in the boarded window of my bedroom.

December 22, 1989. Without looking, I knew that sunbeams sparkled off fresh white surfaces to create such light. We had survived the night unharmed. I hated the thought of leaving the relative warmth of my blankets, but I wanted to see how much snow had fallen. As I lay there procrastinating, scenes flashed in my mind of shooting, screaming, and crawling, the memory of shivering with fear and disbelief. For an instant, it seemed like yesterday's horrors had only been a nightmare. I bolted out of bed and dashed to the hallway's window. I pried the board open wider at the crack and saw the fresh powder in the back yard, the serenity like so many other December mornings.

Back in my room, I dressed quickly, hurried to the front entrance, unbolted our heavy "night" door of solid oak, and then unlocked the outer door with its fancy glass panel—all without stopping to think. I stepped outside onto the small front doorstep. The world seemed calm. The snow was not as deep as I'd expected, only a sheet of new powder. My cherished lilac bushes held pockets of glinting snow among their bare, frozen limbs. It occurred to me that we had probably panicked by boarding up the house and hiding all our valuables. . . .

Then I looked closer at the front steps, at a flaw in the snow. The clear imprint of the sole of a large, ripple-tread boot. And another. And still others. The nearest ones pointed directly toward the door. They were huge. My own shoe looked like a small child's next to them. Even among the police, few men in Sibiu were tall enough to require boots that would leave such prints. Was someone watching me even now? I stared at the prints, following their direction toward the side of the house, but saw no one.

Securitate . . . hulking foreigners . . . Russians . . . Arabs . . . looters . . . rapists . . .

I cupped my ears with my hands like the figure painted by Munch, silently screaming. I could feel my body tightening, pulling itself inward. My legs turned leaden. I was frozen, could not move, much like in my nightmares when I was paralyzed and utterly powerless in the face of danger. There was roaring in my ears, and my vision turned dark.

From the doorway behind me: "Aura! Aura! Please respond!"

The voice was my father's, but it didn't make any sense to me. I felt his strong hands tugging at me, and I managed to raise my head as I stumbled sideways. My father's lips moved as if he were speaking, but I heard nothing. He grabbed my shoulders and shook me.

"Aura? Are you okay?"

Dad tugged me into the doorway and smoothed my hair, caressed my cheek. "Aura? Please . . . Aura!"

"She's in shock," I heard Buni saying. "I've seen this before."

I sat down hard just inside the doorway and willed myself to take a deep breath, Alice returning from Wonderland. "Daddy. . ." was all I could say, as if I were five years old.

"Fanel, what happened? Oh my God, what happened?" Mom was almost screaming from somewhere nearby, deeper in the house. The entry hall. She pushed Buni away and reached for me. Dad moved aside, and Mom dropped to her knees and hugged me hard.

"Aura, honey, sweetheart, what happened? Honey, do you hear me?"

"Yes." I breathed in the vanilla scent that always had seemed to cling to her, either from the Victory sweets lab where she worked or because of the rich desserts she loved to make whenever we could find ingredients on the black market. I sat all the way up. Dad helped me stand and looked out the door, his arms akimbo. He looked back at us.

"Lock the door. Do not open it again until you hear my voice!" He stepped out to the steps.

"But why aren't you—?"

"Do it!" he ordered.

I shut and bolted the inner oak door, while Buni disappeared in the attic.

"Why didn't he come *in?*" My voice was high-pitched. "Why is he still *out* there?"

"He is following the footprints into the back yard," Mom said, "to see if whoever made them is still there."

Still there? Oh, my God . . . I thought of Dad's own shoeprint compared with that of the trespasser's print outside. Dad was fit and strong, but I could not imagine what might happen if the big man or men were still there, and jumped him. As I waited for Dad's signal, I imagined pacing the length and width of the yard in back. What was taking him so long? Our back yard was big enough for another home to be built, plenty of room for someone to hide. I thought about our garden in the half of the yard closest to the house. There we grew lilacs, roses, and hyacinth, and Buni grew her vegetables—potatoes, cabbage, carrots, peas, and spinach. A tall row of bushes divided this section of the yard from the back, where there was a shed. Could someone be hiding back there? Someone who might want to hurt us in order to take refuge in our home?

Buni stormed down the stairs, carrying the ax that usually hung from a nail in the attic. She unbolted the door and ran outside to save Dad, her son, from the unknown. I called after her to please, please, please turn around. Mom held me back from following Buni outside, and again bolted the door. So brave, my dad and grandmother, running toward possible death without hesitation. Tears welled in my eyes, spilled over, and streamed down my face. I made bargains with God. *Keep them safe, God. Keep them safe and I'll do whatever you ask.*

The huge grandfather clock, solid wood with a cherry finish, ticked off the slow seconds. In its mirrored perimeter, the swinging pendulum appeared and disappeared in a steady peek-a-boo that matched the ponderous tick . . . tock . . .

What was that? I thought I heard a *thunk.*

Silence. I waited. Mom and I stood, sat, paced—always straining to hear any indication of what might be happening. The clock's chime nearly short-circuited my nerves.

Ten times it bonged.

Footsteps. Voices outside. I jumped toward the door, but Mom blocked my move. "Aura, don't unlock the door. It can be anybody, anybody! Do you hear me?" Tears flooded her eyes.

From outside came Buni's voice—low and distant, but hers and no one else's. She was all right. In a rush, I jerked the lock aside and opened the door to see my grandma and dad trudging up the front walk. Once inside, Buni set down the ax she had been carrying, and all four of us hugged and kissed.

"There was someone in our yard last night," Dad said. "Footprints everywhere. One person, the way it looks. Soldier, for sure. Very tall. His boots sink deeper than mine, so he's heavy."

Buni added, "He jumped over our front gate and exited through the backyard."

How many more like him were around? Would he come back, or others like him? None of us had to ask these questions out loud. They pumped through our brains with every heartbeat.

4
Up for Grabs

Hoping to learn something new, Dad rushed to the television, but it merely rebroadcast earlier footage: rioting, fighting, Ceauşescu's useless speeches. Dad tried the radio. I fixed a bowl of polenta porridge with reconstituted milk and listened beside him.

Finally, from the BBC, we learned of the astonishing protests that had erupted six days earlier, on December 16. Father Laszlo Tokes of the Hungarian Reformed Church had spoken out publicly against Ceauşescu's plans to demolish more and more peasant villages, transferring all independent farmers to state-built high-rise apartments, razing from the face of the earth people's homes, and taking over their lands. Tokes had incited people in Timisoara, one of the most westernized cities in Romania, to protest. Police tried to put him in custody and a riot ensued. Over the next few days, thousands of Tokes's supporters fought noisy, bloody battles with the police in the streets. Outraged at the fate that might be in store for the much-loved pastor, more and more people had taken to the streets.

Ceauşescu planned to further restrict religious freedom, shut down all ethnic schools, seize all historical archives, and more—but the people were angry, bold, and on the march. The following day, December 17, a hundred thousand people amassed in Timisoara's main square, where they dared to burn oversize portraits of Ceaușescu. What we hadn't seen on TV was the extent to which the army retaliated: firing tear gas, water cannons, and even live bullets into the crowd. The Executive Political Committee in Bucharest had supported the move. The body count was believed to be high, but was as yet unknown.

From Radio Free Europe we learned that the government sent so-called negotiators from Bucharest to Timisoara on December 20, but the move was really only an attempt to buy time so that new elite troops could arrive, provide backup for the securitate, and "crush the rebellion."

"They're sending in foreign soldiers," Dad said, "like the man who left the tracks outside."

"And those two men dressed in black near Piata Mare," I said.

Mom put her head in her hands, but she didn't change the subject as she'd done so many times when Dad talked about the regime. "Now the Russians will come in and take all of what's left of Romania."

It seemed our poor country was up for grabs again.

Our telephone rang with calls from friends, neighbors, and relatives reporting incidents of brutality, beatings, street fighting, bombs exploding, broken windows, fires right there in Sibiu. Romanian Army tanks rolled through the streets. Students were out fighting with anything they could find, from rocks to clubs to homemade bombs, occasionally capturing an enemy's weapon. The airport was shut down, along with the main traffic arteries. In most major cities throughout Romania, there was mass confusion and violence in the streets.

Somehow a call from Uncle Petre in Baden-Baden got through to us. He told Dad that German TV channels showed the resistance spreading to other parts of the country, and that the United States had condemned the Romanian government for its brutal killing of innocent civilians.

"Hello? Hello? Petre? Petre? Hello? Hello?" Dad kept repeating. Finally he gave up. "They intercepted our conversation and cut it off." He seemed more angry and frustrated than worried. We already knew that the jamming of radar, radio, and telephone signals had begun in the government's effort to monitor communication—an electronic warfare. Ironically, while the outside world knew what was happening in our country, we on the inside had to rely on batteries (while they lasted) that connected us to foreign radio.

Each sporadic outburst of gunfire or distant explosion terrified us and made us desperate for distraction. After a quick midday meal, we played dominoes and cards, and then Dad went up to the attic to see what he could see from the windows up there.

Buni and I nestled together next to the stove in the kitchen, snacking nervously. I smoothed her soft, white curls that always smelled so pleasingly of lavender shampoo. One of my pet names for her was *Cretii* (Curly). I caressed her cheeks, rosy over her high Hungarian cheekbones. I pleaded, "Buni, tell me the story of you and Grandpa, please." I had heard this story many times. To me, it was a Romanian twist on *Romeo and Juliet* blended with the sweep of *Gone with the Wind*. Buni didn't dwell in the past, but she loved to revisit the love story between her and my beloved grandfather.

"Transylvania was always the great prize," she said. "It's why I fear the Cossacks will roll in with their tanks." She talked about her people, the Hungarians and their princes, who had ruled Transylvania for centuries when Viennese elegance thrived. She talked of cities, the fertile plateau, forests, mines, the beautiful Carpathians. "Everybody wanted to take Transylvania away from Austria-Hungary. Turks, Germans, Russians, Greeks. Of course, our city of Sibiu was built by Saxon Germans.

"Your father's ancestors came from Athens around 1640 and did well for themselves in their dealings with the Romanians." As usual, Buni could not say this part without revealing her resentment for the wealth, prestige, and property our family had lost to the Communists. She threw aside the blanket that covered us, stood, and put a purloined log on the embers in the stove.

Dad was talking on the phone, while gun volleys erupted from a more northerly direction than before, making me feel like the fighting was surrounding us. I bit my nails, trying to blot out the image of soldiers creeping through our neighborhood. Dad continued talking on the phone, looking toward the sound of the gunfire, though he could not see anything through our boarded-up windows. He asked Uncle Petre, who had called once again, about the militia. The popping sounds stopped, but I wondered how many lives had ended while we huddled for warmth.

"There's nothing more we can do, and being afraid won't help," Buni said as she sat beside me on one of the heavy kitchen chairs, tucking the quilt around us again. She understood war and loss more than anyone should ever have to. "So, back to the Imbarus clan . . ."

"Buni," I said, "did the Imbarus family shun you because you were Hungarian?"

She nodded sadly. "Before World War I, Hungarians held most of the important positions in Transylvania—but after the war, the land was taken away from Austria-Hungary and given to Romania. Hundreds of thousands of Transylvanian Hungarians migrated to Hungary. But not my family. Our roots here were too deep. . . . And in just a few years' time ethnic Hungarians were a minority here. Many Romanians resented us, so they began ignoring the Hungarian language and isolating us. We were no longer welcome in our own homeland. We became invisible and meaningless so that those in power could become more important."

This narrative affected me even more profoundly than usual under our current extraordinary circumstances. Such terrible truths Buni had learned and taught—that governments, in their relentless exertion of power, do not see the humanity of their own citizens. At eighteen, I didn't want to think about such things. College exams, what to wear on an outing, seeing a certain interesting and handsome guy—that's what I wanted to be thinking about.

I leaned against Buni's shoulder and felt even more love and admiration for her than before. Her given name was Irma Balint.

Well informed and well read, she could hold a conversation on topics from history to classical music. It was because of her that I'd fallen in love with opera and the composers Giuseppe Verdi, Giacomo Puccini, Richard Strauss, and Georges Bizet. Her character, accomplishments, and perseverance brought me comfort. Her parents had both worked, so Buni raised her sister and three brothers, making sure they all had proper educations. She worked as a clerk for CFR, Caile Ferate Romane, the railroad department. Her salary was small, but she had organizational skills, dedication, and intelligence. She saved enough to buy a house and pay for it in cash.

"After the war, typhoid hit," she was saying, "and it killed my sister. I was very sick myself. I lost all my hair and nearly died, but I held on. My hair grew back. I regained my health. I swam, ice-skated, skied, and danced."

"And you met Grandpa on a clear day in September," I prompted.

"A warm, sunny fall day in 1928. Your grandpa lived on a street that crossed Ecaterina Teodorescu Street, my street, and we faced each other at the corner that day. He was a little shorter than I, but I looked into his green eyes, and I swear to you, our souls recognized each other."

I loved seeing Buni light up as she told this part. She, always so stoic and pragmatic, so calm, actually blushed a little, revealing a glimpse of the romance she had once allowed into her life.

"Oh, he was a grand young man, rich and well educated, and from an entirely different social stratum than I. The Imbarus name was so well known. The famous Romanian writer and poet—"

"Octavian Goga!" I blurted out, proudly.

"Yes. He mentioned the Imbarus family in one of his books, as did the historian and prime minister Nicolae Iorga. Your grandpa's family had registered its coat of arms in Vienna. They managed banks, owned real estate, many homes, and farms with arable land, vineyards, orchards, hayfields, vegetable gardens, pastures. . . ."

We were both quiet for a moment, imagining walking in an orchard and picking fresh ripe summer plums. The fact that this was no longer possible made my eyes prickle with tears. Couldn't those bastard Communists have left us even one orchard?

Dad climbed back up to the attic, and Buni and I were alone by the stove.

"Ioan courted me and we fell in love. At first I thought I might become the lucky Mrs. Imbarus, but his parents ignored me. They swore to disown him if he were to marry me. For five years, we saw each other almost every day, and I thought our love would cross all boundaries. Ioan was hoping his parents would change their minds when they saw how much he loved me."

"But they didn't."

"No. When I was twenty-nine years old, he told me that the rich woman his parents had selected for him was now his fiancée, and he had to marry her." Buni sighed and then made a *hmmff* sound. "He didn't love me enough to walk away from his inheritance and position. You say I never cry, Aura, but I did then. My tears soaked my pillow every night, and I vowed never to marry."

"But Grandpa was unhappy, too," I said.

"He was. His wife had a baby boy, and he tried to be a good husband, but after four years, he couldn't stand it any longer and divorced the woman. This was a scandal in his family, but he came to me, begging me to take him back. He'd rather be poor with me than wealthy with her."

"But you couldn't forgive him."

"I could not. For one year he begged and even shed tears. I was resentful and didn't want to open myself up to any more heartache, but then his former wife died, and her family insisted on raising the child. There came another day in the fall, the breeze blowing, colorful leaves drifting down. In my mind, I heard Vivaldi playing. Ioan came to see me, got down on his knees and proposed."

We grinned at each other. "And you lived together happily," I said.

"Yes, your great-grandparents realized that intervening in matters of love could prove to have consequences. They trusted their son's heart and accepted his decision to spend his life with me, and gave us the house next to theirs."

I remembered Buni and Grandpa together, always calling each other "dear." She spoke fluent Hungarian, German, Russian, and Romanian. Grandpa spoke primarily Romanian, but he learned basic Hungarian for Buni. She spoke to my grandpa in Hungarian and German, and Grandpa responded in Hungarian or Romanian. They always spoke calmly and respectfully to each other, were always attuned to the other's needs, loved each other until he died when I was seven.

"I was thirty-four when we married," Buni said, "and unhappy that I was too old to have children—but then, when I was thirty-eight, your wonderful father came along. Considering we had to survive World War II, a terrible flood, a devastating earthquake, and the loss of all our family lands, we were happy." She smoothed my hair and squeezed my hand. "I want you to be happy, my darling girl, and to know the love Grandpa and I shared. I wish I could offer you that bright future here in Romania, a future in which you are not terrified by something as small as a boot print."

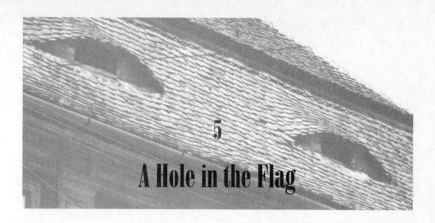

5

A Hole in the Flag

THE SOUND OF GUNFIRE HAD GROWN MORE DISTANT, BUT IT HADN'T stopped, so we stayed barricaded inside our home that day of December 22, 1989. We listened to the sounds of war outside and wondered if our world would end. We did normal things, because what else could we do? Mom and I washed dishes in boiled water. She poured another hot kettle onto laundry soaking in a tin tub. Later, I helped hang them on the clotheslines in the attic, where they solidified into odd, decapitated, ghostly forms. As a child, I would always lose myself in the haunted attic, playing hide-and-seek through the frozen laundry.

We were trying to conserve energy, so one light, or as Mom called it, "the one-eyed bulb," was on in the kitchen where we listened to Radio Free Europe, trying to understand the chaos outside.

As my father had predicted, the government negotiations turned out to be a sham to buy time. The newly formed USLA, the Special Unit for Antiterrorist Action, led by Colonel Ardeleanu, was trained in urban guerilla warfare and heavily armed, ready to intervene in the uprising at Timisoara. All phone links to Timisoara had been cut. Soldiers fired on demonstrators in the street, including parents who'd merely brought their children out to show them the Army troops. People screamed at the soldiers, "You are our brothers!" and "Brothers, don't shoot our children!"

We also listened to VOA and BBC. The reports mentioned clandestine activity of various groups within the Romanian military and security apparatus. Unidentified helicopters, aircraft, and unmanned vehicles were recorded penetrating Romanian airspace. The military was given orders to shoot demonstrators, called "hooligans" and "terrorists" by the Ceauşescu regime.

Somber radio reports announced that the Soviets were monitoring developments closely.

"Maybe those guys we saw dressed in black came in on MiG-29s," I said.

Dad turned on the TV. Ceauşescu had proclaimed martial law, blaming the uprising on Hungarian fascists—obviously referring to Laszlo Tokes, the pastor from Timisoara. And now LIFE, the national news program, showed Ceauşescu addressing a crowd in Bucharest that could not be controlled. We later learned that he'd summoned the people to show support, but only the first few rows applauded as he offered workers a pay raise. The rest of the crowd, which had swelled to over a hundred thousand, began booing and shouting him down.

In the light of our TV we looked at each other, wide-eyed, open-mouthed, ready to speak, but not daring to miss a word. We could barely grasp the implications, the history being made right there in our Romania. The rebels had claimed the media and revealed the true shape of our times. The rebellion unfolded uncensored on national television.

Although the militia arrested many demonstrators, the crowds refused to disperse. Police started using armored cars and gunfire. The death toll rose to what would later be reported as a thousand.

The securitate and militia continued fighting the protesters in Bucharest, and then the news switched back to Timisoara. There, in the vast public square, students wearing open jackets formed lines, swinging from side to side, holding hands and showing their unprotected chests, ready for the incoming bullets. They stood, unafraid of death, in opposition to the young men in the armored tanks.

I gripped Mom's hands, dreading the massacre I was about to see . . . but something else happened.

Eighteen- and nineteen-year-old draftees, mostly recent high school graduates, made up eighty percent of the Romanian Army, which, for centuries, had focused on defending the country's border, not on oppressing its own people as it was now being ordered to do. Though the Communist regime had intentionally created the militia and the securitate to serve the Party, the army still served the people, even after fifty years of Communism. The young cadets were newly enlisted, still attached to their families, not yet brainwashed and indoctrinated by the regime. That day in Timisoara, they let people climb on their tanks, everyone screaming together, "Down with Ceauşescu!"

"*O Istenem!*" Buni cried (My God, in Hungarian). Everyone else said it in Romanian: "*O Doamne Dumnezeule!*"

Dad flipped from Radio Free Europe to VOA to BBC, where we finally learned that the national army, although it had countered protesters earlier in Bucharest, had turned around and sided with the civilians fighting against the militia and securitate in the capital.

"The army is with us!" the crowds chanted.

For the first time we actually believed a revolution could be successful—and in the small fortress of our home we cheered, jumped up and down, and did little Romanian folk dance steps.

An hour later, we watched on TV as the Ceauşescus fled the central committee building in a helicopter. Into the structure swarmed students, soldiers, and workers, all wearing tricolor bands and flying the revolutionary flag: the Romanian flag with the emblematic Communist coat of arms cut out of the yellow center panel.

I immediately found our flag in a kitchen drawer, and a pair of scissors. It was the same red, yellow, and blue flag every Romanian displays on August 23, Romania's National Day during the Communist control, a flag whose colors still inspired pride and love of our homeland. The colors dated back to the fifteenth century, the era of Michael the Brave and Stephen the Great, and even further back to the Dacian standard presented on Trajan's Column in Rome in the first century. The flag, a symbol of the people's strength, had survived many crises, even this wretched Communist regime, and it served as the common denominator for the Romanian people. My heartbeat quickened as I snipped out the Communist emblem. My mom gasped when she saw me, then gave me a nervous hug.

As I cut, I listened to members of the newly formed National Salvation Front deliver anti-Communist speeches. New faces and new promises emerged amid the chaos and violence. Shots could be heard around the central committee building and the national television building.

And then I realized I had been so absorbed in the ongoing events on the TV and radio, I hadn't noticed that the sounds of gunfire in Sibiu had moved far away. Dad and I took claw hammers and pulled the nails from two of the boards across the dining room windows. After peering through the gap for a while, Dad ventured outside. All was quiet, so he opened the dining room shutters. Through the window I saw only a few souls out in the streets, but by around 5:00 PM, people had clustered in front of the neuropsychiatric facility, Hospital Number Three, across the street from our house on Dr. Dumitru Bagdasar Street, named after a neurosurgeon who founded the Romanian School of Neurosurgery.

From what I could see, people seemed to have a lot to say. More and more neighbors joined the group, as if a dead city was waking up, its muscles aching, its brain cells slowly switching on, each of its voices beginning to speak. Ethnic Romanians, Hungarians, and Germans were all going through the same turmoil.

Darkness fell and still the group grew. By 7:00 PM there were at least forty people gathered. The window fogged up, and I wiped it clear so I could look outside at the gray, intoxicating atmosphere underneath the streetlamp, which shone despite the chaos. My warm breath soon fogged the pane again, so I wrote with my finger against the icy glass, "FREEDOM FOR ALL."

Night had always been the time to steal a bit of freedom. As if bred into our Transylvanian blood, we were like vampires who felt a bit of life after sundown. Daylight empowered the securitate to encircle us like starved wolves, so we slipped out mostly at night.

I tucked the flag inside my heavy sweater and left my outpost at the window to join the action.

The temperature was just above freezing, but no one seemed to mind. Everyone buzzed with the events they'd seen on TV and heard on the radio. Faces animated, they shared their personal experiences. No longer was there a sense of impotent helplessness. All these people were united here for the first time for a common goal of confronting the enemy—the Communist regime. My heart pounded with this new surge of hope.

A man ran shouting up Petru Maior Street, a road that ran perpendicular to our street.

"Terrorist! Soviet mercenary!" he cried.

The hour was exactly 9:00 PM.

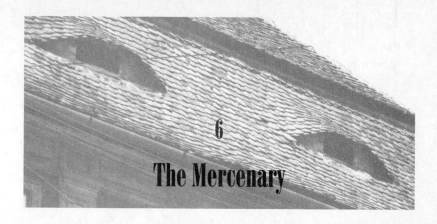

6
The Mercenary

EVERYONE RAN TOWARD THE MAN. LIKE A RIVER OVERFLOWING ITS banks, people whooshed along, footsteps thudding into the snow and ice. Now I recognized him, a neighbor. He had gone to the attic of his house to check on his pork cache. Most Romanians had attics in their brick houses where they stored the food that had to last the whole four months of winter, providing the main source of survival during the harsh blizzards and below zero temperatures. While climbing the stairs, he had bumped into a six foot four inch man dressed in black, smelling like he had not showered in a week. The hulk had pushed past him to leave the house.

"He left stinking piles of shit in our attic!" the neighbor said.

A woman gasped. "Holy Mother of Jesus!"

"And wrappers of protein bars."

"Cosmin, what are protein bars?" another neighbor asked.

Cosmin explained, and added, "These kinds of food don't come from around here."

"Foreigners!" the woman said.

"My God! I heard noises in our attic last night. I thought an owl had gotten in . . ."

"Where is the mercenary now?" Dad asked Cosmin.

"Did you catch him? Tell me you caught him!" added another, wheezing from running in the cold air, hate in his voice.

Cosmin said, "The bastard escaped."

"Why didn't you jump him?" the wheezing man demanded.

Cosmin looked at the man as if he was crazy. "He caught me by surprise! He jumped over the fence into the road, and then in three gigantic steps, jumped into someone else's yard and then was gone. I lost him at the fence."

"Which yard?" asked another man. "Let's find him! Catch the bastard!"

"Don't bother. You don't want to be killed—he has a gun."

I thought about the boot print in our back yard. My whole family could have been killed by one of these "mercenaries," foreigners hiding in our homes, yards, in our town.

"God damn secu! They have guns! I would kill them all right now! Bastards!"

"These aren't the secu," my father said. "These mercenaries are foreigners."

"I say they're Cossacks!" an older man said.

"If they are Soviet special forces," Dad said, "they might send for reinforcements. The Soviets might decide they need to crush a satellite army in open rebellion."

For a moment, no one said anything. I knew we all thought the same thing. We were breathing clean crisp air that felt like freedom. Even though this air was only a few hours old, by God in heaven, it was precious. We would all die before we lost it again, even if it meant throwing ourselves onto Soviet tanks.

"We need patrols," someone said.

That got everyone moving. Patrol units were formed to supervise our district, Terezian, named after Maria Theresa of Austria. An amazing woman, she had been the Holy Roman Empress from 1740 to 1780, and was also known as the Archduchess regnant of Austria, and Queen regnant of Hungary, Croatia and Bohemia. Her statue stood on top of the hospital.

My friends Monika, Ildi, Lulu, Daniela, Adi, and Vicentiu also joined the checkpoint groups. Our assignment was to scout the assigned areas in daytime; our parents would do the night patrols for as long as necessary. Adults instructed us in how to handle unpredictable situations and remain safe.

I was too excited to sleep that night, so I insisted on going on duty with Dad for his shift, which started at 2:00 AM. Standing in the middle of my street among the tall, strong chestnut trees, their icy branches glistening in the streetlights, the hyperactive flashlights, and the candles that many brought, I welled up with hope and love for the potential of my country and my fellow freedom-loving Romanians. I thought about the microphones in the trees and realized no one was listening any more.

I waved the Romanian flag with its hole in the middle. It was my connection to my ancestors, my commitment to the future, my weapon, my protection. These colors united me with my neighbors and other Romanians fighting in the streets. Through the hole I looked at my future with a cautious optimism. In this bleak time and place, when there was nothing we could do and nowhere to go, the colors of the Romanian flag represented an unseen happiness for my country. I was not the only person to modify my flag in this way. The ironic void in a piece of colored cloth brought Romanians together, fighting in the street, willing to spill their last drop of blood for the future.

A neighbor brought tricolor armbands; I got seven of them, for myself and my friends. Proudly, I slid mine over the sleeve of my sweater and felt truly part of the Revolution.

Explosions and gunshots came from the center of town. We all looked uneasily toward the intensified violence. "We need a barricade!" someone shouted.

We hurried to our houses and came back with wood, old furniture, mattresses, whatever we could find to barricade the key streets. More people joined us, raising two fingers in victory signs, and bringing more junk. We created several fortresses along the streets, all with a narrow passageway to allow one car at a time to pass through. We wanted to keep the traffic under control at these checkpoints, and each checkpoint had a password. Ours was *trei* for Hospital Number Three.

I had not slept for hours, but I vibrated with excitement. To raise our morale, some of my neighbors went back to their homes and brought jugs of brandy, homemade wine, *placinte* (pies), wrinkled oranges, and still slightly green, unripe bananas. A real treat for the times. Some women came with small sandwiches with *unsoare* (lard) sprinkled with paprika and hard-boiled eggs sliced as thinly as possible; other sandwiches were spread with margarine, thin soya salami, and a light dusting of *cascaval,* an aged cheese. The margarine on bread with honey was a real treat. My mom had made *scoverzi*—fried, twisted dough sprinkled with powdered sugar—and brought them outside for my friends and me and others nearby. I gobbled one as I sat by a radio that reported a Belgian toxicologist had found traces of poison in the water in Sibiu.

"Stop drinking the water!" I shouted, while jumping to grab the cup holding her chamomile tea from Monika's hand. I felt rage and hate. Dad ran inside the house to tell Mom and Buni not to drink tap water. In the house, fortunately, we always kept bottles of Biborteni and Borsec mineral water, and *sifon* (soda).

"They want to kill us," said Daniela, my childhood friend and neighbor.

"Ceaușescu, burn in hell!"

"Down with the shoemaker!"

"Down with the tyrant!"

"Death to all Communists!"

"Death to securitate!"

I stood watch at our checkpoint with Dad and various friends and neighbors until around 7:00 the next morning, December 23. I was tired and cold when the relief shift arrived, and I dragged myself home and into my bed, heated with the bottles of hot water that Mom placed under my blanket each night. As was so often the case, there was a note underneath my pillow: *"I love you, sweetheart! Mom."*

I smiled. Although the room was almost as cold as the temperature outside, my mother warmed me with her caring. The morning sunlight cast a weak shaft of light through the shutter gap, glinting off the dust mites like tiny fireworks and leaving a pale pink stripe where it hit the rose wall of my bedroom. I was in love with the revolution. I was a part of it. I had dared to cut a hole in the flag and incited others to do it as well. I had stopped people from drinking possibly contaminated water. I had soldiered at my post all night. I'd had a hand in my own future.

My mind kept buzzing, but I needed sleep. I reached for *Twenty Years After*, the sequel to *The Three Musketeers*. Alexander Dumas was one of my favorite authors, an old friend who had lit a spark of romantic adventure alive in my life. I could always escape into my world of dreams where good still prevailed while people fought for their rights. It seemed an appropriate way to honor the day.

As soon as I opened the novel to the page where I'd last stopped reading, my bookmark fell out . . . and looked at me. It was a photo of Michael Chiorean. I stared at it. Handsome Michael Chiorean, the "someone" I always dressed for when heading into town. The someone who interested me more than any of the boys my age at school. He looked like a younger, curly-haired version of Julio Iglesias, and, oh, those warm chocolate brown eyes. He carried his height and muscular body in a way that established a presence I thought of as heroic. He was also a someone who, I told myself, was best forgotten. Yet I hadn't forgotten him. Quite the contrary . . .

I'd met him eleven months earlier. My friend Adriana and I had gone to the Nae Ionescu Jazz Club, even though I was only seventeen. The club featured the music of Dizzy Gillespie and Ray Charles that night, and the promise of such spirited music drew me like a blazing fireplace during a storm, a spot of excitement and liveliness in a cold, drab world. Michael and two other men ran the club. Every seat was filled except the one next to me, and Michael grabbed it. I could tell by the trendy way he dressed he wasn't from Sibiu. He was twenty-six, and I was sure he thought of me as a child. Still, we struck up an intense conversation.

He told me that he had come to Sibiu from Bucharest seven years earlier after his father, a brilliantly educated man who'd earned a top position in the regime, had fallen into disfavor—undoubtedly to his credit as a human being. Michael's father was like many other intelligent people in the 1970s who believed that the Communist Party of Romania, the PCR, would enable a new utopia, and joined its forces. This kind of thinking was part of the reason my own mother had joined: initially, Ceauşescu had been the anti-Soviet crusader who kept the Soviets outside the boundaries of Romania. Presenting himself as a reformer and populist, he appealed to the masses. He created a branch of paramilitary patriotic guards to help counter any Soviet intervention. Enrollment in the PCR nearly doubled to over two and a half million members. In 1970, when Romania was considered *granarul Europei* (the grain basket of Europe), independence and prosperity seemed within reach. Ceauşescu, the former shoemaker, promised egalitarian values and equal distribution of material benefits, attracting inquisitive minds to become part of the ruling tier. Nationalism increased. People wanted to be part of this vision.

Living well in Bucharest, Michael's father was offered the job of a *prim secretar,* equivalent to a regional governor, but he refused it—first, because he thought of himself as a teacher more than an administrator; and second, because of his wife's deteriorating health.

I kept asking Michael questions, and he kept answering. He said his mother died at the same time as his father's relocation to Sibiu, and for a moment, Michael looked away as if hiding a sudden twist of emotion. Then he went on. Before those difficult times, he had included among his friends the sons and daughters of ambassadors and political figures, and hung out with the country's *protipendada*—the social A-list.

"So where do you live now?" I asked.

"With my dad." He told me the street's name.

My jaw probably dropped. "On Nicu Ceaușescu's street?"

"Practically next door to him."

I took this in. There had been a great deal of misinformation spread about the dictator's son, who was rather a dashing figure. Young women all over the country considered him a hunk.

I was attracted to Michael, but I also noticed that he drew continual looks from women determined to make eye contact, and he responded. I gathered he was rebelling against the plotted course of his life. He smoked and laughed about wild parties while tossing back several rounds of whiskey.

At one point in the evening, he pinned me down with his gaze, and I knew he could see the fireworks he ignited in me. In that moment, the beautiful world my heart had constructed around him collapsed, my fantasies a tiny song never to be sung. I knew he was marking me as just another potential conquest. Still, when someone snapped a Polaroid picture of him, I asked if I could have it. Michael smiled and gave it to me, signing it at the bottom: "For a better future! Michael."

I'd held on to this photo ever since, using it to mark the pages of my treasured books. I wondered where Michael was now, in this wild and extraordinary moment in time. Was he excited by the promise of a genuinely better future? Was he all right? Would I ever see him again?

I often placed his picture on my pillow, and did so that morning when I finally put down my book and closed my eyes. The photo still lay there when I woke around noon. I tried to tell myself not to be too concerned for this man. He was probably engaged or something by now. Yet, looking at the photo, I decided that one way or another I would at least find out if he was okay.

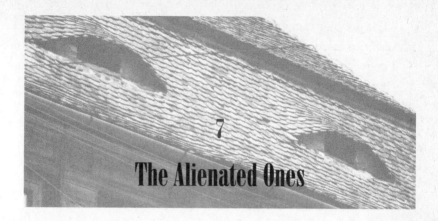

7

The Alienated Ones

I HAD TO REPORT TO THE BARRICADE FOR MY SHIFT IN LESS THAN AN hour, so I wolfed down some of Mom's *cuchele*—milk curd balls, boiled and rolled in bread crumbs, topped with precious drops of melted butter and powdered sugar stolen from her work. I felt secure and comfortable at our old kitchen table, its white and red paint leached away over the years, exposing barren, scratched wood. The peeling white kitchen walls bore the layers and smells of Buni's and Mom's endless cooking.

Dad and Buni sat in the living room, obsessed with news reports.

"Aura!" Buni yelled. "You haven't seen this. Someone got Nicu!"

I'd heard about it while on barricade duty, but hadn't seen the footage. I rushed into the living room to see Nicu Ceaușescu on camera after his capture, saying that some rebel had stabbed him in the abdomen. He was taken to a local hospital, where a spokesman said his condition was stable.

"Wounds to the gut are the worst," Buni said. "Victims last for days of horrible suffering before dying."

"It looks like a mob mentality is taking over," Dad said.

"This is so unfair!" I said. "He was different from his parents."

"The people's rage has been awakened," Buni said. *"A legfagyos-abb teli ejaszakak elesztik a legehesebb farkasokat."*

I knew she was speaking Hungarian and asked for a translation.

"It means, 'Out of the bleakest winter night come the hungriest wolves.'"

Dad nodded. "People haven't seen any logic or justice in years. I hope we still remember what they are."

"How could someone from Sibiu have done this to Nicu?" Mom asked.

And what about Michael? As Nicu's neighbor, was he safe? I kept this fear to myself, but I was even more determined to find out about him.

I recalled the day the previous summer when I saw Nadia Comaneci playing soccer in Nicu Ceauşescu's front yard. My house was in the lower part of the town, much of which my ancestors had once owned and where they had once had many houses. The upper part of town quartered Ceauşescu's securitate and highly ranked officers. Michael and Nicu lived close to Thalia Hall, only a few blocks from my high school.

After school sometimes, my girlfriends and I went to Pacea, the central cinema, or roamed around to catch a glimpse of the best looking guys in town, especially Nicu and Michael. I didn't catch sight of Michael that day, but there was Nadia in shorts, playing soccer with friends. She was in her late twenties by that time, and it was no secret that she and Nicu were involved. Nadia had soared into superstardom at the age of fourteen when she became the first gymnast to score perfect tens at the Montreal Olympics in 1976, and every young girl in Romania idealized her, none more than I. There were rumors that Nicu abused her, and that her fingernails were often black and blue from his smashing her fingers, a reminder that if she left when off competing, he would track her down and pull her nails out one by one—things denied by Nadia herself. I never ever believed those rumors, because from what I saw, he was too nice to complete strangers to do any harm to someone he cared for.

Nadia had been given an eight-room villa in Bucharest and brought in her mother, brother, and several servants. She wore expensive jewelry and drove a Dacia, a Romanian-made Renault, with its license plate of only three digits—allowing the select few who were "more equal" to park anywhere, drive at any speed, and drink all they wanted before getting behind the wheel. I'd seen the Dacia twice before in front of Nicu's house.

Nicu drove his own dark blue Renault around town, wearing dark glasses and black suits that gave him a very diplomatic air. With dark, wavy hair; blackberry eyes; a clean-cut pale round face; Nicu caused double takes wherever he went. Thirty-six years old when he was sent to Sibiu, he gave people something to talk about with his various relationships. Political women, singers, and gymnasts all passed through his bed—then there were the women working at the hotels he stayed in or the restaurants where he dined, the hairdresser who used to cut his hair. He ignored the marriage his mother insisted on, and women were happy to be chosen, usually benefiting in some way beyond the coupling.

Still, despite his playboy lifestyle, Nicu used his position as the prime secretary of Sibiu County, equivalent to a governor, to help people. On the day my friends and I saw Nadia playing soccer, we also saw two desperate-looking people hiding alongside Michael's two-story house so that militia officers patrolling the streets couldn't see them. Each of the three or four times I ventured near the house I would see someone, usually leathery and wrinkled, clothed in rags, with a white envelope trembling in his or her hands. These people took a terrible chance in order to hand Nicu, the son of the cruelest dictator in the Eastern Bloc, a crumpled letter. I had seen Nicu's driver stop, pick a letter up, and hand it to Nicu before leaving the grounds.

Nicu had helped families keep their homes, intervened when someone was arrested for political reasons, helped arrange a complex surgery that required a trip to a Western country. Soon after Nicu's arrival in Sibiu, major changes in the economy and in people's lives took place: monthly rations of meat, butter, eggs, milk, flour, and sugar were increased; electricity and natural gas consumption increased. People realized Nicu was different from his father.

And now he was severely wounded, possibly dying.

"Well," Mom said, "I think *most* people from Sibiu are praying for him."

"But if the new revolution begins with such an injustice, this can't be a good sign," I said. Then I went outside for barricade duty across the street.

The neuropsychiatric facility, Hospital Number Three, had long provided a place for neighborhood teenagers to hang out. As children, we'd played in its vegetable garden and unpaved areas, found roof leaks and windows with broken out panes, peeked into the morgue, explored the many abandoned wings and closed attics where fat rats ran from one corner to another. This hospital was ours, and we were its children. We fed our sick "friends" with candies and waffles that Mom brought home from the Victory sweets factory. I knew patients named Ioan, Sanny, and Ungar. They were mentally unstable but not insane. Their families had abandoned them here so the state would take care of them. We remembered the stories they shared of how they ended up in the cuckoo's nest. We befriended them, teased others, or ran for our lives to escape the patients we bugged too much with our pranks.

Ward Number Nine harbored the most severe psychiatric cases. Their rooms had thick iron bars at the windows and doors, and food was served through a tiny crack in the door. From this place, I had many times heard screams of despair; I had seen people smashing their heads against metal bars; I had seen people laughing or roaring in fury.

The hospital had opened in 1863 as Ospiciu de Alienati, Hospice for the Alienated Ones. New sections for psychiatry were added in the 1950s: neurology, infantile neurology, and recuperation, while a new building housed mentally challenged kids. As teenagers we used to hang out around the bench meant for visitors in front of the hospital, staying until our parents called us inside at night. This was a natural spot to have built the checkpoint barricade. It struck me as apropos for another reason as well: with plenty of "alienated ones" stabbing and sniping at innocent people, life couldn't be much crazier outside the hospital than inside.

"The people in the house across from mine had somebody in their attic that left boot prints all around their yard," Daniela said.

I shuddered and described the enormous prints that had circled my house.

Vicentiu said that their tool shed had been slept in by a man in black who also left boot prints the size of concrete blocks.

Adela, a nineteen-year-old girl, was smoking. "You know that woman with the dyed red hair who hangs out at Suru? I heard one of those mercenary creeps broke into her flat and raped her before heading out on the fire escape."

Looking toward the South, I saw that the wind coming off the mountains had pushed the city's many rising plumes of smoke eastward. Laden with ash, the cold air nipped my cheeks. The staccato clatter of gunshots still reported fighting in the distance. My companions and I checked the IDs of anyone we didn't know who passed through the narrow opening in the barricade. What would we do if an actual mercenary tried to drive through? In our state of mind, perhaps jump on him and beat him to death?

Other friends stopped by to hang out and share their stories, and we took turns doing patrols in pairs. Then the gunfire and explosions in the center of town intensified, and those who didn't have to be there left. The rest of us stood nervously at our posts. Dad came out and hovered for a while, but when the noise died down, he went back inside to check the news for reports. An hour later he popped back out with the news that the BBC had announced that USLA troops loyal to Ceaușescu had confronted unarmed protesters in Sibiu. Victims were clubbed to death, shot at, stabbed. The Romanian Army was fighting back, supported by street fighters.

Night fell early again, and our watch dragged on. I hopped from one foot to the other and slapped my arms, hoping the next shift wouldn't be late. At 6:00 PM, a man in his forties named Luca arrived with others to relieve us. He knew my father. We exchanged news, and I was about to leave when Luca stopped me.

"Tell your father that I'm worried about his friend Gabriel. He was protesting at Casa Sindicatelor with a fellow named Michael Chiorean."

Michael? My heart started pounding. "Luca, tell me what happened." Casa Sindicatelor was the Trade Union Cultural Hall. The day before, some four hundred students had organized a protest there, with thousands of other people gathering by noon. "Gabriel and Michael . . . were they with the students?"

"Yes, with the leaders. I was there, too. The hall has a balcony right above the main entrance, and Gabriel and Michael and the others used it to address the masses with the hall's amplifiers. A hundred or so representatives of different factories from Sibiu followed them inside and took turns shouting out lists of demands and making speeches. Gabriel and Michael were ready to deliver a hopeful speech about Eastern Germany's anti-Communist riots in Leipzig and Berlin and the downfall of Communism."

"But the shooting started," I said. I'd seen the news clips.

"Right. Snipers fired at the speakers on the balcony, and they all rushed to get away. Panic broke out. Gabriel and Michael ran out of the building, and I followed them. It was total chaos. Other snipers were shooting at the securitate's headquarters. A demonstrator very close by me was shot in the leg. We ran towards the militia's building, but there was shooting coming from it, too, as well as from the army building across the way. Machine gun fire and automatic weapons, all shooting at each other! Gabe and Michael were caught in the crossfire. I got away, but in the stampede I lost sight of them. Neither has returned home yet."

I started shivering. I wanted to pray, but what could I ask for if the damage was already done?

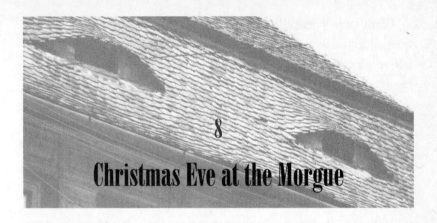

8

Christmas Eve at the Morgue

HAVING A CRUSH ON SOMEONE CREATES A SECRET PLACE TO TURN TO, A little closet world of hope and bright dreams. I knew I was silly to feel that way about Michael, but the fantasies I indulged in had made the grimness of life more bearable. I could withdraw into that world and come out with a smile. I didn't dwell there; it wasn't an opiate, but knowing it existed fed the optimism that allowed me to work to achieve my goals. If anything had happened to Michael, something as precious as our family's jewels would have been torn from my life.

"Honey, honey, honey," Buni said when she saw me. "What's wrong?"

I told her and my parents the bare facts, but Mom saw through the story and into my heart. "Michael is the guy in that picture you carry around . . ."

They pampered me that night. Buni used our last fresh egg and powdered milk to make *friganele* (French toast) for me.

"Oh, Buni, I love you!" I lifted the lids from the pots and pans on the stove and discovered *mamaliga* with *branza de burduf*—polenta with peasant's cheese. I loaded up my plate and took it to my room. Gourmet food couldn't have soothed me any more than this humble feast did, yet I had a hard time swallowing.

Familiar voices called from across the street. I peered between the gap in the wooden boards across my window and saw my best friend Monika talking to her sister, Ildi, in front of the hospital. I ran into our front yard.

"Monika! Ildi! Come inside!" Ildi was my age and Monika a year younger. They lived in one of the nearby houses that had belonged to my family before the Communists took it. The girls were the sisters I never had but wanted. We shared food, clothes, books, school supplies, and, most importantly, confidences about families, boys, hopes, and disillusioned dreams.

Both girls came up to my room, where they shared my *friganele* and listened to the story about Michael and Gabriel. We comforted each other for several hours, when a flashing light from outside made my room pulse red. I knew immediately what it was and aligned one eye with the gap at my window.

"An ambulance?" Monika asked.

"Two. . . . They're headed toward the morgue."

"That's weird . . . ," Ildi said.

I said nothing, thinking of the recurring vision I had of the dark street and the ambulance almost running me down. When had I last had that dream? Only two nights ago.

Monika was staring at me. I knew she was remembering our last caper in the morgue. The morgue had always held a special fascination for us. Everyone knew that Transylvania was one of the most powerful areas in the world in terms of psychic phenomenon. That wasn't a literary invention or a product of Hollywood. I believed it, too. I felt this was because so many had lost their lives needlessly and had returned to live them out, even if as a ghost. Some of our neighbors visited gypsies; others could read the future in tarot cards, coffee grounds, and melted wax. On a windy autumn night the previous year, Monika, Lulu, Daniela, Lili, Adi, Cristi, Titus, and I went into one of the abandoned wings of the hospital to try turning tables, a practice of contacting the dead that seemed to work equally well with a chair. We dragged the essential wooden chair behind us through the cold, slippery cement hallways of the west wing. Tilted, squeaking doors opened onto spider-webbed rooms with broken windows. The thumping of our own shoes raised the hair on my arms. Crows, bats, stray dogs, and rats were the only full- time warm-blooded inhabitants. We knew that here, in this dark, mad world, the spirits would come alive if you called upon them.

We sat on the cold cement, huddled around nine burning white candles, the wooden chair in the middle. Since the name of the recently deceased was Radu, we held hands and started slowly moaning, "Radu, Radu, Radu, come back to the world. Show your presence. Materialize."

We all placed the tips of our fingers on the wooden chair, and soon a strange vibration accompanied our chanting. Three of our candles blew out. A door slammed, but we kept chanting. The chair started to rotate and vibrate; it tilted to one side. Its legs rapped on the floor. I knew that sometimes, Titus and another boy had deliberately tipped the chair, but that night I wasn't so sure.

The feet of the chair slammed to the floor, and the six remaining candles blew out in a howl of wind. We screamed, leaped up, and ran as if goblins were after us, leaving the possessed wooden chair behind. It was all silly, of course . . . but also eerie.

Like tonight.

My friends and I resumed our visit, but after a few minutes the red lights flashed through the slats again. This time Monika peered through the gap at the world outside.

"The ambulances seem like they're in a hurry to get out of there."

A sense of dread overcame me. I told myself this could have nothing to do with Michael. Even if he were dead, he wouldn't be brought to Number Three. Would he? But then, why would *anyone* be brought there, other than patients?

"Something's fishy," I said. "Let's go and check it out."

"Are you crazy?" Ildi said. "It's almost 11:00!"

"And there's this thing called a *revolution* going on," Monika said.

More flashing red lights, more faces pressed against the wood slats over my window. Another ambulance headed for the morgue.

A sick dread settled in my stomach. The small amount of food I'd eaten threatened to rise. "I'm going over there."

"You can't go alone," Monika said. "Let me go home and get a flashlight."

"You're crazy," Ildi said, a statement this time. "Count me out."

They both left, but faithful Monika soon returned with a flashlight. She looked nervous and a bit excited. But just as we were about to step out the front door, Mom appeared.

"Where are you going?" she whispered, obviously to keep Dad from hearing.

I murmured a hasty explanation, and I think she understood I was terrified it might be Michael at the morgue, although I didn't say so. "Please say you're okay with this, Mom. Please? And please don't tell Dad."

"Aura . . ." She held my hand in hers. "I won't tell him. Be careful. Tap on our window when you get back, and I'll unbolt the door. But don't be long, or we'll come after you!"

"Thank you, Mommy. I love you."

Monika and I crossed the street. Under a dense cloudy sky that blocked the moonlight, we slipped past the night watch group at the checkpoint and walked alongside the hospital grounds. This macabre place looked like something from a Poe story. Coated with soot that made parts of the sprawling buildings disappear into the blackness, yet vaguely revealed by the spread of a green fungus, the hospital was especially creepy at night. Cavernous, neglected halls could have housed vampires for all anyone knew. Standing atop the main building, as if to ward off evil, the statue of Maria Theresa kept watch, visible only as an ominous silhouette. I thought about the tales that unfolded on humid summer nights when my friends and I would hide away in dark corners of the hospital grounds, listening to legends about Maria Theresa, such as the one that claimed she was a sex addict who died while having intercourse with a horse. I understand that the same was said of Catherine the Great—probably a victim of the same propagandists.

The morgue lay at the west end of the hospital, close to the Rossbach River and the hated Cooperative Agricole de Productie, where each autumn, the State mandated that students pick potatoes and carrots for a month during school time. This forced us to fall behind in the curriculum in favor of hard, unpaid physical labor. All high school students were also forced to train in the use of guns, especially AK-47 assault rifles, out in the open fields—crawling in trenches, mucking about, girls and boys shoulder to shoulder in the mud. When no one was watching, I preferred to drop my AK-47 on the ground and kick it along rather than carry the hated thing.

Monika was clearly thinking about the same things. "If the revolution is successful," she whispered, looking toward the frozen clods in the fields, "at least we won't have to do any more field training or pick the damn root vegetables."

We were still on Bagdasar Street, but it was unpaved at this end, so the slightest rain created reeking mud everywhere. No one ever cleaned this mess, but fortunately the cold had frozen the stink out of it and enabled us to pass without sinking up to our ankles.

The thick morgue walls had no windows, only a narrow door that barely admitted gurneys to carry in the deceased. Its wood may have been blue at one time, but it had blackened and faded over years of neglect and had developed a vertical crack an inch wide. Frightened yet curious, my palms sweating inside my gloves, I pressed my eye to the crack and peered straight into the second part of my recurring ambulance vision.

Three bloody bodies lay on wooden tables alongside the dirty gray walls. The corpses were of well-built men in their fifties, each with a flickering candle standing near his smashed forehead. They bore bruises on top of bruises, ranging from red to purple, blue, and a sickly yellow. Crimson gashes and scratches showed through their tattered clothing. Their eyelids were shut, but the eyes bulged bizarrely underneath the skin. Their swollen lips had lost their color, whitened in death's eerie grimace. The once-white shirt on one of the men, now murky red, was twisted around his shoulders. Another's hand was missing fingers, and the nails had blackened on those remaining. Broken legs dangled from the tables. I smelled blood, candle wax, putrefying flesh.

I turned away. "Shit . . . Going to throw up."

"Just don't faint here," Monika said, and took my place at the crack. She did not shift away. She was preparing for the medical school entrance exam, so the scene of dead people didn't seem to affect her as profoundly as it did me. "Oh, my God," she whispered. "What has happened to these men?"

Though cold, I was sweating. Tears ran down my cheeks like ice water. At some point snowflakes had started falling, and I inhaled the fresh cold air, focusing on the dainty flakes until I could speak again.

"Monika, these men are *not* patients from the hospital."

"No." She stood and turned toward me, ours breaths sending up small clouds.

"The brutality . . ."

I heard voices inside the morgue. They were getting louder.

Without a word, Monika and I dashed across the street. Luckily, there were two Dacias parked there, and we slid behind them just as the morgue door burst open. A hulky silhouette appeared in the doorframe, staring in our direction.

The nearest streetlight was closer to the main hospital, so I hoped the man couldn't see us—but Moni was panting, and the clouds of her breath could give us away. "Monika, breathe into your coat!" I whispered.

"Oh, God," she whimpered.

"Shhhh!"

Silhouetted by the candlelight in the morgue, the bulky man looked around. He wasn't anyone I'd ever seen at the hospital before, and he didn't seem like a coroner. He looked like a thug. Maybe one of the Dacias was his. How many men like him were inside the morgue? Would they come after us and beat us, break our bones, chop off our fingers?

The man scanned the area. We didn't dare move. Monika's teeth chattered, but she bit into her coat collar.

Out of the silence came the rumble of a distant car engine. It grew louder, and a black van approached the morgue. It stopped in front of the thug, and two other men dressed in dark clothes got out and walked inside. When they reappeared, they were dragging the corpses we had seen by their arms and legs. Each was dumped in the back of the van, thumping like sacks of potatoes.

"We're going to die tonight." Monika's whisper was hysterical.

"Shhhhh. Don't move." My heart pounded like it would burst from my chest and explode. I was afraid that these human shadows would hear it, too.

Monika took my hand into hers like a true sister. This whole experience had turned us into witnesses to something. But what, exactly?

The thug jumped in the front seat of the van along with the other two men, and the van made a U-turn, skidding in the ice a bit, and sped past us.

Monika and I jumped to our feet and ran as if demon-chased toward our homes.

"Mom is going to kill me," I said.

"Well, then you will die tonight, no matter what."

"Let's move! Faster, soldier, faster!" I was teasing, but then I heard many soft footfalls behind us. Without stopping, I turned to see six stray dogs following us, maybe forty feet back. I saw tongues shiny with drool, and ferocious eyes. They accelerated toward us, nails clattering on the cobblestones.

Monika looked back, too, and gasped. We ran harder. So did the dogs. They began to bark, harsh, eager staccatos of sound.

Monika's house appeared. With the dogs ten feet behind us, we vaulted her fence as if it were only a foot tall. I have no idea how I was able to do that. The hounds tried to follow, leaping at the tall pickets and threatening to wake the whole neighborhood with their baying.

"Git!" Monika threw a rock at the most aggressive of the pack.

The dog yelped and slunk back. I found a loose garden brick and heaved it toward a mangy, snarling shepherd. I missed, but our aggression was enough to discourage them. They turned and headed back toward the river.

Monika and I looked at each other, gasping for breath. A quick hug and I left for my own house, three doors down.

Knowing Mom would be waiting for me, I ran to the door. It was open. Sobbing, I rushed into her arms. My words tumbled over one another as I tried to tell her about the bodies, my vision, the men in the van, the feral dogs, and the terror I felt about witnessing the results of what was quite possibly a horrible crime.

"Don't mention this incident to anybody!" Mom's eyes were scary with insistence, her grip on my shoulder a steel clamp. "Nobody! Do you understand me? Nobody!"

She walked me to my room. I tore off my outerwear and hopped into bed. The cold mattress reminded me of the icy ground beneath my bottom as we hid from the thug in the doorway of the morgue. I saw again the contortion of bodies, humans whose families were probably still waiting for them at home to share a bowl of soup. I smelled the blood, mud, sweat, wax, excrement. . . .

"Aura, do you hear me?" Mom jarred me out of my shock.

"Yes . . ."

"Aura, nobody can know about this. Nobody. You didn't see this!"

"But I did!"

"You saw something that could possibly be used against others in power. You don't want to be picked up by securitate tomorrow!"

"There is no securitate anymore. Is there?"

"We don't know that yet. Time has to pass to really see who is behind this revolution. So promise me now, Aura! You tell no one!"

"Okay, Mom, I promise. I'll warn Monika, too. She can keep secrets."

"Aura . . ." Mom's voice softened. "Honey, why did you go there?"

I teared up. It had been foolish to take such risks over a silly crush. I was relieved I hadn't seen Michael on one of those morgue tables, of course, but in truth, I probably would have gone even if I hadn't worried about him. My vision had compelled me. "I just knew something was up," I said. "I was curious. You know me."

"Aura, you must not be so impetuous." She smoothed the hair away from my forehead.

I shook and sweated.

"It's Christmas Eve," she said.

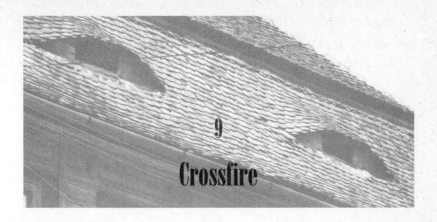

9

Crossfire

I AGAIN FELL ASLEEP LOOKING AT MICHAEL'S PICTURE. WHEN I WOKE at noon, no one had a thought for normal Christmas Eve traditions. The television covered the demonstrations in the streets of Sibiu. Hundreds upon hundreds of people were gathering in the streets with posters and handmade signs.

My impetuous nature took over again. I don't know what I thought I could do, but I suddenly felt like a soldier who belonged in the streets. I had to know how things stood. I wanted news of Michael, my friends, and their families. I dressed in my gray wool clothes, sturdy boots, cap and mittens, and headed for the door.

"And where do you think you're going?" Mom asked.

"I can't sit cooped up in the house and watch TV like a pensioner when so much is happening. I must be a part of it."

"Haven't you learned not to just dash out into danger?" Mom looked at me pointedly.

"Aura, don't be foolish," Buni said.

"This is history! The turning point in our lives! I'm going, even if I have to sneak out the window."

"All right, all right," Dad said. "I'll go, too."

"Wait!" Mom said. "I can't stand worrying about you. I'll change and go, too!"

Buni sighed. "I'll cook something hot for you to come home to."

Dad made a few phone calls and learned that the demonstrations were taking place on Balcescu Street and Corso. "Don't worry," he said to Buni. "I would die before I let anything happen to my girls."

Buni nodded. "I'll be watching at the window every five minutes."

The iron gray sky hung low over us as we headed out on Rusciorului Street. Three days ago we'd taken the same route, thinking that it would be a day like any other. Now, fires, bullet holes, and overturned cars made what had already been grim look even worse. As we passed Suru, the corner bar, a dense acidic smell of urine combined with ash and diesel fumes poured out. It sickened me. The bar had been boarded up, and graffiti spread like a white winter fungus on top of the ugliness.

> Down with the murderer!
> Death to Communists!
> We are the people!
> Liberty for all!
> Kill Dracula!

Paper strips fluttered on the trees. "What are those?" I asked.

We walked closer and saw paper stained with blood. The first one had a name on it, as did the second. One paper had four names on it.

"I think these are the names of people who have been shot," Mom said.

A woman stood by one of the trees, sobbing. She screamed a name, and then cried, "My son! My boy!" Other mourners stood by the trees or wandered aimlessly, calling out their dead loved ones' names. Three children were crying in the street while their older siblings looked for their parents. Had they been killed? A woman befriended them, promising to help. Some people carried candles that flickered in the soft wind that now carried snowflakes. I felt sad, furious, proud. Revolutionaries had died for a better Romania, entombed in the rubble, but enshrined in our souls forever.

Broken bottles and iron trashcans littered the Cibin River. The factories were empty and silent. Independenta wasn't manufacturing road-building equipment and industrial furnaces; Libertatea was producing no textiles. Men with coal-blackened, exhausted faces and bulging muscles had left their jobs to join the revolution. They prowled about restlessly that afternoon. Ceauşescu's buildings had weathered the assaults well, unfortunately. Small and cold, made from drab gray cement, they still stood, uglier than ever. Ceauşescu had razed hundreds of thousands of impressive old houses, replacing them with blocks of apartments so he could move the farmers off their lands and into towns where they could work in the factories. We passed burned and overturned cars, a blackened flag, trashed billboards with Ceauşescu's image torn or burned out. I stopped to stare at a single bloody leather shoe, a woman's, and wondered if its owner was still alive.

The closer we got to the center of town, the more bullet holes marred the buildings. Machine guns pointed in all directions, and small tanks sat on the cobblestones, blocking the entrance to the center of town, the main passageway to the plazas, churches, shops, and the most famous hotels. From the tops of their armored cars, soldiers of the Romanian Army waved the new flag with a hole in the middle. Signs and posters appeared everywhere with anti-Ceauşescu slogans: *Jos cu dictatorul!* (Down with the dictator!) *Moarte criminalului!* (Death to the murderer!) *Noi suntem poporul!* (We are the people!)

Mom shivered. "Let's go home," she said.

I was hoping to get a glimpse of Michael, or at least see some faces from the jazz club, so I could ask if he was okay. "Just a little longer," I pleaded.

"We should at least try Balcescu Street," Dad said.

We trudged on to the remains of the once impressive Imparatul Romanilor, the Roman Emperor's Hotel, now blackened with so many holes blasted in its walls that a car could drive through. Shards of glass everywhere. The shop where foreigners could use their own currency . . . gone. On Corso, the main street, people walked in all directions. "Where can I find a safe place for the night?" they asked. "Where can I find my friends and family members?" "Where can I go to best help the cause?" A small group formed in front of Pacea, the central cinema, and solicited donations for the families of those who had died in the revolution. This great shuffling din, the dull roar of massed humanity, the moans of those in grief, left me feeling faint.

At 3:00 PM the heavy sky sank into an early nightfall. People improvised shrines out of wax, and the heavy smell made me cough. We neared the Continental Hotel . . . and nothing I'd already seen prepared me for the sight.

Several floors of the hotel had been blown away entirely, and a mountain of shattered glass lay at the foot of the monster. Inside, more glass, a ravaged lounge, and porous, blackened walls mocked the elitism that had two days earlier characterized this decadent refuge for the rich and powerful, those who had oppressed the Romanian people. Manned and unmanned machine guns and more small tanks guarded the building. The securitate and militia buildings were almost demolished. Paramilitary units were stationed at various points, ever vigilant.

My zeal for the revolution faded a bit as I witnessed the consequences of defying the Regime. I saw the faces of "savages" around me. People looked like they hadn't slept for days, and many wore filthy, blood-stained clothes, their hair uncombed and dirty, the men with unshaven faces. This was the image of a starved nation, of a freedom-deprived country, not one with a rich, strong history of warriors and leaders. One of the bedraggled faces caused me to take a second glance. The unshaven young man walked toward us on the other side of the street. He was dressed in black corduroys, a black jacket, black leather gloves and an *ushanka*—a Russian hat with earflaps designed for heavy winters. His hat was of dark brown, almost black, rabbit fur. He reminded me of one of the hulking mercenaries seen around town, but it was Michael Chiorean.

"Michael!" I yelled.

To my surprise, he waved at me.

"Mom! Dad! Let's go and talk to him!" My voice trembled with excitement. "You can ask about Gabriel."

Dad said, "This is not the time or the place to have social conversations. We need to get home."

But Michael moved toward us, and I stepped off the curb toward him. "Hey, Michael!"

He crossed the street. "Aura?"

He remembered my name. I introduced him to my parents.

"Are you okay, Michael?" I asked.

"Now I am—after forty-eight hours of no sleep and almost being killed. Now I'm fine."

"What happened?" I asked, looking at his unshaven beard and the dark circles under his eyes.

"I was arrested by the Army. Taken as a mercenary."

"What are you saying there, Michael?" Dad asked. "Gabi's friend said you'd been caught in a crossfire at the protest demonstration."

"I was, Mr. Imbarus, but what I've been through since then. . . . Let's just say I'm thankful to still be alive." He shook his head. "I was shot at from all directions and then mistaken for a mercenary and spent two nights as a prisoner scheduled for execution."

We stared at him, trying to make his words fit with our concept of all that was happening.

"Well, you do look like a mercenary . . ." Mom said. I frowned at her, and she added, "A little."

Michael blew his breath out. "If I'd known what the well-dressed mercenary would be wearing, I would have dressed differently that morning."

I smiled and he returned it.

"Here's what I want to understand," my dad said. "Who was
doing all the shooting at the demonstration?"

Michael's gaze grew distant. "Sniper fire first came from the
securitate's headquarters. Gabriel and I ran about six hundred feet
away into crossfire from the militia building and the Hotel Continental. A guy close to us was shot in the leg. Beyond that point, I
couldn't tell. All hell broke loose, people shooting at each other
and at anyone still around. Gabriel and I ran for our lives. This
was not like the Leipzig protest I was going to speak about at the
demonstration. The bullets flying everywhere weren't rubber."

We turned toward a concrete bench beside a flattened bus-stop
sign outside the front of the Teatrul de Stat Sibiu—the Sibiu State
Theatre. Never appealing, it now looked like a monster's head with
missing teeth. Chipped gray walls were peppered with bullet holes,
and the burned-out second story had blackened windows. As if
watching a grim documentary, we sat on the bench, listening to
and visualizing Michael's story of gunfire and ricocheting bullets.
His and Gabriel's only hope for shelter had been a locked photo
shop. Gabriel pounded the glass out of the door with his elbow
and unlocked the door, allowing six or eight people to take shelter. After a few minutes, when the heaviest fighting ebbed, everyone fled through a back door.

"Was the Army there? Did they stop the fight?" Dad needed
explanations.

"I don't know. The information we got was very confusing."
Michael described the vandalism to militia cars, the acts of retaliation, the subsequent acts of revenge for the retaliation. "And then
things got even uglier. Another crowd gathered, shouting and
screaming in sheer animal fear and hatred. I hoisted myself up
onto a window casement and saw the most inhumane, cowardly
actions imaginable." He put his head in his hands.

We sat there stunned, curious but not wanting to prod him. He seemed to need to talk, though. After a moment he described watching a hapless militia sergeant brutally beaten as the hysterical crowd cheered.

"To see another human being beaten to death before your eyes is . . . I can't get the sights and sounds and *smell* out of my mind." He shook his head and looked up. "Gabriel and I wanted to run away from it, but I knew we had to do something. . . . Human . . . compassion, I guess, took over. We went out there, and the crowd let us through. I think they thought we wanted in on the bloodbath."

"Oh, my God, Michael." My hoarse voice barely registered. The mob could just as easily have turned on them.

He and Gabriel had managed to pull back the three or four main aggressors who were taking turns punching and kicking the militia man. The victim lay on the pavement, his face was unrecognizable . . . but he had white in his hair, and his hands were aged. Hundreds of bare-knuckle punches had turned his head into a swollen cauliflower, his ears and eyes mere bloodied lines. People screamed at Michael and Gabriel to kill the bloodsucker, kill the bastard.

I could barely breathe. He had just described the condition of the bodies I'd seen in the morgue. This made me feel bizarrely but deeply connected to him.

Michael went on. "We screamed back, 'He's just an old guy, could be your father! He looks like a desk guy, a bureaucrat!'" His voice quavered and tears beaded his thick lashes. "I couldn't live with the idea that I might have let someone get killed in cold blood. We *are* Christians, aren't we?"

10

Meet Me Tonight

THROUGH MICHAEL'S EYES I COULD SEE THE TURMOIL IN THE STREET, the blood painting the cement and reddening the spaces between the cobblestones. I heard through his ears the screams of desperation flung at the sky.

"What did you say to them?" Mom asked him, her tone conveying both shock and gentleness.

"I yelled louder than I ever had in my life, telling them that they didn't want more blood on their hands. 'You don't want to be remembered as a criminal instead of a revolutionist!' is what I said."

Gabriel and Michael managed to save another six men, already badly beaten, from death. I wondered if Michael had been thinking about his father, a member of the Communist Party even if not in good standing. I wondered if he imagined his father lying bloodied on the cobblestones. A military sedan had slowed to pass through the clogged intersection. Michael and Gabi told the driver they had a militia man in critical condition, and others at risk. Half an hour later, a military truck showed up and took the militia men into custody.

"It was just in time, because people had started yelling that

Gabriel and I had let militia men escape through the back door of the photo shop. They just couldn't think straight."

Michael had seen the ugly human side of this Armageddon and had the courage to do the right thing. I was more in awe of him than ever.

Even saving the men wasn't enough. Michael and Gabi had decided to go to the hospital to find out what happened to them. Michael apparently itched with the same kind of curiosity that plagued me, because after failing to find them in the hospitals— also scenes of disaster and chaos—he paid a visit to the morgue. The men weren't there, either, but in the interior court of the morgue, lying directly on the ground, were twenty bodies in grey-blue militia uniforms. Several had been severely beaten, but bullet wounds had killed most of them.

"I stopped at a face I recognized, Lieutenant Corlaciu. He worked for the traffic division, a man I'm sure women found handsome. Last year he pulled me over and gave me a speeding ticket—which I deserved." Michael looked up at us, weary, resembling a man in his late thirties more than in his mid-twenties. "Did he deserve to die?"

"At the very worst, he deserved a trial," Dad said.

I thought of the beaten men at the morgue in my vision, and those I'd seen in real life the night before, and felt chilled to the marrow. I knew it was past time to leave, but I wanted more of Michael. Actually, I wanted him all to myself.

A sharp scream rose from the passageway underneath the street that linked the Continental Hotel and Trades Union Hall to the now-ruined Dumbrava shops. A woman ran out of the tunnel and crashed into the arms of a middle-aged gentleman. "No, God, please, no! Not my son. Why? Why?"

The man tried to calm her, but all he could do was to keep her from falling to the ground. Another woman, who had followed her, spoke to us.

"Poor woman. Her neighbor just recognized her son at the morgue."

Michael looked stunned a moment, then said, "I need to leave. My parents are probably looking for me in the same place. Then I'm going to grab some sleep . . ."

"Oh, my! Of course!" Mom said.

"We've overstayed our intentions, as well," Dad said. "I wish you luck, young man." He shook hands with Michael, took my mom's arm, and began the walk back home.

I stalled. "I wanted to hear about your capture," I said to Michael. "You didn't get to that part."

That smile I'd seen earlier returned. "I'll be at the University tonight. We're patrolling the buildings, taking turns." He looked at me directly, as if trying to let his eyes say what he probably should not. "My watch starts at 9:00. You could stop by. A group of us will be there. . . ."

"Great!" My heartbeat did a drum roll. "I'll be there."

I caught up to my parents, who wondered if I'd gone insane, plotting to wander the streets at night during a revolution. We walked home from Corso, analyzing each detail of what Michael had said, trying to figure out how the revolution had really started.

It was only 4:30 but already quite dark. In daylight, the streets that were blocked hadn't been too great an obstacle, but by night we had to grope around, walking many blocks out of our way to find unfamiliar alternate routes. Soldiers could still be a danger since we didn't know who'd be in control of the country when the fighting stopped. Shadows moved around us, and I jerked each time to see what created them: a bicycle headlamp bouncing along behind us, a stray cat darting into an alley, someone carrying a flashlight. Our footsteps echoed in the dark streets. At one point, Dad stopped to listen. I heard nothing except the noise of a lone military transport several blocks distant. A certain sickly sweet smell still hung in the cold evening air. I didn't know if it was from unburied dead or not, but it could have been. It was the kind of night where you half-expected old Vlad the Impaler to step out from behind a tree.

"Let's pick up the pace," Dad said, scanning the darkening streets.

Snow began to fall, each flake on my face a cold ghost-kiss.

It took over half an hour before we got home. I could see Buni's curly white hair. She stood at her usual position at the third window on the right, her post at 3:45 PM when she waited for me to come home from school, and at 10:30 PM when she waited for my Mom to come home from work.

Warmth and the smell of good food greeted us as we stepped inside.

"Where in the world were you?" Buni asked. "What took you so long?"

"Oh, you are so good to come home to, Cretii." I hugged her, and Dad explained about meeting Michael.

I noticed that she'd chopped down the small pine sapling from the backyard behind the fenced garden, brought it inside, and wrapped cookies in colored paper to hang on it. She set out bowls of hearty lentil and barley soup served with hot bread and beet pickles. We wolfed the food down, telling her more of what we'd seen.

The airport needed Dad at work that night, so I wrapped a few small gifts and helped decorate the tree until he was gone. Buni went to bed early, leaving Mom and me in the kitchen.

"Mom, there's a watch at the university tonight. Michael asked me to meet him there. I told him I would."

"Aura, dear," Mom said. "That's just foolish. This time I insist. You must not go out tonight."

I knew this was my chance with Michael, and I couldn't let it pass, but I didn't want to fight with my mother on Christmas Eve. I thought of a guy named Dan who attended the university and lived on our street. He'd been at the barricades with me, so I called him to see if he wanted to help man the watch at the Engineering University at Sibiu. He was with a friend, Nicu, who also attended the university, and they both decided to go over and help . . . and yes, I could walk with them.

Mom looked at me as if I were a lost cause . . . and agreed.

The streetlights had not come on that night, so Dan carried a flashlight as the three of us left our neighborhood. Because of all the roadblocks, we decided not to take the Corso to get to the university. Instead, we walked through the farmers' market, hiding from the occasional cars that passed. I heard a pack of dogs, chasing something . . . and killing it, by the sound of the yelping.

All was dark, cold, unfamiliar. I started feeling like the hopeless idiot Mom thought I was. What if Michael wasn't even there? What if he had fallen asleep and decided to just keep on sleeping? He must have been exhausted.

Several hundred students were gathered in front of the university's main entrance on the corner of Dr. Ion Ratiu Street. Dan and Nicu joined them immediately, leaving me alone, but then I spotted Michael and another guy standing by lanterns at opposite ends of the steps, walkie-talkies in their hands. Several pretty girls stood near Michael, flirting. Yes, Mom was right. I qualified as a bona fide idiot.

I felt a piece of paper in the pocket of my coat and held it up to the dim light.

"*You are my aura.*" Another of Mom's notes, telling me that as foolish as I sometimes was, I carried the aura of love for her and from her. Her words reminded me to, as she often said, "craft the highest vision of yourself and stay true to it."

I walked by the front of the building and crossed to the other side of the street. I so wanted to talk to Michael, but I didn't want to give him the impression I was just another girl throwing myself at him.

Instead, I stared in fascination at the concrete walls of the university. No matter how stripped of individuality the place had become under the pragmatic hands of Ceaușescu's architects, the very structure of the building imposed its dream of higher learning. Students carrying lanterns clustered at intervals to replace the dark streetlights. Their dedication reminded me that I might have a future there, too. I wanted to be part of the educated class, among those who had been given the reins of the country. Maybe I wasn't an idiot after all. Maybe pushing myself to come there that night served a higher purpose than I had thought or intended.

Now I could return home. As I passed by the front of the building again, I thought I heard someone call my name. I turned.

"Aura!"

Michael was waving at me. The butterflies that had been fluttering in my stomach since my arrival lifted in nervous flight.

I crossed the street to meet him.

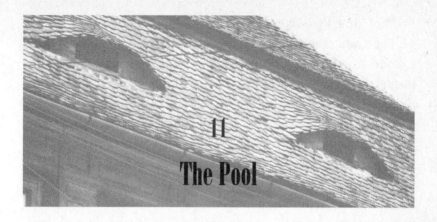

11
The Pool

"So good. You came after all," Michael said. He was standing with a few colleagues. One was telling the others what happened to him after the shooting at the Trades Union Hall. He finished the tale of his narrow escape by saying to Michael, "But what about you? I heard you were picked up at the military academy."

Michael motioned for me to step closer. "Yes, I was. Aura wanted to hear this, too." He made quick introductions.

Michael grew less tired-looking and more animated as he told his story. Perhaps needing to share these moments from the revolution was why he had felt the need to be there that night.

He said he was near the army's military school when he heard shooting coming from that direction, and went to investigate. He heard footsteps and saw a man's silhouette following him down the unlit street. The man rushed at him. Michael scrambled up and over an eight-foot cement wall, landing inside the grounds of the school. Two cadets on guard immediately took him into custody.

Michael, now dressed in blue jeans and a brown parka, described the black clothing he'd been wearing.

"So, they thought you were a terrorist, then?" the other girl in the group asked.

"Exactly my problem."

The cadets and an officer hauled Michael to the office of Colonel Aurel Dragomir, the school's commander, and shoved him inside. But Dragomir was busy, out defending the city against what he called "the securitate's rebel forces"—the terrorists who attacked innocent people. "In other words, he was out there to catch guys who looked like me," Michael said. The soldiers stripped and searched him. Michael tried to explain who he was, but the cadets ignored him. They ordered him to put his clothing back on, then tied his hands behind him and pushed him through a dark corridor and into a brightly lit gymnasium. On the hardwood floor, marked with colored lines for different sports, two groups of prisoners sat tied up, facing twenty or so armed cadets. Michael recognized the groups immediately. Those in uniform were militia officers; those in civilian suits were none other than securitate. Secu personnel always wore impeccable suits along with their arrogance.

The soldiers jabbed a gun into Michael's ribs, and he stopped close to the militia group. He noticed that while many of the militia officers had been beaten, none of the secu guys showed signs of having been roughed up. Michael sat down.

Later, Colonel Dragomir appeared, and a gray-haired, overweight secu struggled to stand. "Colonel," he said in a calm but forceful voice, "stop this charade!"

The students in the group listening to Michael reacted with surprise: "No kidding!" "Wow!" "He said *that?*"

"He did," Michael said, "and then he said, 'Stop instigating these poor tired, hungry kids against us! They're exhausted. They could easily shoot at us while falling asleep!'"

Dragomir responded with a threatening tirade, but the secu didn't flinch. The cadets became fully alert. Michael prayed that none of them would get any funny ideas about impressing their commander by firing at the unrepentant secu and starting a bloodbath.

Dragomir ranted about terrorists in the city shooting innocent people fighting for freedom, but the secu man said, "Stop lying about this! The whole securitate department was in the basement. We did not shoot! We didn't attack anyone, so find other scape-goats!"

"Liar!" Dragomir cried. "*Your* people started this chaos!"

"You know I'm telling the truth, because *you* picked us up from our headquarters' basement! *You* have the department's roster!"

"Wait a minute, Michael," one of the students listening to Michael's story interrupted. "You're saying that the secu guys were all accounted for. Right?"

"Right," Michael said, "and still the shooting went on."

"Unbelievable! Unbelievable!" said another student. "We thought the securitate were the ones doing the shooting."

"So who *was* shooting, then?" I asked. "Was it the militia?"

"No, they were all in the same place as me," Michael said. "Except the ones who had been executed by the Army at noon. They were apparently shot without any warning while they tried to surrender and get protection inside the military school."

So who had done all the shooting? Mercenaries? Terrorists? People called them different things, but their real nature remained a mystery.

Michael had spent that long night talking to the militia men. Eventually he told them that twenty or so of their colleagues were dead at the morgue and described how he and Gabriel had tried to save others from the same fate. Michael hoped none of the prisoners would try to revolt and start the guards firing.

At 9:00 AM December 23, some civilians came into the room, wearing tricolor armbands. They were revolutionaries and looked at the prisoners with hatred in their eyes. Some had AK-47s slung over their shoulders.

A militia man told Michael this was his chance to make contact with the outside world, but Michael didn't recognize any of the revolutionaries. He got closer to them and started mentioning the names of his friends. Finally, three of the revolutionaries said they'd call his parents, and another told him that if he met anyone from the University, he'd pass the information along.

Around noon, the school's second-in-command arrived, a calm man. He listened to Michael's story and promised he'd try to call Michael's father. Michael felt hopeful, but by evening, nothing had happened.

Dragomir returned to check on the captives. He seemed calmer, so Michael dared to approach him. He explained how he had been arrested and noted that he was the only civilian in the room. Someone handed Dragomir Michael's ID. Dragomir looked it over. "You live on the same street as Nicu Ceaușescu," he said, and walked away as if Michael's sins were obvious.

Night came. There had been no food or water in all this time. At least the prisoners' body heat kept the gym from freezing, so Michael slept a little. Then Dragomir and his entourage strode back in and accused the prisoners of having colleagues hiding around town poisoning the city's water system. "You murderers!" he yelled. A huge military barrel used to transport liquids had been filled with public water. The cadets pointed their guns at the prisoners as they were lined up and forced them to drink from the barrel. Michael had no doubt that the water was fine and felt grateful to finally get a drink.

Later that night more prisoners were brought in, two brutally beaten. Many of them had been arrested in their homes.

At around four in the morning, the rapid fire of automatic weapons sounded very close to the gymnasium, which was about twelve feet from the wall that separated the Military School from the civilian world. Heavy artillery fire followed, and some of the upper windows shattered. The cadets jumped to their feet. Sporadic outbursts of gunfire sounded from varying distances. Artillery explosions sent more windows crashing to the floor. The lights went out and only the dim white and green emergency exit lights provided illumination.

Dragomir appeared yet again, now wearing a combat outfit and holding an AKM. Two platoons rushed in behind him, soldiers in their early twenties. He ordered them to take positions against the outside wall. Then he turned toward the younger cadets and ordered them to arm their automatic weapons and be ready to kill if the platoons couldn't defend the building. "We are under direct attack! Enemy forces across the street are trying to free the prisoners. We will never surrender! We will waste all you murderers first!"

He left the gymnasium, and the gunfire slowed down. Michael heard the sinister sound of the heavy armor rolling nearby, and felt the vibration the tanks caused. Then the shooting ceased. Michael heard voices exchanging information and assumed the tank's officers were talking to the men from the platoons.

At dawn, Dragomir appeared again and announced proudly that "the terrorists" had been chased by his troops into a house next door, and surrounded. He never bothered to give further explanations, so no one ever found out who the so-called terrorists were, or if they were mercenaries, who they were working for. No one even verified their existence.

Around 7:00 AM on December 24, Michael and the other prisoners were escorted from the gymnasium at gunpoint. Dragomir had decided to move them to a more secure area. They entered an even bigger building that housed an Olympic-sized pool, drained of water. Piles of mattresses lined the pool's edge. The prisoners were told to throw the mattresses inside the basin and lie on them.

Michael descended into the dry pool with a hundred and fifty other prisoners. Forty armed guards stood around them. Militia and securitate prisoners were supposed to be judged by the military court, but was a bloodbath considered a simpler alternative? Hungry, thirsty, exhausted, and feeling abandoned, Michael was more depressed than he'd been since he'd gotten arrested.

Finally, in the early afternoon, his name was called. He had to work his way to the ladder to get out of the pool. Some of the old militia guys wished him good luck. One asked Michael to tell everybody what had happened there. Another one said to tell people they were innocent, that all this was a charade, all Dragomir's fault.

Michael's friend Gabriel had come with Nicolae, a close friend of Michael's family, to vouch for Michael, insisting that he not only wasn't a mercenary or terrorist but was actually part of the revolution, a man who had helped to organize the protest rally at the Trades Union Hall. They were allowed to take him off the grounds.

People cheered at the end of Michael's story and swamped him with questions. Michael had often turned to look at me during the telling—more than at anyone else, I thought.

A little before midnight, Dan and Nicu found me and said they were ready to leave.

Michael heard. "Glad you came," he said, and gave me a light kiss on the cheek.

I thought about that kiss all the way home.

12

Red Christmas

I STILL FELT IT ON MY CHEEK WHEN I AWOKE LATE ON CHRISTMAS DAY to find the family gathered, not around our Christmas tree, but around the TV set. Knees contorted, a dead body on the screen lay face up in a black coat and navy blue suit, white shirt, and red tie, a distinctive black Astrakhan hat lying next to him. The sight of Nicolae Ceaușescu's big forehead, white hair sticking up, and darkened blood at his temple shocked me. His neck was twisted to one side, leaving no doubt that the man I'd hated and feared since childhood was dead. The camera shifted from Ceaușescu's corpse to that of his wife, fallen in the opposite direction after their execution. Blood streaked Elena's hair and had formed a grotesque little rivulet at a right angle to her body. Their hands had been tied behind their backs, and they looked like wax dummies.

Apparently Elena and Nicolae Ceaușescu and their entire Central Committee had been caught the day before while trying to flee the country in a helicopter. According to the TV news anchormen, they had been found guilty of genocide, massacring unarmed civilians, stealing billions of dollars and hiding it in foreign banks, and destroying Romania's economy, people's lives, and communal properties. The military tribunal charged them, and the firing squad mowed them down.

This was the end of Ceaușescu's tyranny, and hopefully, the end of Communism in Romania. The tyrant and his wife were dead, but their hasty court-martial and its delayed news release aroused a flurry of unanswered questions.

I felt an overwhelming happiness and relief, but at the same time, a bleak sadness for all who lost their lives during this memorable holiday. How could I celebrate the birth of Jesus Christ when people were burying their loved ones?

Christmas was not white that year. Christmas was red.

Yet, we couldn't help ourselves. We were thrilled the Ceaușescus were gone. Our modest Christmas tree was decorated with cookies and a few red glass ornaments. Mom had bought some small gifts for everyone from the bonus money she made at her job. Beneath the tree lay small homemade chocolates and opera wafers, wrapped in colorful paper also from Mom's work. Christmas carols, normally heard in the streets, were missing, but we listened to some on our cassette recorder, the one Uncle Nelu had bought for us at "The Shop" using Deutsche marks.

Sarmale—stuffed cabbage with meat and rice—paired up with polenta and sour cream represented our Christmas dinner, along with homemade pickles, the pork we had to roast before it spoiled, and homemade red wine for Mom and Buni. Dad had never touched alcohol in his life, and I made the same choice. We ate our modest feast with quiet cheer, so grateful to be together, celebrating and unharmed. No one pointed out that there was no guarantee that whoever came to power next would offer any improvement, yet we all silently wondered, *How could we trust a revolution whose original agents never showed themselves? A revolution that left people in charge who carried out immediate executions and controlled the news releases?*

After that shocking holiday, Romania stood up, dusted itself off, and went back to work. We had gas and electricity. Our water was pronounced safe to drink. I heard the distant roar and mournful whistles of freight trains. Buses ran. A few businesses reopened. Anarchy had not set in, yet no one really knew what to expect next.

I vowed I'd plunge back into studying for my university entrance exam in July. I'd always hitched my dreams to education's star, but the combination of revolution and being near Michael had addled my sense of the future. In high school I'd originally selected a science emphasis, although literature, both Romanian and English, was my true passion. My English teacher in the seventh grade, Liliana Ciocoi-Pop, had made her classes so interesting with her positive attitude and knowledge of the world beyond Romania's borders that I hoped to choose foreign languages— especially English—as my major area in high school. Not only was Ms. Ciocoi-Pop attractive and charismatic, she dressed in high fashion—despite the strictures of the Communist regime. Everybody turned to watch her walk through the corridors. I wanted to be like her. In high school, however, the only major offered that was even close to what I wanted was philology, an area of scholarship combining linguistics with literary studies.

Anything concerning foreign languages was frowned upon at the time. Ceaușescu had essentially closed Romania's borders, and so, he reasoned, why would anyone ever need to know a foreign language, let alone the literary heritage of another country? Besides, to be truly employable, one needed a background in science, math, or engineering. So I'd chosen science. I knew, though, that in college I'd want to return to the humanities. In my senior year, I decided to cram a four-year program into seven months so I could take the college entrance exams in July.

When I was invited to a New Year's Eve party, I declined. I had to study.

Charles Dickens lay open before me. *Bleak House*. I read the same page three times, and then slammed the book shut. What was the point? Would the new regime tolerate literature more than the old one? Would they even support education? For all I knew, admittance standards to universities might become even more stringent due to scarcity of resources. So much had been destroyed, and who knew how Romania would get the capital to rebuild? If a university diploma still twinkled up there in my destiny, it hid behind a cloud of uncertainty.

And then there was Michael. I knew he liked me, but in retrospect it seemed that his "good night" had held an edge of "goodbye." His kiss, while not exactly brotherly, suggested he thought I was a child. At eighteen, I was still a virgin. I wanted to turn twenty-one, and then sleep with the love of my life—Michael. Yet, of course, a grown man like Michael couldn't be expected to wait for a girl to grow up. He would be with other women. . . . Oh, I didn't like that thought at all.

Four days of nearly useless study passed. I tossed my books aside and looked at myself in the mirror, a halo of celebrity stickers around my image. Michael Jackson, Kim Wilde, Duran Duran, Sandra, Don Johnson, Kylie Minogue, Jennifer Grey, Eros Ramazotti—all saying the same thing: "Live your life; make something happen; seize the day; seize the night; do *something!*"

I had to get out of the house. Perhaps my gym, Obor, had reopened. Dressed in my sweats, I took off jogging toward it, passing Suru. The boards over the windows had come down, and the zombie crowd had gathered again—except now they were a bit raucous, celebrating the revolution, the end of a ghastly decade, and the impending new year. Romania's alcohol consumption had long since soared above that of Western European countries where people had to drink responsibly in order to keep jobs and pay mortgages and save for vacations. None of these issues concerned Romanians, who under the Communist regime had held jobs for life, though they might be transferred for poor performance. Romanians could keep houses that were inherited before 1947, or else pay low rent on state-owned apartments. Traveling outside the Communist bloc wasn't allowed, and ninety percent of the population didn't earn enough money to afford it in any case. So drinking and smoking were Romanians' main recreations.

To my grateful surprise, the gym had opened its doors. I worked out like an Olympic athlete, trying to lift, pull, push, run, and sweat my fears and confusion away. Romania's national body-building team had trained at Obor for years, and I'd learned a few tricks from the pros. Posters of Arnold Schwarzenegger hung all over the training room, and I'd started paying attention to the success he created for himself through bodybuilding, courage, and persistence.

I loved the way athletics always gave me an emotional boost. I'd been swimming since I was three and speed-skating since I was seven; I took ballet classes in grades one through eight, played on the volleyball team in high school, and went out for track and field as well. I had learned to trust my own strength, stamina, and self-discipline.

My best friend, Monika, and her sister made me want to carry physical fitness even further into self-defense. They practiced *kyokushin kaikan*, a style of stand-up, full-contact karate, rooted in a philosophy of self-improvement, discipline, and hard training that included realistic combat and physical toughness—all done in total secrecy, because the Communist regime forbade martial arts. Monika moved fast from one belt to another by passing rigorous exams, and she shared with me some of the concepts, inspiring me with the power of concentration and purpose.

As a result, I didn't ordinarily fear the dark or people who were older and stronger than I was. I often jogged the unlit streets of Sibiu after my school sports practices late in the evenings. I went to jazz and folk concerts at the stadium and returned by myself at 2:00 AM, walking home in the middle of the road, though my parents admonished me for my "pointless bravery," perhaps a diplomatic way of saying "foolhardiness."

Jogging home in the cold December evening after my workout, I felt better, until I remembered I had nothing but books waiting for me. I needed something to look forward to. When I got home, I called one of the sisters of the guy who was throwing the New Year's Eve party I had been invited to.

"I decided I need a break from studying," I said to his sister, "and if the offer is still open, I'd like to come to the party."

"Oh, great! Peter will be especially glad!" There was a certain lilt in her voice.

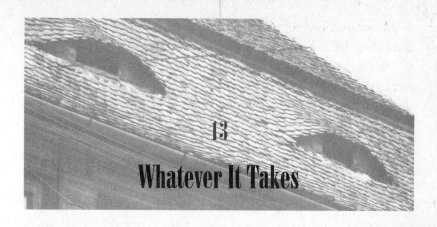

13
Whatever It Takes

P ETER . I SIGHED . P ETER HAD A BIT OF A CRUSH ON ME . I HAD NEVER
been shy, and many young fellows took me out on dates, but they
typified the boring young Communists that aspired to government
jobs. Peter was one of them, and though I was close to his sisters
and had considered them all as friends of my family for the last
ten years, none of this would put Peter's picture on my pillow in
place of Michael's.

Mom understood my dilemma and turned to her grapevine.
After work the next day, she came home with something in her
purse she'd bought from a coworker at the Victory factory. "I told
Veronika I wanted you to have a new party outfit. She said she'd
bought a really special one from one of her relatives in Germany.
When she told me the color, I thought it would be stunning with
your hair."

"Emerald green?" At the time, my hair was long, curly, and
dyed dark brown with red accents.

"No. . ." She removed three small folded garments, all a lavender knit, shimmering with woven silver. "Oh, dear. Veronika said
she couldn't fit into the outfit anymore. I can see why."

She handed me a skirt and top that looked like a girl of ten might wear comfortably and *iegari* (leggings). And then I realized the potential. I quickly pulled on the super-tight leggings and slipped on the matching puffed mini-skirt, which tightened into a band at mid-thigh. The tight top featured little off-shoulder puffed sleeves. When I moved, silver gleamed along my curves.

Mom's mouth dropped open. "Buni!" she called. "Come see this!"

Mom disappeared as Buni rushed in the room. Buni, who'd helped me design and sew many a trendy outfit, eyed me worriedly. "Oh, it's truly *you!* But it might be best not to let Fanel see you in this. You'll have to wear your coat to get out of the house!"

I hugged her, and Mom hurried back into my room, carrying the highest pair of pointed-toe stilettos I'd ever seen. They were glossy with black lace on top. I'd forgotten she had them because there was hardly ever an occasion to wear them. She'd bought them from another friend who, in turn, had bought them from someone in France.

Even though at five feet seven inches I was taller than Mom, her shoes only pinched a tiny bit when I slipped them on. They also elevated me to a height of five feet ten. I strutted a few dance moves before the mirror and, excited about life again, I called Dana, my friend since first grade, a neighbor until eighth grade.

"What time are you going to the party?" I asked her.

"Nine," she answered. Most New Year's Eve parties started late and then went on until 4:00 or 5:00 in the morning. People would crash on the floor, then wake to continue the party on into the next night.

I explained about my studies. "I'd love to go with you, though, Dana. Would you settle for going over for three hours or so? Leaving about 10:30?"

She seemed glad not to have to stay for the whole marathon.

On December 31, I studied during the day while a gentle rain fell. By nightfall, ice coated everything, creating a festive sparkle from passing headlights. Dana loved my outfit, but understood why I didn't want to walk even a short distance on ice in the stilettos, so we called a cab.

Only the previous week, before the revolution, traveling in Romania had been very difficult. My parents had never owned a car. Gas was always beyond our budget and driving was overly regulated. Ceaușescu's government, afraid of big crowds getting together and plotting against him, had allowed drivers to travel only every other weekend, depending on whether their license number was odd or even. As a result, people were forced to plan their outings well ahead of time, often only with those friends whose license numbers were compatible with their own. Getting a cab had been almost as difficult, entailing at least a forty-five minute wait.

But all that had changed. Already taxicabs abounded. Dana and I climbed inside one and promptly put our lives in danger. On the main streets, cars were sliding from one side to the other, as if the pavement had become an ice-skating rink.

Somehow we arrived safely at the two-story house Peter's family had just given him. His sister told me the place was still spartan inside, and he was having a housewarming party that coinciding with the New Year's Eve celebration. Two couches, one black and one white, had been pushed against the wall of the first floor's sizable living room, allowing partiers plenty of space. Despite the temptations of a pool table and bar, people were already sliding their shoes to a Michael Jackson tune. Colored paper streamers hung from a dim lamp in the ceiling, and a few Christmas decorations and candles added a bit of festivity to an otherwise empty room with stark white walls.

The warmth inside the house made coats uncomfortable, so Dana and I hung ours up in the entry closet. The silver in my outfit glittered in the semi-darkness, making me a focal point, and all eyes were on me. A circle formed around me. Would I like a beer? Homemade wine? Tuica? "Thank you, no; maybe later." Pepsi? Borsec mineral water? "I'm fine, thanks." Would I like to dance?

"Actually, I'm starving," I said, "so I'll just check out the refreshments, thanks. Excuse me." I smiled as I headed toward the open kitchen, squeezing between two fellows.

Peter and his sisters had presented a respectable spread, and many guests had undoubtedly brought food as well. Generous trays covered the countertops: biscuits beside thin slices of hard-boiled eggs and ham cut so thinly you could see through it; modest sandwiches of *parizer* (similar to bologna) sprinkled with Schweitzer cheese and bits of pickle; pizza made with canned mushrooms, a black market delicacy; cookies, lemon pie, chocolate cake.

My plate loaded with goodies, I joined Dana, who was gossiping with Peter's sisters.

With some alcohol in their blood, partiers became world travelers. A tape of Dixieland jazz took us to Bourbon Street in New Orleans. Duran Duran and the Police took us to England. We rocked to Tina Turner and Michael Jackson. Music had the power to free our imaginations and take us anywhere in the world. No passports, visas, or money needed.

I began to regret wearing my tight outfit. Young men stared brashly at me as they downed glass after glass, and their behavior turned a little cheeky. I had dressed to dazzle, but I was beginning to feel more like prey. I felt tremendous relief when Peter materialized in front of me. Everyone else backed off. Peter was militaristic in his posture and haircut, with bulging muscles and prominent veins: a body-builder. He stood over six feet tall, and his powerful voice commanded attention. Aged twenty-three, with black hair and deep blue eyes, he was definitely boyfriend material, yet there was simply no fascination on my part. "Hey, beautiful," he said. "Can I give you a tour of the house?"

"I would like that."

I gratefully followed him upstairs. He showed me a small room, then another larger one, both with only a few pieces of furniture and three carpets rolled up and standing in a corner. Two new chairs were still wrapped in plastic, probably to remain this way for years. Romanians were careful with their furniture because they would probably be using it for three generations.

He led me into his own bedroom with its bed, another rolled rug lying against a wall, an unlit gas stove, and next to the bed, a stool that held a bottle of red wine and two glasses. *He had planned this.* Smiling, Peter poured wine into the glasses.

"To say cheers," he said, "and drink to my new house."

I was beginning to think that wasn't all he was after.

I smiled and pretended to take a sip of the wine. He downed his, poured himself another and placed the bottle unsteadily back on the stool. His eyes were bloodshot. I took a step toward the door, my alarms definitely going off.

"Nice house, with a huge potential," I said. "So happy for you!"

Peter stepped toward me, smiling only with his lips. "Well, you can make me even happier tonight."

My skin tightened, but I kept my tone light. "I thought you were happy because I came to your party." I made it to the door.

He moved closer. "Aura. The moment you sleep with me, this house will be yours, too." Wine spilled from his glass and dribbled over his knuckles.

I pulled on the handle; the door did not move. There was no key in the lock. I was trapped. I turned to face him.

"Peter, is this a bad joke? Give me the key."

He was no longer smiling. "Take off your clothes," he said.

All I could think at first was that this was ridiculous. We'd never even gone out on a *date.*

"Now! Take your clothes off *now.* You will make love to me."

"Peter." I kept my voice calm, reasonable. Inside I felt stupid. "Peter, I am a virgin still."

"I know that, but because I will be the first one, you will love me *after.*"

"Peter . . . we've always been friends." With every word, it was harder to maintain the soothing voice. The walls of the house muffled all sound, music, voices. "I like you as a *friend.* And I want to be your *friend* in the future. Making love to you is not appropriate. I intend to be a virgin until I turn twenty-one. Please just understand my wish. I know you care for me, so you will consider it."

He stared at me, eyes red, face flushed.

Someone knocked at the door. "Aura, are you there?" Dana's voice. Peter's eyes narrowed.

"Aura, are you there? Answer me."

As I opened my mouth, Peter's two huge palms covered half my face, squeezing my lips and nose, blocking my airways. I heard Dana's footsteps retreating. Peter's eyes stared into mine, inches away, the cruel, uncaring eyes of a predator. Then, like a stalker who knows it's in charge, he released me. A cat with a mouse. I backed toward the window.

He might have been twice my size, but he was also drunk and thick-headed with desire. I had to think. "I can't breathe," I gasped. "I need air." I opened the window and looked down to see icy concrete: broken bones, serious injury. Still, that was better than—

Peter grabbed me from behind, lifted me, and hurled me on the bed. He started pulling off his shirt, looming over me.

I tried the voice of a pouty kitten. "Peter, I'm cold. It's too cold to take my clothes off."

He blinked, drunkenly confused. I gave him a timid smile. In my head I heard Monika's karate master's words. *Focus on your purpose. Find a way, no matter what.*

Peter turned and staggered toward the stove. He was still between me and the door, but in order to light the stove he would have to adjust the burner with one hand while turning on the gas with the other. In that moment I would leap over, push his face against the burner and set him on fire. In that moment, I felt no mercy, as if my blood carried fury through my veins. There was no way I was wasting my eighteen years of virginity on this beast; before that happened, one of us would die.

Abruptly, Peter swung around; he had figured out my ruse. Looking even more barbaric, veins popping out at his temples, he trudged toward me, then stopped—and turned off the light.

In the sudden darkness, I hated him fiercely and knew I'd fight to the death over my honor. But before I could move he had lunged through the gloom and pinned me to the bed, his weight and strength far too much for me. Grunting like a beast, he pulled off my shoes, tore off my blouse and skirt. But the leggings were too tight for him; he couldn't get a grip on them. This enraged him, and his hot winey breath suffocated me as he clawed at the fabric. *Find a way. Find a way.* My heart beat faster. My leg muscles tightened with gathering strength. I arched my back, and with a burst of power, drew my legs up and thrust them against his chest. Unprepared, shocked, he grabbed at empty air and hurtled backward to the floor with a great *thunk.*

Topless, I jumped out of bed and groped through the blackness for a weapon. My hand found the wine bottle on the stool, and I smashed it on the edge. Wine gushed down my legs. Gripping the jagged neck of the bottle top in my right hand, I touched the cold wall with my left hand and braced myself.

Muffled footfalls, the smell of sour breath and sweat. My stomach churned, but I dared not throw up or run. I made myself wait. I heard harsh breathing, right in front of me. Without thinking, I thrust the jagged edge of the bottle neck forward as hard as I could. It struck something, and Peter screamed. His hand groped past me; I felt the wind of it. Bending lower, I lunged again.

"Aughhh!" Peter cried. "What did you do to me? Oh God, I'm bleeding . . ."

Then, silence.

I held the broken bottle at my chest, ready to attack again.

Heavy footsteps moved away from me. The light flipped on, and I blinked, as blinded by the light as I had been by the dark. The first thing that came into focus was the blood on the floor and the wall, its smell bizarrely intoxicating. I'd never done anything like this before, but I felt powerful for drawing this blood. The morgue scene flashed in my mind. I pictured Peter's body there, and wished it were so.

Peter stood in the light, still between me and the door. He looked astonished at the two cuts on his body, one in his right side at the waist, and the other on his right thigh. Blood ran freely from both. He grabbed a white shawl off the bed and tied it around his waist. He tore his white T-shirt to bandage his leg.

He glared at me, anger all but steaming off of him. "You are not going to leave this room alive."

"Try me," I said. The sight of his blood built my confidence. "The next time you drink water, you won't be able to hold it inside you because of all the holes I'll gouge in you, you filthy bastard."

"You're out of your mind!"

"Thanks to you."

He took two steps toward me.

I raised the bottle neck; blood dripped off the end. "Stop. I'm not joking."

He halted, scowled, then looked at the T-shirt on his thigh. Completely red. Blood dripped onto the floor.

"Pass me the key to the door," I said. "Now."

"Come and get it," he said.

"Put it on the floor and push it toward me," I said. "You're the one running out of time, not me."

His improvised bandages were a bloody mess. His face had taken on a greenish tint. All at once he bent down, put the key on the wooden floor and pushed it toward me. I picked it up, and somehow managed to dress myself in my shredded clothes without ever taking my eyes off him or lowering my weapon. Bedraggled, bloodied, torn, wine-stained.

"Step away from the door."

"You wish."

"I'm not playing games," I said. "I have no remorse. I will kill you. Step aside."

Finally, he lumbered back over to the heater. I slipped around him and unlocked the door.

Dana stood on the other side. Pale and shivering, she looked at me, then at the broken bottle in my hand, then at Peter. "Aura, are you okay? Oh, my God. Did he . . . ?"

"I'll tell you on our way home."

"I'll get your coat." She dashed downstairs.

Peter's friend's head popped through the doorway. The way his gaze shifted told me he'd known about the whole setup. I pointed over my shoulder with the broken bottle. "Call an ambulance or drive him to the emergency room." I looked back at Peter. He stood in a surly hunch, pale, bleeding, naked. Remorseless. Stupid.

Dana returned with my coat, and I pulled it on. I grabbed her arm and walked downstairs carefully in my stilettos. The music still blared, but I sensed eyes on us as we headed outside. I looked at no one. We walked away in the icy darkness. I shivered and concentrated on not slipping.

"I guess it's New Year's Day," I finally said.

"Welcome to 1990," she said. "Oh, my God, Aura, I am so sorry!" Tears rolled down her cheeks. "You should go to the militia tonight. Right now. I'll go with you."

"No. I'll only tell my Mom. My Dad would kill Peter. I don't want Dad to go to jail. I can't let Peter ruin my family. We need to forget about this. If we complain to the militia and sue Peter, his father will just get a certificate from a psychiatrist saying that Peter's mentally disturbed, but *nothing* will happen to him. And the whole city will know about me. Nobody will believe that the attempt was unsuccessful. I don't want people's pity."

"Aura, you're so brave," she said, putting her arm around me for comfort. "I would not have been able to stop him from raping me."

"I could have killed him, Dana." *Whatever it takes.*

Part II

After the Bleakest Night

"Out of the bleakest winter nights
come the hungriest wolves."

—*Imbarus family proverb*

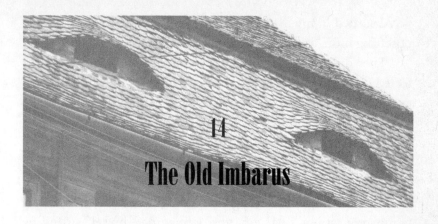

14
The Old Imbarus

On January 1, 1990, I woke to the sound of bells ringing. I lay for a while, listening. I hadn't even known the bells existed. Later, I found out that they had rung from a previously hidden chapel in the mental hospital.

I could hear Mom's voice in the kitchen. Her beautiful high-heeled shoes lay on the floor, but now they looked silly to me. I dressed in my jeans and my revolution boots, but although freedom rang in the lives of all Romanians, a zombie would have seemed more alive than I felt that morning. I didn't feel like celebrating. The irony was just too much. I had played a tiny part in the revolution, but I hadn't been wounded during it or had to hurt anyone else. And then, when the revolution's worst danger was over, I was attacked—by a "friend." Only then did I draw blood. And now I felt . . . at once empty and grimly powerful, dull and hyper-alert. And angry! An anger I couldn't show to my loved ones. If my zombie self couldn't choke it back, I would erupt into a biting, clawing, kicking, screaming rage.

My father was oblivious to the disaster at the party; he didn't notice my internal turmoil. When Buni left the room, he threw the paper down. "I just read that the cemetery is a disaster. Rebels took cover there while fighting Ceaușescu's canine units."

Absorbed in my own problems, I didn't understand what was upsetting him. "Why did the rebels want to hurt the dogs?"

"They didn't. They wanted to destroy the elite teams that protected the tovarasi. What I'm worried about is your grandfather's grave. I don't want Buni to know. Your mom and I are going to the cemetery to see, and to pay respects. I hope you'll come, too."

The graveyard sounded like the right spot for a zombie like me. I would go for Buni, who couldn't walk that far. She missed Grandpa so much I sometimes worried about her, though she always showed me her strong side. Like Buni, I had to show my family my strong side, too, and I imagined myself sitting by Grandpa's headstone, mentally spilling my troubles and listening to what he might advise. Oddly, I knew the graveyard might be the only place that would soothe the violent thing inside me that day.

In the backyard, Buni cut holly branches with a few red berries still clinging to them, and wrapped them in newsprint for me so I could take them to arrange on Grandpa's grave.

As my parents and I walked to the central cemetery at the edge of the city, memories of the previous night began to shift into the background, displaced by memories of Grandpa.

My closeness to Grandpa formed a connection that I would later understand as having a mystical side, although at the time I had no idea what that meant. I actually remember things from when I was a baby. I was eleven months old, sitting outside on my favorite pink blanket with white fluffy clouds on it. I looked up and saw the same clouds above me, except that they were on a blue background. I can still remember my concentration as I slowly gathered my strength to rise closer to those clouds in that vast blue above me. When I stood, I remember feeling some kind of pure baby rapture. I was later told my dad was nearby, working out with his exercise bars, but I have no memory of that. I heard the main gate's rattle and click, and saw Grandpa. He looked at me with delight, dropping the two bags of produce from the farmers' market. He moved toward me, reaching out, an assurance that I could take my first steps toward him without fear. I wobbled over to him, and he grabbed me in his arms, tears in his eyes, beaming with joy.

Grandpa carried a nice cane of carved wood, more as a prop of distinction than for actual support. After I started walking, I would pick it up and help myself walk with it. Whatever Grandpa touched seemed to me like a talisman that carried protective powers.

He walked to the markets several times a week and pampered me each time with a small surprise: a chocolate, a paper doll, a ribbon, a little ring. He pulled me on my sled in the winter. And yet he also treated me as if I were grown up. He and Buni both taught me to look forward to the future, one befitting an inquisitive, energetic achiever. Even at a young age, I wanted that future.

Buni and Grandpa thought I was the darling of the world. They taught me to read and write by the time I was four years old. Grandpa took me on endless walks down sunny streets and through parks, chatting on and on, explaining the rules of physics, chemistry, Darwin's theory and DNA. Often we returned to our row of chestnuts, still holding hands, having dissected the roots of existentialism and the ontological question: why? Grandpa had Sisyphean patience to clearly explain a concept at the level a five-year-old child could not only understand, but also use to light small fires of curiosity. I assaulted Grandpa with questions about all the tricks of nature, from the production of chlorophyll to the system of human arteries and veins.

My early childhood with him was an adventure where we played the roles of Apaches, discovering tracks in the mud. For me a footprint was not just an indentation. It became the imprint of a history. I would try to read how long the print had been there, how tall or heavy the person was who left it. Evidence and meaning lay all around us, and it was our challenge and delight to decipher it. The warmth of his hands, his low, calm, self-composed voice, the small steps he would take to make me comfortable at my own little pace—all of these gifts from my grandfather nurtured in me an excitement for and a love of life.

This was a man who had once known wealth and elegance, a man whose worldly treasures had been stolen by dictators. Yet he still found joy in his love for Buni and his family, and especially in my achievements. I think I embodied hope for him. When I received handmade crowns of roses in recognition of my achievements at school, it brought smiles to my family's dispirited faces and special hugs and cheers from my grandparents. When Dad would come home from the grind of work, aggravated by the office politics involved in working with Communist Party members, I would pester him with endless questions. Sometimes he shooed me away, and Grandpa would say in his gentle voice, "Enjoy this, Fanel. A child is a gift from heaven." Grandpa's words always calmed and soothed everyone.

If Buni and Mom gossiped about our married neighbor coming home with another man, Grandpa would cut the conversation short, asking, "And how is this helping us? This is a negative cloud you are gathering. We don't need that on this house."

I sat with him on a park bench one day, both of us silent, when something happened that I later considered remarkable. It was as if the air had become serene and pure, not something to breathe, but something that filled every cell of my body. Without looking at Grandpa, I knew he was experiencing it, too. I don't know how long we sat that way together. The only word I ever heard that attempted to capture such a sensation was *transcendental*. This happened often with me and Grandpa after that—whether we were sitting under a tree or on a chair by the window. If I went into the kitchen after such an experience, Mom and Buni's chatter sounded like a railway station with many voices echoing left and right.

I remember, to the instant, when our bond came to an end.

I was in the first grade and sitting in class when a pain rose in my chest. This wasn't one of my asthma pains, though it took my breath away. I always knew with asthma that there was pollen in the air, or mold, or that it came because I just couldn't get warm. But this day the pain went deep, and I knew it had nothing to do with the world outside. It was 9:00 AM, and my desk, the teacher, the other students—all disappeared. I saw only Grandpa, as if in a waking dream. He was waving goodbye to me.

I don't know how I got through school that morning. On the road home for lunch, my vision of Grandpa changed. I saw him over and over again, waving farewell, and I knew something terrible had happened. When I opened the door at home, Mom was in tears, unable to finish a sentence. I knew that my beloved Grandpa had died, and Mom eventually told me it had happened at 9:00 that morning.

A bomb exploding next to our house couldn't have affected me more. The empty shaft his death left in my childhood was like the side of a house blown away, leaving a sudden exposure to the harshness around me that I hadn't seen before. And yet, with his death also came visions, dreams, déjà vu, and eerie certainties of events before they happened, events that always came true in some form. I can't explain these things, yet they seemed connected to something vast, as if our souls marched through time together, changing bodies and circumstances, but always recognizing an uncanny bond, like that of Buni who bumped into Grandpa and felt that her soul and his had somehow identified each other. Or like that of a baby standing independently for the first time, reaching for the cosmos, fearless in her first steps because of the love of one who would always be with her, throughout time.

As we passed along the edge of the Dumbrava Forest, tears flowed down my cheeks. Mom gave me a little hug. Dad asked, "Thinking about Grandpa?"

I nodded, imagining sitting by his grave, listening for his words of wisdom, his vision for me and my future. If I didn't pass the upcoming exams, I'd be disappointing him, giving him no return for his investment of patience, his gifts of brilliance, his lessons of life's fascinations. I so wished he could speak to me again.

"I wish he'd lived to see Ceauşescu's defeat," Dad said.

The cemetery lay ahead on our left. We could already see severed trees that had slammed down onto vaults, shattering the stone slabs. We crossed the road, and from inside the gates, saw wooden crosses riddled with bullet holes, tombstones cracked and shattered, cement walkways broken up. Crypts and tombs had been excavated and coffins destroyed, the outcome of a wrath so powerful it extended to the dead.

Many of the tovarasi—who were so much more "equal" than the rest of us—had been buried in the fancier graves. In the past, when we visited this city of the dead, a recent interment in a marble-lined crypt would provoke a comment like, "Ah, a tovarasi, gone to meet the Maker in whom he didn't believe." The tovarasi lay mostly in the Romanian section, because the dead insisted on segregation. Romanians wouldn't live near Hungarians or Germans. The deceased Jews rested in a gated ghetto. No matter that they were all equally dead.

Not one neighborhood of the old necropolis had escaped destruction. The only place that looked at all peaceful was a hastily-built new section.

Though we'd heard news that common graves for unclaimed victims of the revolution were necessary in Timisoara and Bucharest, in Sibiu there were specific plots in a small area labeled *Heroes of the Revolution,* where hundreds were interred in humble coffins. Only God knew who they really were or if the uniformly modest cement markers really sheltered the one named, a body thought to correspond with the names of people on the "missing" lists.

On this New Year's Day of mixed emotions, many others had come to the cemetery. They all registered shock and sorrow at the devastation of a place that had protected their loved ones' eternities. Crews of gravediggers excavated the frozen land, lamenting. They had never seen so much suffering, they said.

We passed a mother imploring God: "Please take me instead. Please, give my son back. He was only nineteen."

The gravediggers stopped for a minute as if waiting for God's response as well. Other mourners looked equally willing to cross death's boundaries in the absence of their dear ones. I heard cries of desperation, saw a fist raised to an invisible God. How much suffering could this country endure?

We searched among the broken, slanted, or missing headstones for Grandpa's resting place. Nothing looked familiar. As if in a maze, the three of us wandered among the scattered memorials. The Communist regime had taken away our properties, and now the revolution seemed to have taken away our dead.

Where was my grandfather? I needed to reconnect with him and his reminder of my powerful family; I needed him to brighten my wounded spirits. I needed something to chase what had happened the previous night completely from my mind.

"Do you know where the Imbarus plot is?" Mom asked one of the gravediggers.

"Imbarus . . . ?" The fellow set his pick down. "Oh, ma'am, you're far from the site. It's way over there." He pointed to our left. "I knew the old Imbarus. What a gentleman. He always used to give me spare money when he would come to pay his respects to his family. All buried in the same place . . ." He looked around at the chaos. "May they rest in peace." He crossed himself and pointed again to where we should go. "See that far stand of pines? Just south of them. . . . There's a lot of damage . . ."

"Thank you." Mom put a coin in his hand.

We found Grandpa's headstone undamaged, along with those of other Imbarus ancestors, but the everlasting wreaths were gone. No vases. None of the fat candles or their holders. Broken bits of other headstones lay around, and shattered glass. Frozen boot prints showed that the ground had been trampled. I thought of Grandpa telling me to learn from the prints. They matched those at our front door.

"Mercenaries were here, too." Dad had noticed, too. He hung his head, fists clenched.

"I hope whoever did this . . ." Mom couldn't finish the thought, but added, "If nothing is sacred, how can a new revolution offer any more hope than the old regime?"

I lay Buni's holly—unarranged, without a vase—beside the stone.

I felt violated. Again.

15

Fata Morgana

STATISTICS FROM THE REVOLUTION TALLIED UP THE CHAOS AND MISERY: 1,104 dead and 3,352 wounded. The National Museum of Art in Bucharest had been severely burned, as had the Central University Library. Millions of bullets had been fired by "mercenaries" from tactical positions, hidden corners, and armored transports; young people were found shot in the head; burned human bodies and their ashes were thrown in canals. The ultimate losses and destruction were never totaled. The National Salvation Front had played the major role in overthrowing the Communist regime and had attracted the world's attention and sympathy.

And then the questions began. Had we truly erupted in revolution, or just been manipulated into legitimizing a coup d'état?

Certain western journalists would conclude that Romania dealt with a popular revolt. When I gazed into the eyes of the revolution's widows and son-less mothers, it seemed like one; when I looked at the frozen spatters of blood and the single bloody shoes trampled by tanks, it seemed like that; when I listened to the endless cries echoing off the walls of decrepit buildings eaten up by mold from unheated winters, it felt like that. But there was something that didn't quite fit.

The beaten men in my vision, the ones who felt unjustly accused—were they the ones I'd seen in the morgue? The ones Michael had tried to save? I knew in my bones there was something unjust in all this.

The National Salvation Front had appeared eight months before the revolution and not been crushed by the merciless Ceaușescu. Why not?

Who else—besides the people—wanted to get rid of Ceaușescu? Was it the Romanian Communist Party Executive Council that had tried unsuccessfully to force the Communist leadership to resign en masse, allowing a new government to emerge peacefully—one that was more in step with the Gorbachev-approved reforms? Had a group of military officers staged a conspiracy against Ceaușescu and his regime? Had the KGB been involved? The CIA? *Who had sent in the mercenaries?*

Was this Revolution real or was it what Romanians call a Fata Morgana?

Fata Morgana—the Italian name for Morgan le Fay, the fairy shape-shifting half-sister of King Arthur—referred to a mirage, an optical phenomenon, resulting from distant temperature inversions. Clouds and islands beyond the horizon are reflected upside-down above the horizon, as if the inversion layer were a mirror, creating far pavilions, palisades, castles in the air. Oh, we wanted to believe in a glorious Romanian Revolution, but those pesky questions persisted. A layer of truth seemed inverted.

What kind of world did I inhabit where my dreams and déjà vu proved true but a revolution involving millions of people turned into a mass illusion?

Later, people at my school sang a little rhyme:

Cine-a tras în noi 16–22?
Cine-a tras în noi după 22?
Doamne, cât o să mai minți
Copilașii prin părinți?

Doamne, cat o să mai ții
Ucigașii de copii?

Who fired on us on the 16–22?
Who fired on us after the 22?
God, how much longer will you allow the lies?
And kids to hear lies through their parents?
God, how much longer will you harbor
The killers of children?

I tried to focus on finishing my last year of high school and studying for exams, but our country's drama of power rushing in to fill a vacuum demanded attention and created more uncertainty. To make things even more unsettling, the revolution and my own near-rape had become entwined in my mind. Was everything about the strong trying to force their will upon the weak?

I watched the news constantly, and attended speeches and rallies at the university. I always looked for Michael, but he seemed to have disappeared—although not from my pillow. I needed to say good night to someone gentle like him, a man who would never, ever try to rape a woman. His picture saw me through this rough time.

At the end of January, five thousand miners went to Victoria Square in Bucharest in support of the National Salvation Front. The front's leader, Ion Iliescu, was a former leading member of the Communist Party and a Ceaușescu ally before falling from the dictator's grace in the early 1980s. Was it merely a coincidence that Iliescu studied at Moscow University, serving as the president of foreign students when his friend Mikhail Gorbachev was the president of Russian students?

"Escu" or "escu"—did the prefixes matter? "Ceauș-" or "Ili-"? This became a new slogan.

Since the revolution, no fewer than twenty-nine different political parties had formed, but the National Salvation Front quickly assumed control over the state institutions, including TV and radio networks. I could not believe my eyes as I watched the vitriolic attacks they made on their opponents. They did promise free elections in April, however, so we still hoped for the best.

In April, Ion Iliescu was elected president. Another slogan arose: *Aceeasi Marie cu alta palarie.* The same kind of Mary with a different hat.

June. Six months had passed since the revolution, and Communists still held official positions under the new president. Political reforms were barely noticeable, except that shops had opened up and now sold imported goods. Romanians were not producing anything though, so there was little money with which to buy the new products. Italians, Germans, Spaniards, and Austrians started purchasing factories. They made money—and drove prices up. Romanians enjoyed more heat and electricity in their homes, but spent most of their salaries on food. At least my family was able to unbury our jewels and bring the rest of our nice things out of hiding. I wrote a bit of poetry about facets, that our lives were like faceted jewels. We'd hidden what was precious, and now we dared to mark a new facet of our lives by bringing them out again.

I had only one more month to prepare for my entrance exam to the university. My studies had been sporadic and a bit halfhearted during the worst of the political turmoil, and I had refused to allow my parents to spend hard-earned money on a tutor for me. Many families went into catastrophic debt hiring such tutors. Also, I was just stubborn enough to think I knew as well as any tutor the best way I should study. This made my dad rather nervous. My first oral examination and interview would be on July 2. I would have my first exam, the qualifying—and exclusion—round, on my birthday. If I passed that one, I'd go on to take three written exams: American and British literature, Romanian literature, and Romanian and English grammar. With the deadline approaching, I knew I should redouble my efforts, but still I could barely focus.

My sweet Mom had stood with me through all of my endeav-

ors in life. She had attended all of my ballet practices and per-
formances. Now she encouraged me day and night while I was
studying, slipping notes of encouragement into my books, waking
up in the middle of the night to bake my favorite sweets to nour-
ish my brain. I began to feel a sense of progress—but then, on June
13, 1990, massive riots protesting President Iliescu's regime shook
the capital. Was another revolution in process?

Protesters and hunger strikers demanded the government get
rid of the former Communist agents. People starved themselves
to be noticed by the new government. Around two hundred people were killed in clashes with the militia. Iliescu declared a state
of emergency to deal with the so-called *golani* (rascals) or *huligani*
(hooligans). He called the miners down from Valea Jiului to end
the uprising. Miners clashed with demonstrators many times over
the next several months, extending the chaos. Would the university exams even be held?

I felt desperate, stifled. I needed my future! I needed my freedom! But I wasn't going to get them any time soon, because Romania had moved in a terrible new direction. I was beginning to
wonder if I belonged in this new Romania any more than I had
thrived in the old.

Just as I got home from school one evening and was unlocking
the front gate, a brand new Toyota zoomed by on the street.

When I got inside, I said, "Mom, did you see that silver car? It
looked expensive!"

"That's the new car Vali bought for her daughter."

"Who?"

"Vali . . . my *hair*dresser!" She gave me a what's-wrong-with-
this-picture look.

"So how does a hairdresser come up with twenty thousand dollars? It cannot be her car."

"No, it's hers. I'm positive. Adela, the daughter, came to pick
Vali up from our house last time she did my hair."

"How much does she charge? She can't possibly cut that much
hair!"

"Well, her husband got money from the government for being a revolutionist. I heard he would get a parcel of land, too."

She explained that the government was trying to win popularity by rewarding the revolutionaries. So false "revolutionists" were appearing overnight, mushrooming in the rain of government handouts. They created myths about themselves and received a revolutionist ID that entitled them to extra income, land, and tax exemptions. Had they actually fought for the new society more than anyone else? The truth is, those who were exploiting the system, like Vali's husband, had not gone anywhere near the massacre sites; they had watched the drama unfold on TV, safe in their own living rooms.

This pretense, this new, false society, bothered me as much as the Communist regime had.

On that day, I realized that what I wanted most was to find an entirely different country to live in.

A few days later, another passing car bothered me, this time for a different reason. It was a convertible, and I saw Michael sitting in its back seat. I started to call out and wave, but then I noticed the pretty woman sitting beside him. In the few seconds it took for them to pass by, I saw a look of love between them.

16
The Return of the Rebel

I TUCKED MICHAEL'S PHOTO AWAY IN A DRAWER AND SHRUGGED OFF my secret, childish dream world. I ignored the beauty of the chestnuts' early summer leaves, the lilacs and roses in bloom. With joyless determination, I labored over my studies. As I had determined my own course of study, I decided to try D. H. Lawrence's steamy novel, *Lady Chatterley's Lover,* hoping it would add a little spark to my long hours. It was a mistake. With my dream of Michael gone and the near-rape experience still haunting my nightmares, I wasn't particularly interested in sex scenes, and the novel's pessimistic view that life and love are so hopelessly overshadowed by social forces like war and labor strikes pushed me even deeper into depression.

I heard Mom call, "Buni! Buni!" and then, "Aura!"

I gladly shut my book and stood as Mom cried out, "Nelu and Petre are at the gate!"

I hurtled out of the room, thrilled. Now that Communism was gone, my father's cousins—my "uncles"—were able to visit their motherland freely. "Maria sends her love," they said, "and . . ." They handed us boxes of Milka and Ritter chocolates, tins of Jacobs coffee, and from Maria, Rexona spray perfume.

We hugged and carried on about how wonderful it was to see each other, and they exclaimed over my growth. In their early forties, they looked fit and wonderful.

Mom and Buni set to work preparing a feast, and we all sat around reliving the richness of our lives as a family, the cruelties of the Ceauşescu regime, my uncles' escape attempts, prison, the revolution, the new regime. My uncles didn't want the Imbarus heritage to die; Uncle Petre had married but had yet to have children.

Later we all went for a walk around the neighborhood, and they saw what the house they'd lived in was like now, after the revolution. It had been well cared for, but the gardens would never be the same. Nothing would be the same. Up until I was five years old, Bagdasar Street had offered a bastion of Imbarus solidarity. Visiting back and forth among the three houses, I had heard a hundred laughs a day, despite the dour Communist regime. Each family had been allowed to keep a single home, usually one they already lived in. Bettie, the daughter of Grandpa's sister, had lived on one side of us, and on the other were the two sons and daughter of Grandpa's brother. Although Grandpa had been disinherited for choosing Buni, his brother, Iosif, and sister, Aurelia, had earned the blessings of my great-grandparents in their choice of mates. The proud Ioan Imbarus and his wife, Maria, allowed German spouses into the family, but not a Hungarian. Iosif's wife, my great aunt Mathilda, was born in Germany. Tante Tilli had kept her home and property in a manner that never failed to lure me, and Uncle Petre had contributed a special element to that magic.

A low wooden fence with a charming garden gate had separated Tante Tilli's property from ours. As a child I would always cross over into their yard, and Tante Tilli would welcome me and fuss over me. I often spoke German with her.

Her yard had been a riot of flowers: pansies in yellow, orange, violet, rich red, white, and a velvety purple so dark it looked black; graceful ferns; and, rising almost four feet above them all, *regina noptii* (the queen of the night) who shied from the sunshine that would evaporate her exotic perfume and scorch the lustrous trumpet petals that flared open into stars. But it was Tante Tilli's field of poppies that I remembered best, because their black eyes hid and peeked from many of the oil and acrylic paintings Petre created there. I had often sat beside him on my small wooden stool, watching in complete fascination as he painted. He was six foot four and handsome, my first glimpse of an Adonis. He had graduated from the University of Bucharest with a major in arts, which nurtured his talents not only in painting, but also in sculpting with iron, wood, marble, and porcelain. Though their house was no mansion viewed from the outside, Tante Tilli's place looked like a Versailles museum inside, with all the pieces done by Petre. She had also somehow preserved from the Communists her collection of silver cutlery and plates, porcelain china, crystal glasses, decanters, and heirloom steins. Antique furniture made of cherry, mahogany, and walnut sat elegantly atop Persian rugs. She draped rich furs over dark leather couches, suggesting the opulence of the family's past. Tante let me try on necklaces of diamond, ruby, and pearl. Golden watches still ticked away the hours as though the times hadn't changed since her youth. And as if the patriarch still watched over his domain, portraits of Ioan Imbarus and other ancestors hung on the walls in stunning gilt frames.

I was very young, but I remembered the times the whole family gathered in her house at Easter or at Karnival, wearing costumes. Petre and Nelu's sister, Maria, would return from Bucharest where she worked for the Ministry of Education. She spoke French, English, German, and Romanian fluently. I so admired her—a slim, classy, tall, blonde with light blue eyes and pale skin. In later years, when I saw pictures of Michelle Pfeiffer, I would be reminded of Aunt Maria and the way she embodied aristocratic elegance. Petre and Nelu would be there, rallying everyone into a game of some sort. They, along with my dad, were super fit, and enjoyed competing with each other in kayaking, sailing, soccer, and bodybuilding.

Even though the world outside us grew bleaker every year, the Imbarus clan managed to keep alive a little of the joy and graciousness of earlier times.

Then came 1974, when Petre and Nelu began making their escape attempts, and the full attention of the securitate fell on the family. In addition to periodically questioning my father in the dead of night, they harassed Tante Tilli mercilessly. In Bucharest, Maria was also put under scrutiny because of her brothers. Essentially hounded out of her job, she moved to Sibiu to take care of Tante Tilli, whose health had begun to fail from all the worry about her sons.

Five years later, Tante Tilli died. Not wanting to live alone in the big house, Aunt Maria applied to join her brothers in Germany. Permission was granted, and the moment Aunt Maria was gone, the government swooped in to take possession of her beautiful house and sell it.

Now we, the remnants of the Imbarus family, could only look at it from the outside.

This was a large part of how Ceaușescu had destroyed a nation: ruining its people's careers and reputations and wiping out the intelligentsia—the descendants of the landed aristocracy who had been artists, writers, musicians, lawyers, professors, and doctors. People like my ancestors. People like my family members. People like me.

Such a government could never tolerate spirited rebels like Uncle Petre. His refusal to live on Communist terms had always inspired me. My grandpa would have been so proud of his courage, his rebellious will, his stamina, and his perseverance.

I thought about my behavior over the past few months: the nightmares, the inability to concentrate, the depression. Yet here was my Uncle Petre, a man who had endured storms at sea, torture, imprisonment, and starvation, all in defiant support of his dreams. A true Imbarus.

When it was time to say goodbye, he hugged me. "Aura, you should never forget what was taken from us. Never. We endured so much. We went through so many things, and still we survived. Now it's your turn to make our family proud."

"I will," I promised him. "I will."

When I returned to my studies, I put *Lady Chatterley* aside and opened Emerson's "Self-Reliance."

"It is easy in the world to live after the world's opinion; it is easy in solitude to live after our own; but the great man is he who in the midst of the crowd keeps with perfect sweetness the independence of solitude!"

Surely Emerson meant the great *woman* as well. Petre's choices and integrity moved me deeply, and challenged me. Was not I, too, a rebel? Grandpa's investment of knowledge and hope in me would pay off. From now on I would build my own future—starting with my exams.

The university could only accommodate about ten percent of the several hundred applicants. Put another way, I would have to be better than ninety percent of the best and brightest in Romania.

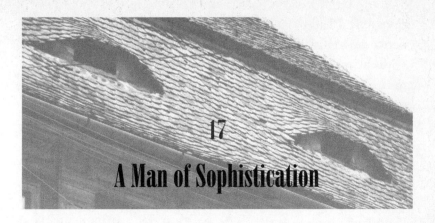

17

A Man of Sophistication

AFTER MY UNCLES LEFT, I STUDIED UNTIL MY EYES BURNED TO MAKE up for lost time. Tomorrow was both my birthday and the day of the first oral interview, so birthday plans were not an option.

Mom came to my room, caressed my hair, and laid a package on my bed. "This is to honor you for all your hard work. You are my pure ten!"

She pulled the package open, revealing an album that held all the awards I'd made when I used to play "Olympics" with the neighborhood kids—or my dolls when everyone else was tired of it. She picked up a ribbon with a cardboard medallion painted gold and hung it around my neck. "You are my Nadia, baby!"

I had made certificates, and medals of gold, silver and bronze, all due to my fascination with Nadia Comaneci and the Romanian school of gymnastics. My friends and neighbors came into my yard, and we improvised the beam, the floor, and the vault beside my dad's exercise bars. Because of Nadia's influence, I'd taken ballet for eight years and been good enough to qualify for the art school in Cluj, although my father preferred for me to follow a more rigorous academic program. Still, with her perfect tens at age fourteen, Nadia had proven it was possible to accomplish the impossible. I had practically worshipped her for the dreams she'd opened up in my life.

Mom was not only honoring my effort, she was reigniting in me the Olympic flame that had burned in me as a child, and I hugged her in gratitude.

Mom went with me to register for the tests at Lucian Blaga University—in fact, she sacrificed a vacation with Dad for doing so. I received my exam number: 217, meaning I was the two hundred and seventeenth person waiting in line to be interviewed. I checked to see who would preside over the screening panel and recognized a surname that gave me hope: Ciocoi-Pop—the last name of my English teacher in the seventh grade, the one who'd awakened in me a love of literature. Dumitru Ciocoi-Pop would preside over my inquisition. I hoped he was my teacher's husband.

After I had waited four hours, the assistant called, "Number 217!"

Mom squeezed my hand, and I entered a room where Professor Dumitru Ciocoi-Pop sat at a table, flanked by the rest of the screening panel. A dapper and distinguished-looking man, who could have been Clark Gable's clean-shaven brother, rifled through papers in quick movements that suggested efficiency and energy. He smiled at me with perfect white teeth.

"Aura Imbarus." He made direct eye contact. "Shall we begin?"

Using different books, the five members of the panel asked me to translate from Romanian into English and vice-versa. I had to give immediate answers. And then they gave me an immediate answer.

I left the room and spotted Mom shivering with anxiety, even though it was summer. Her eyebrows shot up when she saw me.

I ran over and kissed her cheeks. "I passed! I can move on to the written tests!"

We left hand in hand and visited Perla, the bakery in Piata Mare, where we celebrated by ordering profiteroles, served cold with a vanilla filling and topped with chocolate and caramel sauce. A Cordon Bleu pastry chef couldn't have outdone them.

And then I returned home and focused on the upcoming written exams: English and American literature and language, Romanian literature, and a separate exam for Romanian grammar.

I meditated every day. I used synesthesia, assigning numbers, colors, scents, music—whatever I could think of to connect me to the subject matter. When studying American writers, I listened to Igor Stravinsky and associated Twain with white and vanilla; Poe was black and musk. Ludwig van Beethoven's *Missa Solemnis* and *Ninth Symphony* helped me with British writers; Dickens was gray and lead, while D. H. Lawrence was lavender and coal. Vivaldi's *Four Seasons* accompanied the Romanian writers. On my door, I hung a sign: BUSY. DO NOT DISTURB!

The night before the test, I went to bed at eleven and dreamed of the test. The examiner was a mere shadow, but I saw clearly the bench where I would sit. The examiner announced that there were twenty openings available, and wrote an analytical question about the Romanian poet George Cosbuc on the blackboard. A second assignment appeared on the chalkboard: Give an analysis of Charles Dickens's *Bleak House*. My dream then jumped forward, showing the test results posted on a wall. I read through eighteen names, none of them mine. And then the nineteenth name: Aura Imbarus. I awoke at 2:00 AM.

This was not my first such dream. Four years earlier, I had announced to my family that I would get into high school in the first space as a result of my score on the entrance exam and my Romanian exams. And so I did. Then, in tenth grade, I woke up at exactly 3:00 on the morning of an elimination exam in molecular chemistry, with the formulas bouncing around in my head so clearly it was as if I were seeing them with open eyes. I got up and started writing them down. It was as if I'd stepped into a future bubble where someone whispered the solutions to all my chemistry problems. My pencil could barely keep pace with my insanity—or mystical power. Mom, tired and sleepy, saw my light on and came to check on me. "Aura? What are you doing? You should be asleep."

The bubble popped. I was stunned to see that I'd written four pages of formulas. They were all accurate, and I aced the test.

Never did I have doubts about my premonitions. Never did they fail me.

So I took this new dream seriously. Cosbuc, I thought, that would be no problem. But *Bleak House?* Ugh. I hadn't studied it nearly enough.

What should I do? I needed to sleep in order to be fresh for this crucial test, but instead of rolling over, I scrounged through my books for the Dickens novel and started rereading. At breakfast the next morning, I told my parents and Buni that I would pass all my tests and get in on the nineteenth spot out of twenty.

As always, Dad was skeptical about the dream but optimistic about my abilities.

When I entered the testing room, there stood the bench I'd seen in my dream. I sat on it and began my first test—on Cosbuc. When the American and British literature topic was given to me, I had to hide a shout of glee—I was supposed to analyze the symbol of fog in Charles Dickens's novel *Bleak House.*

A few days later, the results came in. Dad read them aloud. "Aura got in!" His voice trembled as he added, ". . . in the nineteenth spot!" He shook his head. ". . . *exactly* the way she said."

I barely heard his last comment because we were all screaming so loudly a passerby on the street might have suspected mayhem. I ended up passing all my exams—Romanian, British, and American literature, as well as Romanian and English grammar—but the relief of passing this first exam is what I remember most.

Thy will be done on Earth, as it is in Heaven . . .

This powerful line in the Lord's Prayer could be an explanation for my mysterious dreams, but I have a slightly different interpretation. I see them as evidence that each of us carries much potential, some leading us on one path, others in a different direction. Yet some of these potentials must be closer to what God—or whatever humans want to call a creative Source—wants to manifest in us. Or perhaps there are parallel dimensions that we sometimes glimpse, as if seeing our reflections in the windows of a passing train. For me, it seems that such a parallel universe sometimes intersects with the earthly level.

Even as a child, metaphysics had always fascinated me. I read books on meditation, chakras, the Upanishads, the Kabbalah, karma, Hinduism, and Buddhism. A true daughter of Transylvania, I enjoyed the esoteric from an early age, turning to Juno Jordan's numerology, Atlantis, or the zodiac when other kids were playing hide-and-seek outside. Grandpa had taught me to delve, and the more I did, the more I wanted greater understanding and knowledge.

When I started classes at the university, I longed to feel a sense of connection with the highest thought and expression that civilization had produced. Dr. Dumitru Ciocoi-Pop turned out to be my high school teacher's husband, and his classes delivered the heady intellectual excitement I'd been craving. He represented an avant-garde generation I wanted to become part of. Was it possible for me to find someone like him on a personal level as well? I wanted someone older, versatile, and well-traveled. I imagined having brilliant conversations with a man who would explore with me the boundaries of the human brain or the evolution of ancient civilizations. Good-looking men were attracted to me, but I never fell for them just because of their looks. Intelligence, sophistication, and charm drew me more powerfully, but such assets were rare in a male-dominated society like Romania's where a woman's role rarely extended beyond domesticity.

The thought of picking up someone else's reeking socks disgusted me. Surely, if any place attracted the kind of man I wanted, it would be the university.

That seemed obvious. It was also wrong.

4

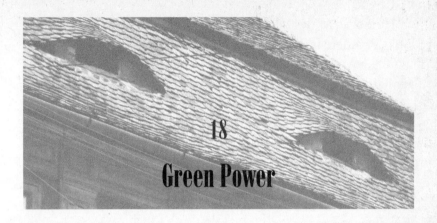

18

Green Power

MY HAIR WAS GREEN THE DAY I FOUND A NEW DIRECTION FOR MY LIFE. Actually, my hair had been green for almost two months, ever since I'd heard through the grapevine that Michael Chiorean had been with his current girlfriend, Mihaela, for longer than he'd been with any other woman. This news affected me deeply. I was twenty-one and had recently ended my own first serious romance after only two years. I had thought it would last forever. First that, and now this. Clearly there was only one thing for me to do: renounce romance entirely. I whacked off my curls, leaving short, fringy dark hair that I dyed black. Flat black. Helpful girlfriends told me I could get a pretty bluish tint to it if I rinsed it with a blue throat disinfectant spray. I did so, leaving the liquid on extra long to really set the color. When I looked in the mirror, my hair was green. Not just green, forest green. I shampooed it over and over, but the coniferous shade persisted.

I took to wearing berets and "newsboy" caps, but a few tufts still stuck out like evergreen sprigs on the day I ran across Liviu in Piata Mare. I hadn't seen him for a while and wasn't expecting to see him then, but I decided to seize the moment.

"Liviu!" I called.

He looked at me and grinned. "Hi, Aura." His gaze shifted. "You look . . . different."

"Oh, my mom's crazy hairdresser tried to tone down the red in my hair. She got a little carried away."

"I see. You're alone today? Where's—"

"I don't know. We broke up a couple of months ago." I had been anticipating the question, because Liviu was friends with the man I had recently broken up with. I had not found this marvel at the university after all; he was a businessman operating out of Germany. Handsome, intelligent, eleven years older than I. On our first date we rode around in his beautiful red Toyota convertible, listening to Vivaldi's *Four Seasons*. On subsequent dates we discussed the themes of post-modernism in painting: Dadaism, Cubism, and Expressionism, with Kandinsky as a special favorite. We talked about mysticism and astral projection. He dissected the Kabbala with me. But could he make me forget Michael Chiorean forever?

"I'm so sorry," Liviu said. "You seemed like such a happy couple."

I shrugged. "Turns out he wanted more of a ménage a trois."

"Oh, Aura, I'm so sorry."

"Don't be, Liviu, I'm totally okay. No regrets. Really."

I had cut the man out of my life completely, and he had stalked me as I walked to and from the university; he had even shown up at my Uncle Petre's house in Baden-Baden when I was visiting there. There were the late-night phone calls—at first only hangups, but later a strange man's voice, harsh and unfamiliar, telling me terribly intimate things about myself . . . things only a lover should know.

At first I was terrified. Then I was angry. This was like Peter all over again: a man who was not who he pretended to be, trying to force me to do something I did not want to do. I couldn't stab this one with a broken bottle, but I could still fight back. I placed a newspaper ad with my ex's home phone number that offered two precious burial plots for sale. *Call after 9:00 PM.* I eventually heard he'd had to have his phone number changed.

The calls stopped then.

It was clear that Liviu knew none of this, and that was good, because there was something I wanted to ask of him.

But he asked it first.

"Aura, listen, I know you're still a student, but you speak several foreign languages, yes?"

"Yes."

"Would you be interested in working for Radio Contact?"

For a moment I couldn't speak. With the downfall of Communism, private radio stations had started to appear all over Romania. The broadcasting profession seemed custom-made for me, and I had been considering ways to break into the field. Liviu and Radio Contact had topped my list of contacts.

"Of course I'm interested," I said.

"Four, three, two, one. . . . Good morning, and thank you for listening to the morning news with Aura Imbarus, here at Radio Contact," said Andy Gisoiu, and turned the microphone over to me.

That was how most of my mornings began now. After clearing a variety of application hurdles, I had been hired at Radio Contact. Each morning, I had a little over an hour to analyze the wire services' articles and deliver the 7:00 AM morning press show. I gave the first news bulletin at 7:30, the second an hour later, and the third an hour after that. Then, during the school term, I had to rush to campus for classes between 10:00 and 3:00, with an occasional night class thrown in to keep things interesting.

Once a week, I also hosted *Thursday Night Conversation* with guests like the mayor of Sibiu, the governor, famous writers, politicians, singers, ambassadors, and, someone important to me personally, the president of Lucian Blaga University. It was not until Dr. Dumitru Ciocoi-Pop took the reins of the university after the revolution that this small, unknown college proliferated into a citadel of both academia and social renewal. The college's motto, *mens agitat molem* (mind moves matter) was taken from the *Aeneid*.

Mind moves matter. It was true. In addition to famous Romanians, I interviewed foreign celebrities like Danielle Mitterrand and Helmut Kohl. Day by day, my horizons expanded beyond anything I had considered possible. What else might I accomplish if I set my mind to it?

After graduating in 1995, I took the summer off before starting my master's degree program, and received the most fateful assignment of all from Radio Contact: to cover the International Jazz Festival that would be held in Sibiu that year. My contact's name was Michael Chiorean.

My Michael . . .

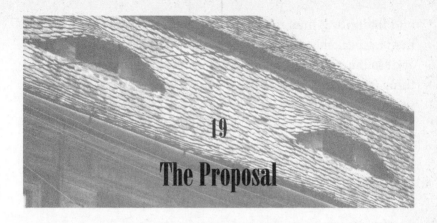

19

The Proposal

I DIDN'T WANT THE ASSIGNMENT. I TOLD MY BOSS THERE WERE SEVERAL others who knew far more about jazz than I did. I'd have to do a lot of research. I didn't add that Michael was practically married and seeing him would just remind me of what I couldn't have.

My boss didn't understand, of course.

On the morning of Michael's first press briefing I got up as usual at 4:45 AM and dressed with care in my arty silk print pants and open jacket. Red and pink swirled among blooming yellow over orange stripes, all on a blue background. I didn't want to be missed. With the end of government-owned garment stores that sold drabness in small, medium, and large, you could almost hear the scream of bright colors on young women—especially me. Buni and I put some fabulous outfits together.

I sprayed myself with the fresh scent of Rexona and dashed out to meet the car that Radio Contact sent over at 5:30 every morning. I aired my usual broadcasts that day and had to keep an appointment at the mayor's office, sneaking glances at my watch every five minutes. The thought of seeing Michael left me a bit breathless.

Twenty minutes late, and trailing a hint of fragrance, I hurried into the Trades Union Hall, the same building where Michael had tried to speak during the 1989 Revolution. He'd already started his spiel to the rest of the media about festival logistics over the next three weeks before the actual event. Now I wished I'd worn black so I could have slipped in unnoticed. Heads turned, nodding, and hands waved. Everybody knew me, and I knew them. I was home, my media home. Whether working for the TV stations Antenna 1 or Pro TV, other radio stations, or the written press, we were all colleagues.

Michael looked at me. "I see Radio Contact has joined us, so now we can move on. Any questions so far?"

I'm sure I was blushing. Did I dare open my mouth?

Michael gave me a nod. "I'll clue you in after the meeting."

I listened and took notes, worrying during the half-hour session that I had irritated him. He had a way of seeming very aloof until you were engaged in an actual conversation with him.

"Aura!" Michael waved me over afterwards.

"I'm sorry for being late," I said. "I was stuck in the mayor's office going over their monthly agenda."

"Aura, listen . . ." He hadn't looked up, nose in schedules and rosters. "I need a PR director to be in charge of all the media licensing for the big event." He looked up, smiling. "Interested?"

Oh, yeah. . . . That smile. But PR director? I hadn't done anything like this before, but how hard could it be? I knew the local media people. The national and foreign press couldn't be too different. Licenses were just forms, and I was a fast learner.

"Sure," I said. "Love to!"

"In addition to your job at Radio Contact, you'd be working fifteen, sixteen hours some days."

Near you. . . . "No problem whatsoever. I can handle it."

During the summer the whole city came to life. Planter boxes gushed with color underneath paned windows. Brightly painted chairs surrounded tables with flowered tablecloths on terraces crowded with blooming flowers in pots. The planters in the central squares erupted in lilies and annuals, and children chased each other around the water fountains, splashing and laughing. The stereo system in the main square played jazz to herald the approaching festival. Michael had arranged for a huge tent to be erected, and workers hammered, sawed, and assembled, anchoring the main stage to the Piata Mare's cobblestones. Passersby stopped and admired the bustle and scurry. Summer breezes cooled them as they sipped cappuccinos and Lavazza coffee. The Italian pizzerias and gelaterias did a thriving business. Posters hung on every storefront, announcing Jan Garbarek as the festival headliner.

"Like 'em?" Michael asked.

It turned out he'd designed the posters, the billboards, the fliers, and all the promotional materials for the event. "Aren't you the artsy guy! These are amazing!"

Side by side, Michael and I spent hours going over the program and budget, purchasing airplane tickets for the musicians, talking to their agents, booking hotel rooms. I had no idea so much work went into these events. Twenty-four hours in a day weren't enough.

And the damned alarm kept going off at 4:45 AM.

Four days into my festival job, Michael and I were sitting in his car—aka, his office—in front of my house, going over the musicians' names, budgets, promo events, and marketing strategies. It was 2:00 AM on a Sunday morning. I was very aware of Michael's closeness, the scent of Aramis he wore, the way his muscles moved under his shirt. He'd never acted like anything but a man already in a committed relationship, however. He smiled at me and complimented me once in a while, but he never came on to me. I'd seen him flirt with women years ago in the jazz club, so I knew he knew how. The fact that he didn't flirt with me made me think he was truly in love with Mihaela.

Michael grew silent a moment and looked at me. "I broke up with Mihaela," he said.

"And I'm done with Horia," I said, referring to this sweet guy I had known since my childhood. There hadn't been anything going on there anyway, but I didn't want Michael to think I was unwanted. Then one serious implication of what Michael was saying hit me. "So . . . will you and Mihaela still be . . . roommates?"

"I can't live with her anymore. I have to move out of her apartment. I asked my Dad if I could move in with him and Olguta, my stepmother, for the duration of the jazz festival, but he said that both of them are too old to deal with my late-night hours. I can't disturb their sleep."

"So where will you go?"

"The campground. I'll rent a little cabin there for the festival, and then afterwards, I'll find an apartment to lease."

He made no moves in my direction, nor I in his, and we said good night.

I'd been looking forward to sleeping in for once, but Michael's situation set me to thinking. He'd broken up with Mihaela. He wanted me to know it. This could lead to something. Yet I wasn't sure he felt any genuine attraction to me.

I spent the night unable to slow the spinning wheels in my brain. Michael needed a place to stay. I just wanted to help him out, I told myself. I wanted to cut down on the late-night hours spent sitting in his car, I reasoned. His temporarily moving in with us would only be logical, I convinced myself. I couldn't quite admit that I was thrilled at the idea of having him near me at night as well as by day.

Of course, I could only make such a proposal if my family approved. The whole night I twisted the sheet and punched the pillow, never able to stop creating a scenario I could present to Mom, Dad, and Buni on Michael's behalf. *Just for the jazz festival. He'll sleep on the sofa-bed. Think of all the time I'll save.*

I'd barely dozed off when I heard Buni in the kitchen and smelled coffee and *friganele*. I snoozed a bit longer and heard Mom and Dad go in for breakfast. This would be the best time to approach them. I threw on some jogging clothes and joined my family.

"Can I have a word with you guys?" I asked.

They sat around the dining table with "uh-oh-here-it-comes" expressions on their faces.

I told them about Michael's situation and my recommended solution.

"Are you involved with him?" Buni asked bluntly.

"Nope. Hmm . . . not yet," I said, smiling. "I do like him, but we've never even kissed."

Everybody exchanged looks, and we hashed it over some more. To their credit, none of them brought up my former "soul mate."

Dad had the final word. "Just for the jazz festival. After that, we'll reconsider."

Once again, my family was supporting me and my ideas. I hugged them all.

It was still early, so I hiked over to the campground to look for Michael. His car wasn't near the cabins. I finally found it in a picnic area. He was sleeping inside. I tapped on his window, and he woke up, got out, and stretched. He was still wearing his clothes from the day before.

"Why are you sleeping in your car?" I asked.

"I wanted to pay for a cabin last night, but it seems there's some crazy jazz festival about to happen." He smiled an adorably sleepy smile. "They have a waiting list to get in. I was too tired to drive back to town to find a hotel. Which would probably have been booked as well."

"Michael, this is the first and the last night you're sleeping in your car." I explained the whole arrangement to him.

He seemed stunned and pleased, and very grateful, but not in any way romantic. "I cannot believe you're doing this for me. You barely know me."

"We're practically joined at the hip at work," I said.

Which was true. Over the next few days we worked long hours together, drumming up last-minute potential sponsors. Because of the endless town meetings I'd attended, I was as familiar with the mayor's office as I was my own living room. I called in my chips, getting several thousand-dollar pledges. Michael brought in major sponsorship money from his employer, the New York office of Pepsi-Cola. He was a branch manager for all of Transylvania. He served in a similar capacity for Prigat, an Israeli company marketing natural juices, which was another corporate sponsor. In exchange for being listed in the programs and applauded at the festival, sponsors signed contracts—but with just over two weeks to go, the concert was still underfunded.

At night Michael and I were housemates and nothing more. I slept in my room with the door dutifully closed; he slept on the couch. On Thursday night, long after Buni was asleep, Michael and I were working in the hallway, sitting on two black chairs outside my bedroom door. Sometimes I didn't hear what he was saying because I was so intent on the flecks of warm brown in his coffee-colored eyes, or in watching the beautiful way his mouth formed words. At just such a moment, he leaned over and kissed my cheek. A quick kiss.

"I just wanted to thank you for all your hard work," he said.

I confess I left the door open to my room that night. I wore a lacy camisole top and matching shorts. I couldn't sleep, listening for any sound coming from the living room, something to reveal that he couldn't sleep either for wanting me, a spring creaking or footfalls headed toward my room.

Nothing happened.

Maybe he really didn't feel the same attraction I felt for him. He appreciated me, and that was it. I felt crushed. I didn't see why fate had practically thrown us together. I had been doing fine without Michael before the festival assignment. But now . . .

Another tortured night.

20

Jazz Festival

GETTING THROUGH THE NEXT DAY WITH MY USUAL SPARK PROVED A
bit more than I could manage. Yet the festival carried its own electricity, energizing the whole town.

I didn't give up on Michael. The next night I wore my lacy night
things again, and left the door open.

My room hadn't changed since I was young girl: its dark, glossy
wood furniture, carved with scrolls and flowers, and a crimson Persian carpet still looked elegant, while a dropped chandelier lent a
bit of sophistication to the rosy pink walls of my childhood. The
chestnuts outside filled my two big open windows with moon-dap-
pled rustling in the summer night. One of Petre's beautiful paintings hung above my bed, an autumn scene with crimson trees, leaves
falling on an endless road. When I pictured the road of my life, I
remembered this scene. I sat reading on fresh baby-blue cotton
sheets on my comfortable queen-size bed. So when the door opened
wider that night, and Michael's curly head appeared, the setting
didn't detract from what was about to happen.

His smile, confident and amused, dazzled me.

"Aura, I have something for you," he whispered as if Buni might
hear.

In blue boxers and a blue and white T-shirt, his tanned, muscular physique set my pulse racing like one of Marilyn Mazur's hot percussion riffs. This was *it*.

He was holding something behind his back and moved closer, sitting on the side of the bed. I restrained myself from swooning over his Aramis cologne. He gave me a box of Priscilla Presley's Moments perfume.

"I know how much you love Elvis," he said. "So I thought you might like something associated with his world."

"Wow! You really pay attention . . ." I sprayed the American perfume on my hands. I thought I detected a hint of jasmine and something juicy, then woodsy and wild underneath. Lovely.

Michael ran his fingers along my palm to collect the fragrance and trailed it over the back of my neck . . . my shoulders . . . he started caressing me, kissing me . . .

Thank God it was Saturday and the alarm didn't go off; I got a few hours of sound sleep. Still, I rose before ten and hurried into the kitchen.

"Do you like him, Mom?"

"I do. His soul is open, and he's such a caring person. I trust your instincts." She kissed my forehead. "I want you to be happy."

I tutored clients that day, and Michael had to tend to his regular employees through Pepsi and Prigat while fielding phone calls and handling crises with the festival.

When I came home, Dad took me aside. "So, as I feared, things have changed between you and Michael. Are you aware of his reputation? He's a playboy, just like that last one. Is that what you want again? What *can* you be thinking?"

I kissed Dad on the cheek. "I don't know all the details yet, but I know that something happened in Michael's life a while ago that made him stop drinking and smoking. It made him want to settle down. Dad, I'm happy right now, and I hope you can be happy for me."

"Aura, I'm your father. I will always be at the guardrail of your life, keeping you from going over. And if you do, I'll jump off and catch you at the bottom. It's my nature. It's my job."

I wanted to tell him I had a nature, too. I wanted to tell him I had not needed his help when Peter tried to rape me or when I was receiving harassing phone calls in the middle of the night. But of course, I couldn't tell him these things. I simply said, "Thank you, Dad. I'll be okay. You'll see. I love you."

That evening I did a phone interview with one of the musicians for the festival, and Michael and I worked late into the night. The next day, Sunday, July 2, was my twenty-fourth birthday. I had plenty of paperwork to catch up on, so I worked in my room until 1:00 PM.

At 1:01 I stepped into the entry hall to find a huge bouquet of assorted flowers. Michael had bought four separate bunches of flowers from the farmer's market and created an arrangement any florist would have been proud to claim. Actually, the whole place looked like a flower shop. He'd also bought a huge bouquet of red roses for Mom and another for Buni. Meanwhile Mom, not knowing about Michael's extravagance, had cut mostly red flowers from the garden and placed several bouquets in vases, the biggest on the dining room table set with a red tablecloth and red napkins. Red and white candles scented the rooms with cinnamon and vanilla. Mom had worked the day before and all morning to prepare a *boef salade,* quiche, cheese and meat roulades, crudités, eggplant salad, fish egg salad, Florentine eggs, and more. The desserts included several types of cakes, pies, and my favorites, tiramisu torte and *cremeschnitte.* Several friends, relatives on Mom's side, and various neighbors would be helping us devour all this food.

I felt so blessed to have both such a family and my new dream lover. The only cloud over what should have been one of the happiest days in my life was Buni. For once, she hadn't done much of the cooking, and had to stay in her room during the party. Hard to believe, but my beloved Buni was beginning to show the signs of aging. She just didn't have the energy she used to have.

Later, I took her a huge piece of cake. "Cretii, look what I brought you."

I sat on the edge of her mattress and caressed her soft, curly white hair. With a faraway look in her eyes, she talked of Grandpa and how she wished he could have seen this day. I'd bought her a new dress, but she didn't feel like getting out of her robe. Her room always smelled of lavender because of the bars of lavender soap or dried sachets she tucked in drawers between the clothes and dainty handkerchiefs embroidered with the initials IB: Irma Balint, her maiden name.

Michael joined me, bringing Buni her red roses. That made her perk up; she had already grown attached to him. They chatted in Hungarian—which I didn't speak—and he made her laugh. They wouldn't tell me what was so funny.

The next day was Monday, which meant we had four more days until the festival began. After a series of radio shows and meetings, I spent intense hours going over the TV and radio stations' accreditation. We hadn't received the funds we'd contracted for from the city officials, so I played phone tag all day. What was stopping these people from paying what they had promised?

Over the next few days I saw more and more aspects of Michael's capabilities as the final set-up for the festival gelled: curtains, lights, and sound system; concessions, parking, portable bathrooms; and a thousand other logistics. I saw how special he was: so impassioned, yet substantial, ethical, brilliant, artistic, exciting, kind.

We were at home having an evening meal with my parents, Buni still in her bedroom, when the phone rang. I jumped up to answer it.

"Is Michael there?" asked a sexy woman's voice.

Girlfriends? Playboy? "Just like that last one?" Was Dad right?

"Just a minute," I said sweetly. Then, without covering the receiver, I called out, "Michael, I think it's one of your old girlfriends," and gave him a wicked smile.

He took the phone. "Yes? Who?" He looked at me. "No . . . No
. . . I'm with *her,* so . . . *no.*" He hung up and looked at me sheep-
ishly. "Sorry. This won't happen again."

But it did.

Dad took me aside again. "You see? I knew this would happen.
After the festival, don't count on his staying around!"

I disagreed. From everything I could tell about Michael, he was
a man of his word. I felt like I'd be the first to know if Michael's
interest in me was waning, if his eyes were wandering. If that happened, I wouldn't want him, and that would be that. Arguing with
Dad was useless, though.

The evening before the opening night of the festival, Michael's
parents invited us to their house for dinner. I knew them only from
his stories and a few conversations I'd had with Olguta on the
phone. We didn't really have time for a social evening, but this was
important, so we simply elbowed it into the schedule. I so wanted
them to like me.

The night was a bit cool for summer, so I wore my favorite long
green dress with the fur-trimmed collar and sleeves. It had slits at
the legs to show off my cutaway summer boots. I had designed the
dress, and Buni had helped me sew it.

Mihail Chiorean invited us in. He and Michael shared the same
height, body frame, curly hair, cheekbones, and eyebrows. I was
stunned at how alike they looked. A good-looking blonde with stunning blue eyes introduced herself as Olguta Chiorean. They were
both refined and intelligent. They offered an elegant meal in an
array of flavors, colors, and aromas. Clearly Olguta, like my Mom,
loved to cook. More than that, I felt an immediate connection with
her. And I could see that I could learn so much from Mihail.

"They adored you," Michael said afterwards.

On the opening night of the festival, Mom, Dad, and Michael's
parents all showed up to support us. I was thrilled to see my father
there—he still had his reservations about Michael—and even more
thrilled to see all the parents sit together.

The music began.

"Incandescent!"

Virtually every media review used this word. Hundreds had gathered in the Piata Mare. Throughout the Communist years, people from widely different social classes—high school students to pensioners—had clung to jazz music as one of the few vivid experiences available in a gray totalitarian landscape, and they were still loyal to it. Dozens of jazz clubs, bands, and fans had gathered for three days to free their minds and spirits, listening to the music that had for decades been our country's only link to America—the land of freedom. Poet Adrian Paunescu called Sibiu "the Jazz Capital of Romania."

Jan Garbarek and Marilyn Mazur were the most prestigious artists to perform that year. Garbarek, the Norwegian tenor and soprano sax player, was the lead performer for the ECM record label. His sharp-edged tone electrified; his long, keening notes mesmerized like a hypnotic call to prayer. Marilyn Mazur's percussion gave the festival its heartbeat, and other artists wowed the crowds as well.

After three days, the concerts ended on a high note. Incandescent.

The only problem was that not all the contracted musicians had been paid. While Michael supervised the deconstruction and cleanup, I pursued sponsors for the money they had promised. "Gee," secretaries said. "He just stepped out, and nobody knows when he'll be back." I tried hourly phone calls. When I did finally reach a sponsor, many said they didn't remember agreeing to anything . . . even when shown the signed contract. In the case of public officials, they *were* the legal system, so we couldn't sue them.

Prestigious musicians demanded their money.

We simply had to come up with it.

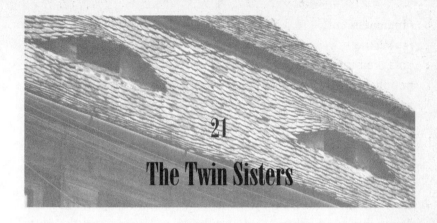

21

The Twin Sisters

ONE OF THE LEAD ORGANIZERS OF THE SIBIU JAZZ FESTIVAL, EMILIAN Tantana from Austria, wired us three thousand dollars to make the final payments to the musicians. We would have to pay him back from our meager salaries, however.

In the end Michael paid a huge price for his dream. I had signed on to be with him and to help, and did everything I could for him. We were happy with each other, if not with some of our sponsors. Even Dad seemed impressed; he didn't mention reevaluating Michael's living arrangements.

An emotional letdown after the thrilling month of the concert was probably inevitable, but what I felt was much more than that. So many of the public officials I quoted regularly in my news reports or interviewed for local current events on Radio Contact had looked me in the eye and promised to sponsor the jazz festival, and signed contracts that, in the end, meant nothing. I felt not only cheated, but betrayed. Going back on the news beat and reading press releases about these self-congratulatory hypocrites took the excitement of my job away from me. I realized I'd been trying to look at the new Romania through rose-colored glasses, but this insult grabbed me by the hair and shoved my nose into the real stink of things—the very things I couldn't report on.

Take, for example, the factory where my mother worked. A permissible news brief would go something like this: "A public auction was held today to sell the formerly state-owned company Victoria. The major portion of shares was bought by Maria So-and-so and her daughter, Adina. Maria is now the new general manager." Ah, well, nepotism is everywhere. Yet there was another side to this story, one I could never report. Maria had once been a coworker of my mother's, earning the same wage. But she and her daughter, Adina, had claimed to be revolutionists and were given the revolutionist certificate that entitled Maria to apply for and receive bank loans for vast sums of money. The truth was that these women had done nothing at all during the revolution. What they *had* done was maintain some highly placed, ex-Communist tovarsi connections. When the auction to sell the Victoria factory was held, only a few people—Maria and Adina among them—showed up. This was because no one else knew about the auction. There was no announcement, no public posting of the information. Therefore, Maria and Adina became the major shareholders of Victoria overnight. They'd also recently opened up a spa, although they had no more experience in that field than my mother did.

Were we supposed to believe that all this had been accomplished on a mere worker's salary? No.

People I had known to be total losers in high school became GMs of factories. Here were Mircea and Valentin, who couldn't link two sentences together, running multimillion dollar companies. I couldn't report on any of these stories honestly, and more and more I hated being a part of what I saw as public deception.

After five years, the country was barely recovering from so many more years of Communism. The people with money were the same former Communists who had placed foreign currency in Swiss banks. Now they were free to withdraw these funds and live the same lavish lifestyle they had enjoyed during Ceauşescu's regime. They flaunted their wealth, wearing designer clothes, driving expensive cars, enjoying exorbitant vacations abroad. Sudden wealth clustered to the bank accounts of the few, while most Romanians were striking it poor. I saw the wrinkled faces of the poor every day on the streets; I smelled their bad breath and noted their lack of teeth. And I asked the same question I had asked before the revolution: What is going to happen to them?

Because Michael and I were so busy, we didn't have many family meals together, but when we did, we spoke of these things. While none of us wanted to go back to Ceaușescu's Communism, the current, pervasive corruption was almost as bad. In fact, people on the street were beginning to mutter something I would have believed unthinkable, although no one would say his name. *Mai bine era pe vreamea lui Raposatu.* (It was better during the Deceased One's time.) Or *Gaseai mai multe pe vremea lui Impuscatu.* (You were able to find more during the Shot One's time.)

Buni used to have a lot to say during any political discussion, but lately she'd grown much quieter, her clothes hanging loose on her once Amazonian frame. One Sunday evening something in her eyes spoke to me, and I knew I'd better spend some extra time with her after dinner.

I went to her room, where she was massaging her hands and legs with menthol to soothe the pain of her arthritis. "Let me, Cretii," I said, and took over the job for her. I had always told her that she was so healthy, she would live forever. She used to wake every morning at 5:30 AM, stretch, exercise, take a cold shower for better blood circulation, and prepare breakfast by 7:00 AM, looking fresh and glowing. She'd instilled this same exercise regimen in my father.

But there was no question that in recent months, Buni's vigor had begun to fade. That night as I rubbed her soft skin she said, "Aura, I will pray for you even in my grave. I will pray for you to be healthy, happy, and lucky."

"Oh, Buni . . ." I hugged her. "You're strong. I love you so much."

Throughout my childhood, I had suffered from severe allergies that brought on asthma attacks. When I was eight years old, Mom and Dad took me to the resort of Constanta on the Black Sea, where the salt air was supposedly beneficial for respiratory problems. But a powerful dust storm blew in, clogging my sinuses and airways. That night, I had an asthma attack so severe that I turned purple. My parents thought I was dying. They rushed me to the hospital where a novice doctor had no idea how to treat such an attack. Fighting for air, I cried, "I want to see my Buni." I begged my parents to take me home. I did not want to die in a hospital by the Black Sea, so far from my grandmother.

Dad called a cab, and we went to the airport only to learn that the next flight to Sibiu did not leave for twelve hours. Dad hired the cab for the ten-hour drive to Sibiu and urged the driver to make it in nine. The cabbie had to charge for a round trip, a small fortune. Dad called our family physician, Dr. Bogdan, who said to come straight to his house with me, no matter what time we arrived at Sibiu. He also said that my crisis might pass when we left the stormy seaside.

Dad sat next to the driver, while Mom held me in her arms in the back seat over the long and exhausting ride up into the Carpathians. My hypoxic color still terrified my parents when we arrived in Sinaia, a beautiful mountain resort built around the lovely old Sinaia monastery, named after the biblical Mount Sinai. If it hadn't been dark at the time, and if I hadn't been so sick, I'm sure I would have loved King Carol's beautiful summer home there, Peles Castle, built a hundred years earlier and looking like it belonged in a German fairy tale. The area attracted hikers in summer and skiers in winter, along with those who believed the waters and vapors possessed curative powers. I can't argue against those claims, because as we passed through the locale, my pain began to abate and my constricted airways opened. Dr. Bogdan had predicted that the fresh mountain air might bring me around, but it nevertheless seemed miraculous.

I woke up in Sibiu at 5:30 in the morning, lying in Buni's arms. Her lavender smell and soft skin against my cheeks, her strong hands supporting me, brought me intense joy. As I listened to her prayers and words of encouragement, I felt as if I were drawing strength from her to go on living.

When I left Buni's room that night in August of 1995 and stood outside her door, I thought about how thin she had felt when I hugged her, as if I'd break a rib if I squeezed any harder. I wished that through my hug I could have sent her my own health and strength, the way she had for me when I needed it.

A week later, as Michael and I lay sleeping at around 8:30 AM, Mom rushed in to tell me that Buni was dying.

I jumped up and hurried to Buni's sweetly scented room with its glossy black furniture. All looked clean and perfect, except that Dad sat on Buni's bed, holding her in his arms. Michael stood at the doorway while I went straight to their side. It looked like Buni had eaten the breakfast Mom had given her a half hour earlier, but while I watched, the breakfast simply came back up. Her breath was faint and her eyes were closed.

Please, God, help her! I didn't want her to go. I caressed her hands and ran my fingers through her lavender smelling hair, her locks a bit tangled, not letting go of me. I couldn't imagine not seeing Buni's striking figure ruling the Imbarus household on Bagdasar Street, cooking her secret recipes, waiting at the window for Mom and me to come home, listening to all the inanities I rambled on about for hours while she pretended she wasn't tired.

I pressed my cheek against her blanket. I felt as if the whole room was levitating, and time had stopped. I seemed locked in a perpetual moment that would end only when I also died. I was aware of an aura of warmth around Buni, and a barely perceptible glow on her face. I held her hand tightly, senses as acute as if my every vein dilated to absorb this last connection more fully. A faintly cool breath of air fanned over me, softer than a summer breeze.

In that endless moment life and death were twin sisters, the beginning and end of each other. And I was a witness, lingering between the two ends of creation.

"Aura, don't cry." Dad's voice reached me as if from another dimension. "Let her go."

Tears rolled down my cheeks as if they would do so forever.

"Aura, please let her go," Mom said. "God needs her. Don't keep her here."

Warmth emanated from Buni's hand, and I jolted as if a current had traveled from her body into mine. Then cold ran down my spine like an icy rain dripping off the eaves. Buni's hand released mine. . . .

22
Palm Trees

MICHAEL AND DAD ARRANGED FOR CANDLE ARRAYS AT THE FUNERAL, and then a lunch was served, attended by a hundred people who arrived by bus.

Michael lay next to me in bed when I couldn't stop crying and hid myself in my room so as not to upset Mom and Dad. He caressed me and wiped my tears and talked to me for hours to soothe my pain. I tried to take comfort in the thought that Buni was with Grandpa now, but wherever I looked in the house, I could see her. There she was, dusting the crystal and china she'd guarded so fiercely, insisting the Communists wouldn't take them from her. Well, she had at last left them behind. The kitchen was so empty, not just of Buni but of all the mouth-watering aromas, the clatter of spoon on pan, the kettle's boil and whistle. The house I lived in was her world, and whatever I touched brought her back to me. I often sensed her presence beside me. And she visited my dreams.

In one such dream, she simply said, "Go."

Go? Where? This message seemed particularly powerful, and I pondered its meaning for weeks. Then, in broad daylight, a vision came to me: I was standing near tall palm trees, gazing up at the clear blue sky in strong sunshine. In this vision I felt at home in a land that was far from Romania. Later, I would remember that I had had this exact same vision as a child. I had even announced it to my family: "I'm going to live somewhere that has palm trees." A ridiculous claim in the dark days of the Communist regime.

I had forgotten about that, and I forgot it now as I struggled to deal with everyday life. I missed Buni, and when I wasn't thinking of her I was grumbling to Michael about Iliescu's government. Private universities were opening doors throughout the country. Few of them provided a good education, but the Ministry of Education accredited most of them anyway—for a fee. Candidates barred from attending a public university by failing the tough entrance exams could easily gain admittance to a private university, again for a fee. They bought their diplomas. Monika and I shook our heads and rolled our eyes. She had almost finished medical school at Targu Mures, one of the best in the country. Her sister, Ildiko, had earned her degree in chemistry. Since childhood all my friends had competed with each other, and the competition spurred us on to greater achievements. Lulu had become an emergency room doctor, and Vicentiu a neurosurgeon. Adrian was an engineer. All of us had sweated through years of hard work to graduate from a public university, but now it seemed that any ninny could earn a diploma. For a fee.

"Go," Buni said to me in my dreams again that night. I could smell her lavender scent, feel the warm touch of her hand. "Go."

When I saw commercials or photos from the West, when I saw palm trees and blue skies, I experienced déjà vu, as if I were more a part of that world than my own.

My own world was plenty busy. I finished my MA in American and British studies of the twentieth century, started work on my Ph.D., and began teaching English courses for the Engineering College and Economical Studies College at Lucian Blaga University—my alma mater. On Saturdays, I continued working for a private foreign language school called Lexis, tutoring children in English. I enjoyed teaching, but still worked for Radio Contact, too. I also wrote for the Sibiu branch of the National Journal and conducted surveys for the American company Gallup.

I could say that I fragmented my life like this because no single job paid enough, but the truth was that I loved cramming as much activity and accomplishment into twenty-four hours as possible, striving to live up to my highest potential. It was what my family expected of me, and what I expected of myself. Fortunately, I'd inherited plenty of energy and stamina from Buni and my father.

Still, despite all this activity and my rich relationship with Michael, I did not feel happy. In idle moments, I found my mind wandering back to Nadia Comaneci, who had always been a symbol in Romania. The Communist government had tried to use her as an example of the heights to be achieved under Communism. She had scored perfect 10s in the Olympics. She had an eight-room villa in Bucharest, wore expensive jewelry, and drove a Dacia. But there was a dark side to Nadia's life—and unfortunately for the government, it was just as symbolic as her achievements.

Sure, she was given a job with the gymnastics federation, but her wages were heavily docked because she was childless; everyone had heard how every three months she went to the clinic for a pregnancy test. The government was trying to force her to have a baby! She had also been guarded constantly for over a decade, and some said in the early '80s she was so desperate to get out, she drank bleach to kill herself.

Growing up, I had focused on Nadia's status as a positive symbol of Romania, her determination, her achievements. But now, more and more often, I thought of the negative side: Nadia had been a prisoner in her own country, her life totally controlled. My life wasn't *totally* controlled, but sometimes I felt like a prisoner, with few options and little freedom. We heard rumors that Nadia had escaped Romania about a month before the revolution, and I was beginning to think that I, too, was going to have to escape.

Romania also continued to torment me with its corruption. For Radio Contact I interviewed officials with false smiles, executives with fake identities. Those who had been informants under Ceauşescu were now exploiters and connivers under the new regime. As under Communism, many only pretended to work, yet continued to draw paychecks and get promotions. I had so hoped that the promises made after the revolution would come true, but an egalitarian society was still far from actuality. Filled with bitterness, I believed that the many people who'd lost their lives fighting for a better society had died in vain. I wanted more from my vision of the future.

"I would wash dishes wherever there is freedom in this wide world," I said, "but I don't want to live in this country anymore."

Michael held me in his arms. "And I would go with you anywhere in the world."

I started looking for scholarships and jobs abroad. One day I bumped into the family's photographer, whom I hadn't seen in a long time. As with the casual connection with Liviu almost three years earlier, this meeting would also change my life. I asked about Petrana, his daughter, and learned that she was living in the US. I'd heard stories of people immigrating there illegally by paying an American citizen a fee and signing a fictitious marriage license. I would never do that and assumed Petrana wouldn't either. I asked her father how she'd gotten in. He said she'd won the green card lottery, a series of drawings held once per year, and published in *Evenimentul Zilei* in Bucharest. He offered to bring me the newspaper when the information for the next lottery came out in the spring.

America, I thought. Home of jazz music, Michael Jackson, Hollywood. Hollywood with its palm trees and blue skies.

Go.

Busy, busy, busy. I'd actually forgotten the photographer's offer when, five months later, he showed up at one of my classes with the promised newspaper. I took it home and discussed the green card lottery with Michael.

I told him how I'd always wanted to learn more about the roots of African-American jazz and the country style of Johnny Cash, and simply to be in a country capable of giving rise to Elvis Presley and Michael Jackson. I wanted to eat Cajun food and walk down famous Sunset Boulevard and see billboards of the Marlboro cowboy. And see those palm trees for myself.

Michael shared these desires, and we both decided to apply for the lottery. I didn't mention it to my parents. It wasn't that they would be surprised—I had first announced my desire to leave Romania when I was seven—it was just that the odds of winning were miniscule.

The application was simple, but filing it—making an attempt to disinherit myself from my homeland—made me take another look at Sibiu. Could I really leave it? Though mainly a manufacturing area, the Lower Town had been the crib of my multicultural family. Upper Town, built along the east bank of the Cibin River, was a romantic island of heritage and beauty, an exciting mix of cultures. Even though Communist contempt for Old World roots had chipped Sibiu's colors and caked it with grime, the neglect hadn't completely stolen its storybook appeal. I adored the cobblestone streets, the medieval huddle of buildings around the squares, the elegant Viennese baroque façades, gothic roofs and spires, the architectural mélange that reached back through time, merging into Renaissance foundations and Romanesque archways—layer upon layer of history. The blue color of many buildings reminded me of *albastru de Voronet,* so predominant in Moldova's monasteries. My city was a piece of antique jewelry neatly tucked at the flare of the Carpathian ruffles circling Transylvania.

The city's post-Communist administration had pretended to be involved in restoring the architectural charm, but even there, corruption had ruled the effort, and the real vision went unrealized. Every narrow street led to frustration. Still, Sibiu was and would always be my first love . . . but it was an impossible love, for we could never be together.

I'd grown and changed. Buni was gone, so I could also leave now.

Still, I forgot about the lottery. I was working toward my PhD, and

Michael was considering a position with Pepsi in Bucharest. Life went on while we lived together and loved each other, saving so we could eat out occasionally and give each other small gifts. He brought home flowers, and we evolved pet names for each other. I called him Mickey, Bubu, Bumbii; he called me Bobo (doll in Hungarian, which I loved) and Pushkin—a bit sickening to others, I suppose, but we made each other laugh. He picked up my mom's habit of leaving little notes in my purse, along with flowers perched on the seat of my beat-up old Ford, perfume bottles under my pillow, aroma candles on the dresser.

Artistic Michael spotted a bolt of woolen fabric in rainbow stripes. We both loved it. He had wanted to buy me something smashing to wear, but we couldn't afford anything, so Michael amazed me by designing and sewing a poncho that I could wear a bit like a scarf over a tailored mid-thigh coat of the same fabric, all lined in red. To create the poncho's fringe we sat for several evenings pulling strings of fabric away. How I loved wearing the set over skirts or pants. Michael's style was avant-garde in clothing, music, the articles and books he read. He not only agreed with my feminist ideas and actions, he supported them. I was truly lucky to have him in my life.

On August 25, 1996, I picked up the mail and found an oversized envelope from the US that had come via Holland. *Hmm,* I didn't know anybody in the US or in Holland. Maybe it was a pyramid scam like Caritas—the Ponzi scheme that had involved public officials, drawn up to five billion dollars in investments, then collapsed in 1994, owing 450 million dollars. I opened the envelope to see.

> Congratulations! You were randomly selected by the computer as a winner for the 1997 Green Card Lottery! There have been 8 million people, and you are one of the lucky 100,000 selected for the first round. Please don't leave your job, don't sell anything. The decision is not final. Fill out the following forms and send them by October 1, 1996.

I had won. *My dear God!* I called Michael at work. "Michael, Bumbii, oh, my God . . .you will not believe it. Oh, my God, Mickey . . ."

"Aura? What's wrong? Are you all right? Aura?"

"Mickey . . . I can't believe . . ."

"Aura, please, I implore you . . . calm down and tell me what happened."

I took a deep breath. "I won the green card lottery! We can leave Romania . . . I think. Can you come home from work?"

"I'll be right there."

In the living room, I checked the big grandfather clock to see what time this miracle had occurred. Nine o'clock? I looked at my watch: 1:35 PM. The grandfather clock must have stopped. . . . My breath caught. The clock had stopped at 9:00 AM that morning, August 25, exactly one year to the hour since Buni passed away. "Go!" she had said in my dream. I started sobbing again. I felt it was Buni who had somehow unchained me, giving me this chance to leave Romania, to fly freely, legally, to go to America. From the other side, she was still helping me.

"There is one major issue," I told Michael after he got home, and I managed to stop blubbering for a moment. "For you to come with me, you'll have to be my legal husband."

He kissed my lips. "Well, now, Pushkin." He held my arm out and kissed my palm. "Shall I ask for your hand in marriage?"

I sighed. "I'm already married to you in heart, body, and soul. But I guess we'll have to be slightly more married than that."

A few more kisses, and then he stopped.

"So . . ." His beautiful brows fretted. "We'd better tell our families."

"Yeah." I leaned back on the sofa. "I'm dreading this, though. You know, Dad is so . . ."

"Overprotective? Possessive?"

"Yes." But I wanted Michael to understand that underneath his ferocity was love. I told him about the times Dad cut gossipy relatives off in mid-sentence when they made unkind remarks about me. "I know who my daughter is," he would say, "and I don't need your innuendos!" I told about the time when I was in grade school and came home crying because, although I had earned an A in a subject, on my report card the grade had been changed to a C. The teacher had lowered my grade to boost the grade of the daughter of a Communist official. Dad had put on his suit, charged over to the school and straight into the principal's office, demanding things be set right.

"And did the grade get changed?" Michael asked.

"Definitely."

We decided that Michael would take the afternoon off, and I would take a break from my PhD research. Michael inspected the many bottles in the dining room hutch. Not for himself—he'd stopped drinking well before I reconnected with him at the jazz festival, and Dad and I never did drink. Mom, however, had once traveled on a wine-tasting tour through Russia and into Mongolia with Monika's mother, a chemistry teacher from Octavian Goga High School. The trip conferred a certification in wine tasting. Mom could judge the age and alcohol content just by looking at the wine. She also blended "women's drinks," liqueurs made by adding alcohol from the Victoria factory to creams of chocolate, vanilla, burnt sugar, coffee, and even an eggnog-like mixture. Under Communism, ordinary folks had had no money to buy alcohol for personal use, so everyone made their own wines, brandies, ales—anything alcoholic. In Romania, you never visited anyone without such a gift. No one ever came to your home without being offered a drink of some home brew. At that moment, a wood tub of cherries recently picked from the garden sat fermenting for Mom's cherry liqueur. The cherries were almost ripe and ready for her pressing, and there would be more canning and pickling of produce for the winter.

That afternoon, Michael selected a bottle of Murfatlar, a wine from Jidvei, to open for Mom to help soften the shock.

Mom was out in the garden trimming flowers. When I called

her she came in clutching a bouquet of roses, daisies, lilacs, peonies, and lily-of-the-valley. I summoned my dad while Mom put the flowers in a vase. When Dad entered he wore a look of skepticism on his face. He knew that if he had to be summoned, the news couldn't be to his liking. Mom shook her head at the proffered wine. I put the bottle back unopened.

Michael and I looked at each other. For once, I had no clue how to start a conversation. Michael's open palms and raised eyebrows said, *They're your parents. You start the show.*

An invisible weight pressed down on my shoulders, but I drew a deep breath. "Michael and I need to get married right away."

Dad's eyes almost popped from their sockets. "You don't have to marry someone just because you are pregnant. You just started your PhD program. That's the most important thing. You'll have a career to rely on. Everything else can wait." He spoke only to me, as if Michael weren't present.

Michael looked offended but said nothing.

"Aura," Mom said softly, "we aren't against you getting married, but why the rush?"

I tried to break the news gently. I reminded them of the palm tree vision I'd had as a child, and told them I was still having it. I described my ongoing dream about Buni's command to me. I explained about Dad's photographer friend and the green card lottery and how Michael and I had both applied, thinking it was sort of a lark, and then forgotten about it. I went on about my acceptance letter and the date and the clock stopping at nine in the morning.

"I still might not get selected," I said "There are other procedures, but if I am cleared . . . well, I can't take Michael with me just as a boyfriend. Don't you see?"

"What is this thing about America?" Dad sounded like he was asking about a trip to prison.

I tried to explain. Freedom, jazz, palm trees. All my dreams and visions coming together in one place.

Mom's cheeks and lips were pale. Tears gathered in the corners of her dark eyes, and her hands shook. She hid them behind her. I reminded my parents that they'd always known I wanted to emigrate; it wasn't just a lark or some sudden impulse. "I've prepared my whole life by learning foreign languages and reading about different cultures and religions. I'm hoping that the time has finally come."

My parents could not seem to comprehend. Of course, it was a lot to take in, especially since they had never even heard of the green card lottery. Bit by bit, Mom hardened into a stone, lost in thought. Dad also fell silent, but I could see his jaws clenching. I tried not to cry. Leaving them would be hard on me, too. I always wanted them nearby . . . but not at the price of a dreary future. The closer I came to the idea of living in freedom, the more I wanted it.

"Won't you say something?" I asked.

Mom's voice quavered. "Aura, I know it was a dream of yours to leave this country, but why didn't you tell us what you had in mind? You've always been so close to us. What happened? Why didn't you share this thing with us?"

Before I could speak, Dad turned and pointed at Michael. "It is all because of him!"

Michael stiffened. "What are you talking about?"

"Yes, it is all because of you. Aura has never lied to us. Never! She never hid anything from us before. It is all because of you!"

"You can't blame me for this," Michael said. "You always knew she would leave this country that offers no future. The time has come, that's all."

"Aura does not make arrangements behind my back! It *is* your fault! You're taking her away from us!"

I couldn't speak; I felt like I was choking on guilt.

It was Mom who changed things. She put her hands gently on Dad's arm. "Fanel, calm down. If she wants to leave, let her. We'll be fine here, just the two of us. We have each other."

Dad shrugged off Mom's hand. The veins in his temples stood out like bas-reliefs.

"It is all your fault," he told Michael again in a voice as hard and cold as steel. "Since you came into this family, Aura has changed.

These crazy ideas are only because of you!" His eyes narrowed. "I will kill you. I will not let a stranger ruin this family. *My* family!"

"Of course!" Michael yelled back. "It's always about you. It's not about what Aura wants. It's about what *you* want. Buni, Rica, and Aura have always done whatever *you* want! It is you, and you, and you again. Give me a break!"

Dad's stance shifted. "Don't make me do it. Don't make me go behind bars. I will do it!" His eyes glittered with a frightening combination of fury and tears. He seemed not to notice Mom's arm slipping around him. "Aura is an idiot for falling for you," he snarled. "You are ruining her life and ours, too! Be damned!"

"Bring it on!" Michael said. "Spill all of it out!"

Dad tore himself from Mom's arms and grabbed the unopened bottle of wine. He smashed it against the doorframe. Shards and wine rained onto the floor.

I knew exactly how the neck of that bottle felt in his hand. I knew exactly what it could do. In a fraction of a second, I sprang like a tiger between my father and my lover.

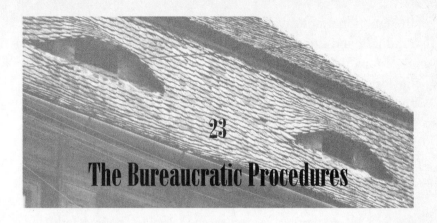

23
The Bureaucratic Procedures

"FANEL, *STOP!*" MOM PUT HER HAND ON DAD'S ARM AGAIN. HIS GAZE shifted from Michael to her, then to me. His chest heaved. "I could have killed you, Michael," he said, almost reluctantly. Mom whispered into his ear. The broken bottle sank lower.

Then my father's gaze snapped to me. "If you're getting married, count me out. I will not come to a liar's wedding." He turned and stalked toward the front door, Mom right behind him.

I followed. "Dad, please, I beg you, try to understand—"

Mom stopped in the entryway and faced me. "This is all we can handle for today."

"Please don't leave like this. I want this chance at a better future, to spread my wings and fly. You raised me to want this! Please, don't make this harder than it already is. I love you the way you love me. I'm going through the same things you are. It's not easy for me either. I would always be close to you, do things for you, call you, come and see you. Please, please come to our marriage ceremony and give me your blessing. I need to know you're okay."

"I am not okay!" Dad yelled and stormed out, slamming the door.

This time, Mom didn't hurry after him. As she looked at me,

the emotional upheaval made her face glow with all its beauty, kindness, and sincerity.

"Mom," I said, "I love you. If I go to the US and make a better life for myself, I can help you, too. I can give you the chance to see the world. I can bring you over there."

"Aura, I will not leave Transylvania. Here is my home, my land. Here I met your Dad and fell in love. Here in this city I gave birth to you. This country, the way it is, is who I am," Mom whispered as the tears ran down her smooth skin. "And my dear Aura, what will you do there? Wash dishes? You are in a PhD program here; you're a 4.0 student; you're smart, good-looking. Why would you want to start again from zero?"

"Mom, this is a one in a million chance. Please try to understand!"

She just looked at me sadly.

"Will you come to the wedding?"

"My baby. Of course, I will come."

"What about Dad?"

"He will come, too."

"But he said—"

"Aura, he will calm down; I will talk to him. I will convince him."

"It means everything to me to have both of you there. Please!"

She kissed me and left the room.

"Well," Michael said. "That went well."

On September 2, 1996, eight days after the arrival of the big envelope from the US, Michael and I climbed into the car and set out for city hall. Just as no document could decree a marriage, to my way of thinking, no white dress could elevate that document above what I held for Michael in my heart. I wore my favorite long green dress with the fur trim and black high heels. Michael, another rebel, wore black pants and a dark glossy shirt.

Michael's parents arrived with a friend of the family. By now even Olguta knew me well enough that she would have been more shocked if I'd shown up in a white outfit than in something of my own creation. She gave me a wondrous three-string pearl necklace as a wedding present and fastened it around my neck. "These belonged to my mother," she said. "I want my new daughter to have them."

Just then a taxi pulled up. I could see my mother inside it, waving. The door behind the driver opened, and out stepped my dad. He'd come. He'd come!

I hurried over to hug him.

Michael's older brother was working in Germany, so only seven people made up our bridal party. A door with white peeling paint opened, and the city officer invited us inside a dingy, formerly white room that smelled of cigarette smoke and old, unheated air that attracted mold. I'd left all the paperwork with them the day before to speed things along. I certainly respected others who revered their weddings, but I couldn't summon any emotion around a bureaucratic procedure. Having our families there was all that mattered.

Some civil servant played a tinny recording of the bridal march, and I signaled to cut it. We were simply jumping through the necessary legal hoops, and I didn't want any element of what we were doing to be romanticized by the government in any way.

"And your last name will be changed to Chiorean?"

"No. It remains Imbarus," I said. "I will not change it or hyphenate it."

Several jaws dropped, but Michael brought my hand to his lips and kissed it. His smile blended delight and amusement. He was so different from all the other guys I'd met. So perfect for me.

The city hall official looked at me as if utterly baffled and then wrote our names on the marriage license. Done. Official. Governments and institutions now condoned our love for each other.

I looked at my watch. One of the classes I taught at the university began in twenty minutes. I would show up in my green dress, and no one would take any special notice because everyone, professors as well as students, dressed with great respect and formality.

Michael would rush back to the Pepsi-Cola branch office. It was a day like any other. My parents left with Michael's parents to go to a restaurant, laughing at our pragmatic priorities. Even Dad. Thank God he had come.

The following day we filled out all the lottery paperwork, attached a copy of our marriage license, and mailed it off to the US.

On a cold Sunday evening in late November, Michael made peppers stuffed with meat and rice in an effort to earn favor with my parents. We set the dining table with silver, china, and crystal. The clink of fork on porcelain seemed unusually loud in the absence of conversation . . . until Dad fired the first volley.

"So, what exactly are you thinking of doing in Los Angeles?" He arched one of his silver eyebrows in an accusation aimed at both of us.

"We'll get jobs and start adapting ourselves to the American lifestyle," I responded pleasantly.

"Oh, I *see.*" Sarcasm suffused each word. He squinted as if he really couldn't see me. "So you'll teach at a university, and Michael will land a dream job with Pepsi as a branch manager the moment you disembark. I get it now." He pretended to have trouble chewing the stuffed pepper.

"You know as well as we do that it's not going to happen just like that." Michael's irritation crept into his tone.

"You're right," Dad snapped. "You will probably wash dishes like any other immigrant."

I looked at Mom, who obviously didn't want to interfere. Her gaze was fixed on the ice-rimmed chestnut trees outside.

"Okay," I said, "yes, we'll start at the bottom. . . ."

"And that's why I gave you all this education, exposure to foreign languages, so you can wash dishes, pour drinks, and clear tables. Are you crazy?"

"That would only be for a while." Michael tried to be patient after I nudged his ankle under the table.

Dad fixed his gaze on Michael. "Again, you know better than all of us. Are you the Oracle of Delphi?"

"Stop it. Please, Dad. This is not taking us anywhere."

"Michael," Mom said, "you're a wonderful chef. These peppers are so tasty."

Dad glared at me. "I thought you'd make better decisions for your life, but obviously I was wrong. Or maybe all this is happening because of Michael."

"Oh, my God, Dad. I have *always* dreamed of going somewhere else. You know my place is not here in Sibiu. Just because you want to get back what the Imbarus family once had, you think I owe it to you to stay and help you reclaim it."

Mom gasped. I had just expressed the truth that underlay all of Dad's hopes for me. I'd never dared before hint that the child in me had never appreciated the responsibility. I was surprised that it came out now. I hadn't planned for it to ever come out.

For a moment Dad was still, then his face registered contempt. "You don't owe me anything. You can leave and *never* come back."

"Fanel!" Mom cried, "How dare you say that?"

Dad rose from the table and strode out of the room.

Almost three months passed with no response from the embassy. Things improved with my parents, possibly because they began to hope that Michael and I hadn't made the final cut. Then, when I came home from Christmas shopping on a day in December, a letter was waiting for me on my bed. Mom had placed it there. My heart pounded in my chest for fear that this might be an official rejection, and with excitement in case the news was good. I tore it open.

> Congratulations, you made the cut once again. From now on, do not write to this address. Your only contact will be the American Embassy in Bucharest. They will contact you shortly. Thank you for applying. We wish you success in your future endeavors.

Our first interview at the American Embassy was scheduled for January 13, 1997. In the meantime we had to go through even more rigorous physical check-ups, have new blood tests done, X-rays, hepatitis C tests, EKGs, fingerprints, and more, all to be completed before the interview. Back and forth we traveled to Bucharest in the middle of winter.

I started preparing ideas for my interview. I'd heard that embassy people didn't like malcontents who badmouthed their native country, so I was not going to mention what I was leaving behind, but instead concentrate on what I wanted to accomplish in the US. I focused on "freedom" and came across a quote by C. Wright Mills that defined the word behind all my ambitions:

> Freedom is not merely the opportunity to do as one pleases; neither is it merely the opportunity to choose between set alternatives. Freedom is, first of all, the chance to formulate the available choices, to argue over them—and then, the opportunity to choose.

That was it. This was the sort of declaration that warranted the wearing of a white dress and being the center of attention in front of witnesses. Emigrating was at least as big a change and commitment as marriage. Why no pomp and ceremony around *it?*

Still, on January 13, 1997, I didn't wear a white dress. My family might understand my eccentricities, but I didn't want to give the embassy people a reason to look askance at me. On a windy, chilly, bleak morning, Michael and I dressed warmly and respectably and waited in line with a hundred others inside the American Embassy in Bucharest. This final interview would decide our future. An unknown interrogator would judge our answers and accept or reject us. I tried to remember the pages of notes I'd made of possible talking points. *What was that Mills quote?* My mind went blank.

An official and bored-sounding voice called out: "Imbarus, Aura, and Chiorean, Michael, please approach the window."

This was it. I gripped Michael's hand as we sat down.

An American officer spoke to us in Romanian, asking routine questions, with special interest in our destination.

"Los Angeles," I said.

"Why?"

"Because of the weather." *And the palm trees.*

"That's a new one. No, really, why there? Do you have any relatives there?"

Michael said, "We have some friends who live in LA, and they offered us room and board for a month until we can rent an apartment."

We signed a form stating that we would not ask for housing, governmental help, or food stamps, so that we would not become a liability for the American taxpayer. We needed to show that we had enough money to support ourselves for at least six months.

"Okay, here's your temporary visa," the man said. "Your green card will be delivered to your LA address two weeks or so after you land on American soil. You have four months to leave Romania. That's by May 13. Good luck to you! Welcome to America!"

That was it? We were done? No questioning our motives? No chance to quote Mills?

"That was quick," Michael said, as we walked away. "Well, I guess this is it. Four months. Wow."

We were in shock. Blitzed with excitement and hope. Ecstatic. Rushed.

We had twelve weeks in which to uproot our lives as we had known them and prepare to become legal aliens in the United States of America.

24
And Now I Leave You

THE GALLOP OF TIME GAVE ME HEADACHES. WEEKS COLLAPSED INTO hours; hours went up in smoke. We had to keep working up to the last minute. Even with both of us working for a total of seven employers a month, we still only brought in about $1,100. We rarely had cash left over. So we had to jam all our preparations into our already crowded schedules.

The house in Sibiu that my parents were living in actually belonged to me, a gift from Aunt Bettie for my helping her through her final years as she died of cancer. I had it appraised at $75,000, though I had no intention of selling it. This satisfied the government, but we would still need money to live on. We had to sell the Ford, which paid for airfare: two thousand for both of us, one way. We'd only be allowed to take two pieces of luggage per person, so I planned to sell some of my unique clothing collection and other possessions. These were my own personal creations, and my friends knew they couldn't get anything quite like them anywhere else, especially Sibiu. My uniqueness, though often gossiped about, gave me status in Sibiu—but in Los Angeles, I didn't want to draw stares until I was sure of my footing. In addition to doing low-wage work, I would be keeping an uncharacteristically low profile.

On the first day of the sale, my smart khaki suit sold first. Forty dollars. My aubergine dress with the huge collar brought in fifty in a tiny bidding war. There went my classy coral dress with a hood for thirty dollars. I sold my arty silk pant outfit that I'd worn on the day I reconnected with Michael. My yellow pantsuit and red nightgown brought high prices. My much-adored outlandish lavender tuxedo made out of a coat and long skirt sold for the price on the tag. Friends started bringing their friends by, and one by one my skirts sold: the leopard one; the zebra; the long, skinny, black skirt; the tiny red one; the stripy one, the checkered—all at good prices.

By the end of the first day, "Aura's Boutique" had brought in five hundred dollars. On the second day I added scarves, handbags, and nighties. The poncho Michael had designed and sewed for me, and its matching coat, were still there. I had refused to sell them before, but now I pictured trying to pack them—the two items alone would fill a suitcase. And would I ever wear them in California's seventy degree weather? Reluctantly, I brought them out and offered them for sale. My friend Gratziela asked how much.

"For you, it is free. I'm so glad you'll be the one wearing it."

She was delighted. "I hope that when you come back for visits, you'll want to borrow it back." I hugged her tearfully.

The sale eventually yielded two thousand dollars—wonderful, but not nearly enough to live on for six months in LA. I simply had to come up with more money.

I had already resigned my teaching post, but Dr. Sever Trifu, my employer, had some advice for me. As a well-rounded intellectual who traveled and taught abroad at multiple universities in the US, Germany, Austria, and France, he'd earned my deepest respect, so his suggestions were more than welcome. Over a cup of coffee in his office, he told me how I could continue to work toward my PhD through Lucian Blaga University, but at the same time transfer my BA and MA for credits in California. Dr. Dumitru Ciocoi-Pop had set up exchange programs with more than fifty universities all over the world, including the University of California system. Besides transcripts and diplomas, I should compile a book containing a translated syllabus from each of my classes, and translated major papers and my master's thesis. Though horrendously time-consuming, I gathered all these materials and paid two graduate students to help me translate everything in two months' time. Each professor had to sign the documents, then the dean stamped and signed every page, and finally the whole book had to be stamped and signed by the president of the university. I worked like a trouper and got it all done.

Since we wouldn't be buying much in LA when we arrived, I had to fit enough to get by on into two suitcases. I knew I couldn't last six months without my most precious books, so I would fill one suitcase with those and other possessions I couldn't live without. As I selected what to take and what to leave, memories of my childhood somersaulted in my mind. An old prayer book brought back admonitions from a pretentious Greek Orthodox priest as my elementary school friends tried to stifle giggles in church. Lili and I had flirted with the choirboys and laughed at the nun's voice shrieking at us for refusing to kneel for prayers. An old arithmetic book brought back a bully from elementary school, still taunting me in some nook of my brain alongside the replay of a devilishly harsh teacher shaming me. I remembered liking the rain for keeping me home from school but hating the hacking coughs and asthmatic wheezes it brought on. I could almost smell the boiled polenta Mom had wrapped up in a rag to slam onto my reddening chest to release the grip of my attacks. I could inhale the tuica Mom boiled to make extra money for doctor bills and to buy clothes for me.

I inspected every room of the house, every cupboard and cranny, every box and chest. I found old woolen stockings Buni had mended to make them last another year, so we wouldn't need to buy new ones. I picked up the faded pink photo album and a thick green one that carried the happy moments we had shared as a family. I gazed at a black-and-white photo of me admiring my beautiful mom when her hair was long and black, a rose in her hand. And there was my Saint Bernard, Benny, and a family snap-shot with my grandparents. Oh, here I was at three, Mom and Dad behind me, a chocolate cake in front of me with *Aura–3 Ani* writ-ten in whipped cream. Aura–3 Years. I wanted to teleport every-thing to America with me. I didn't want to leave anything behind.

So much emotion is embedded in the process of starting over. All these memories collected to form who I was and who I would become.

Finally, the day arrived when Michael had to tell Pepsi's CEO that he was leaving the country and had to resign. I said goodbye to my radio and newspaper jobs. More difficult was explaining the move to the kids I was tutoring. Saying goodbye was hard for me and them that last rainy Saturday in April.

The rain continued into Monday for my appointment with Dr. Sever Trifu at the university. Time for another goodbye.

"Aura," he said, "knowing you as a student and now as a faculty member, I think America will fit you like a glove. You already have the American mentality, the American way of dressing, and with your bubbling personality, you will fit right in."

I told him how much his help had meant to me and how much I'd enjoyed working with him.

Then I made one final stop. One last important goodbye.

On the first sunny morning after the rain, Mom, Dad, and I took a cab to the cemetery and entered through the old iron gates. Overgrown with ivy, the place attracted songbirds and but-terflies.

We wended our way past the tombs and headstones, to Grandpa's and Buni's graves. Dad set about lighting candles. As I filled the heavy vases with water to hold bouquets of hyacinth, lilac, and tulips, a pain sank into my shoulders and back. My hands shook violently. In abandoning my homeland, I was leaving not only the living, but also the dead. Still quaking, I silently prom-ised them this was not a final goodbye; I would be back to visit. I would try, in some small way, to repay my parents and my ancestors for all they had done for me. The calm face of Grandpa and the imposing stature of Buni seemed as clear in my mind as if they stood before me. Even though the lavender wasn't yet in bloom, I smelled it in the air. The scream of an owl startled me, and a high wind set the treetops rustling.

I'll be back, I told my grandparents.

We are not here, they replied, but we will always be with you.

Our last full day in Romania arrived. We took the money out of our bank account and closed it. After all the bills were settled, we paid Tantana a few months in advance on the thousand dollars we still owed him after the jazz festival. This left us with only $1,300 to live on in Los Angeles. It wasn't nearly enough. Reality was setting in, and I felt more nervous than I had when studying for my college entrance exams.

Mom filled the house with the garden's bounty of lilacs, peonies, multicolored roses, and tulips from her garden. Their lovely perfumes intermingled with the scents of cinnamon, vanilla, chocolate, and coffee from the feast she'd prepared.

We shared what would be our last meal together for who knew how long, everyone cordial, a bit strained from holding back emotions. My dad coughed and held out an envelope and a tiny golden box. I opened the envelope first and gasped. It was full of hundred dollar bills in US currency.

"Three thousand dollars," he said. He looked a bit cross. "Count it."

"Why? I believe you. Thank you, Dad. Thank you so much."

"Fanel, this is amazingly generous of you and Rica," Michael said. Like me, he knew the gift had to represent the bulk of my parents' life's savings. "I can only offer you my deepest thanks."

"I want you two to have a roof over your heads in California," Dad said gruffly, then looked at me. "Now the box."

I blinked away my tears and worked the little clasp open. Inside I found a Greek amulet of locks of hair, and I immediately recognized Buni's, Mom's, and Dad's. More tears. Rivulets turning into streams. This was far more important than the money.

That night, I couldn't go to bed even though an arduous trip lay ahead of us. We were packed, ready for the adventure of our lives. But what price had I paid? How much were we sacrificing? Would we ever be able to get jobs as good as the ones we had here? We had a house here and had owned a car, material possessions many impoverished Romanians would fall on their knees in gratitude for.

Not knowing if I would ever see my parents again, not knowing if I'd ever be able to return even a part of the love and opportunity they had showered on me over the years. . . . These thoughts kept my eyes open all night. What if Michael and I were leaving behind all the truly good things life has to offer and leaping into disaster?

I said nothing of this to Michael, who slept soundly. I said nothing, nor did I change my mind about our decision. As tormented as I was, I couldn't let this once-in-a-lifetime opportunity pass me by.

Shortly before dawn on the morning of May 5, 1997, one of my cousins picked us up in a van. Mom and Dad had insisted on coming on the five-hour drive to the airport at Bucharest. The motor and the hum of tires on the pavement lulled me, and my head drooped against Mom's shoulder. I was only dimly aware of driving up and over the cold Carpathians, still blanketed with snow.

The sun's rays on my face woke me as we reached the outskirts of the capital.

Mom pulled a box made of ebony out of her bag and said, "Aura, I'm giving you some pieces of jewelry that you always liked. Keep them, save them, give them to your children. And if you cannot feed yourself, sell them!"

I accepted the box, and, barely breathing, opened the lid. My ruby ring caught the light slanting into the van, as did a white and gold necklace with diamonds and matching earrings and bracelet. An impressive aquamarine pendant necklace with a matching stone set in a ring created prisms when I held them up to show Michael. There lay a beautiful oval sapphire ring, and there, the emerald pinky ring that always reminded me of the movie *Green Ice* with Omar Sharif. Oh, I loved the Egyptian collar necklace. A black cord diamond watch nestled aside an amethyst necklace and two crosses, one amber and the other my Byzantine diamond cross that I'd foolishly worn on the day the revolution started.

"Mom, these are our family's heirlooms. I can't take these with me! They belong here. I can't just uproot them. I cannot . . ."

"Aura, I talked to your dad."

Dad was looking on from the front seat. He nodded. "These pieces belong with you."

Mom said. "Take them!"

The only expensive jewelry I'd risked packing was the pearl necklace Olguta had given me on my wedding day—that and the gold box with the Greek amulet. I was afraid of having things confiscated at the custom's checkpoints or stolen from my luggage. I didn't know what to do. I looked at the jewelry and wanted to return it, but I thought of the poem I wrote after we'd unburied our jewels following the revolution, of how many facets were cut into the jewel of my life. What could be more fitting than to mark a bold new facet than carrying part of my lineage with me?

I kissed Mom. "I will never sell them, no matter how hungry."

I took half the pieces out of the box and placed them in my purse. The rest I sprinkled in my luggage after we stepped out of the car at the airport.

The moment came.

Our bags were already on the plane and the boarding call had been made for our flight. Everything had been said, I thought, all promises made. My father's last hug brought the scent of his cologne. Mom's last kisses carried the fragrance of her perfume. Determined or not, I found it almost impossible to let them go.

Then Michael and I walked outside the airport terminal and onto the wind-swept tarmac, the last passengers to board.

Behind me, Mom called, "Aura, I love you!"

I turned and mouthed, *I love you,* and blew kisses.

Then Mom screamed, "Don't leave me!" I turned again as she sobbed to my father, "Fanel, stop her. . . ." and collapsed against him, the wind whipping her coat and hair.

25
Wings

MICHAEL AND I SAT BUCKLED INTO OUR SEATS ON THE AIR FRANCE
jet with our four pieces of luggage stowed in the hold and a huge
dream of America ahead, but I still couldn't look toward the
future. All I could think of was that last image of Dad holding
Mom, hugging her and wiping the tears I knew were streaming
down her cheeks. The sight would remain a tableau imprinted on
my mind forever. Michael stroked my hair and caressed my arms.
I knew he was thinking that it wasn't quite fair of my parents to
cling this way, and that he was excited about our adventure. His
parents were thrilled about his chance at living in a free and dem-
ocratic country. He completely understood how close I was to my
parents, though, and how terribly hard this moment was for us,
and so he kept any critical comments to himself. I appreciated his
silent support. Goethe's words came to me: "None are more hopelessly enslaved than those who falsely believe they are free." I
wanted to think of myself as embracing freedom, but the ties to
my family let me know I would carry their bonds with me everywhere.

We were headed toward Paris for an overnight layover, and
then on May 6, we would depart for the City of Angels in the New

World. After four hours of flying, we hit weather that matched the conflicted storm of my emotions. This wasn't the first time I'd flown, but it was the first time I felt I would never reach the ground again. Dark, heavy clouds with thunder and lightning surrounded the plane, dwarfing it as if it were a toy. The wings shuddered with great metallic cracking sounds as if the great bird would fly apart. The winds whipped us in drastic lifts and drops. The plane had reached the skies over Paris and was circling the landing area. The flight attendants' faces didn't reassure me with any "oh-this-happens-all-the-time" looks of efficiency. They looked terrified, though a shaky voice announced over the PA system that we should stay calm, and the plane would try to land despite the horrific conditions. My ears popped as the plane lost altitude. I could hear the engines spitting fire. The landing gear was lowered. We were approaching the runway, but then my stomach lurched and my ears popped again as we quickly lifted upward. The plane started gaining altitude again. The pilot was unable to land. Jagged light danced on the wings on both sides of the plane, and thunder boomed. The air crackled and felt electric. The plane quaked, and everybody went quiet.

It seemed as if the wind had simply carried us away. The stomach-in-throat feeling from the extreme turbulence left me nauseated and wheezing in panic. Michael looked terror stricken. Was this the end? Dear God, was this my destiny—to end in a plane crash on my journey to the New World after all our plans and dreams? I forced myself to focus on positive outcomes and urged Michael to do the same.

The plane circled back toward Paris again, dipping, tilting, swinging like a wind-battered kite. I felt trapped in the metal can, thrown like a tennis ball from one side of the court to another. My stomach dropped, lurched upward, then dropped again. The co-pilot announced that we would attempt another landing. Popping sounds came from the wings. People held hands, and many prayed; others held their heads in their palms. Michael kissed me on my cheeks and hugged me. I crushed his fingers as I squeezed his hand. He held me tight against his chest, just as he had all the nights I cried after Buni's death, hiding myself in my room.

"I love you, Bobo," he said.

If we went down, I wanted his black curly hair, his long black eyelashes, his eyes that held my reflection to be the last thing I saw. He was the one I had chosen and would choose again. "I love you, too, Michael."

Another massive explosion of light, a bang and jolt, and we still existed—slightly deafened. I could finally see the earth below, and the airport. We hit the tarmac with a crashing sound and careened along before the pilot finally gained control of the aircraft, holding it steady until we came to a stop.

We had landed. We were safe.

We had left Romania. It no longer defined our future.

I started laughing. Tearing myself away from my roots had almost proved too horrendous an ordeal, but now that we were here in Paris, a new kind of lightning had struck. *Freedom*.

A freezing rain clogged the city, but who knew when we'd ever see it again? Because our luggage remained with Air France for the morning flight to LA, we didn't have another set of clothes, just our pajamas. We had the city almost to ourselves, because sane people found it way too cold to go outside. Michael and I dressed in every piece of clothing we had, including our pajamas, and went walking up and down the avenues of Paris, singing in the rain like two children thrilled to be on a movie set. The top of the Eiffel Tower was as cold as a Romanian winter night, but there we were reborn. We trooped alongside the Seine and down the Champs-Élysées, stopping at a few shops and a café or two, and dropped into bed in a small hotel long after midnight, utterly exhausted.

Back at Charles de Gaulle the next morning, I was a bit nervous about getting on a plane again, but the worst of the storm had passed. Standing in line, a young man in front of us lit up a cigarette in spite of the *No Smoking* sign. I had never smoked, and Michael had given it up after fifteen years. The fumes really bothered us. As I was working up my nerve to say something, an imposing male voice said in an American accent, "Can't you see the 'No Smoking' sign next to you? Get rid of your cigarette."

The guy put out his cigarette. The man who'd asserted himself was no taller than I, nicely dressed, accompanied by a blue-eyed blonde—an athletic-looking couple. I smiled and nodded in appreciation. They both smiled back. It turned out they were on our flight, returning to the States after visiting their son, who had moved to Paris to work for a big American law firm there.

Sam and Leslee Mayo chatted with us during the flight and invited us to visit them in LA—our first American friends, made even before touching US soil. I was amazed and encouraged. This sort of thing never happened in Romania, where no one trusted anyone until they'd known them for a while, and even then, mistrust always lurked on the sidelines because of the era of people informing on others—either currying favor or under threat of prison. The Mayos' openness enchanted me. More and more, I had the sense that I was coming to the country to which I had always belonged.

Part III

Dawn

One need not be a chamber to be haunted;
One need not be a house;
The brain has corridors surpassing
material place.

—Emily Dickinson

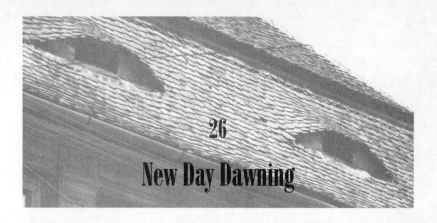

26
New Day Dawning

WE LANDED TWELVE HOURS LATER. THE SUN SHONE IN CLEAR BLUE skies, just as in my vision. Inside the terminal, we stood at one of the vast bay windows and looked out at that sky. Hand over my heart and with tears of joy, I whispered to Michael, "We're in the United States of America. Can you believe it?"

"Just like we dreamed!" he replied, squeezing my hand.

"Oh, Michael, I can hardly contain my feelings! I didn't know you could literally *feel* freedom, but you can. I'm so happy I don't even have words for it!"

"We have every reason to be excited. Our *new* lives begin right now."

And so they had. We hugged and kissed and laughed, happier than a prisoner on death row who'd just won his freedom to begin life anew on the outside.

Mighty LAX. Daunting actually. Its control tower looked like a spaceship hovering over a weave of freeways. People pushing or pulling their luggage, a Babel soundtrack, an array of ethnicities. Asians, Latinos, African-Americans, and Arabs dashed and dodged among those of European ancestry, catching flights, meeting schedules. I had never seen so many cultures and races in one place. Romania, was very homogeneous, like most of Europe, with each and every country keeping its own culture and religion. The races didn't really mix, and the only Arabs I'd ever seen were medical school students. I hadn't seen one single African or Asian in my life, except on TV or in the movies. How could so many people of so many different races get along under the same roof? This was amazing—and exactly what I'd envisioned American freedom to be—diverse people working in concert, creating opportunities to do interesting, important, and positive things.

Beaming, I attracted smiles from others in return. The brightly colored T-shirts and tropical shirts and women's dresses made me wonder if the day were a special occasion. People strode around confidently, no furtive slinking or trudging along with stooped shoulders. What an astonishing difference from what we had been used to all our lives: where our fellow Romanians, inured to the harsh conditions of life under Communism, wore ever-present and deeply carved worry lines on their faces, fearing that someone, anyone, might report you for whatever the reason, and punishment was sure to follow. Here everyone seemed light-hearted, a good-natured demeanor flickered in their eyes.

And oh, the energy; it just knocked me out. I was so ready for life here! I couldn't wait to dig in and get this show on the road! My father had complained that our coming to America would mean that his well-educated daughter better be prepared to "start at the bottom." Well, so be it! This was Horatio Alger's country where a nobody could become a somebody through enough hard work and determination—nobodies like Michael and me.

We proceeded to the luggage area, where a very athletic guy with dark sunglasses and long dark hair pulled into a ponytail, smiling ear to ear, stood with a sign that said, *Michael & Aura: Welcome to America!* It was Michael's friend Tatomir Pitariu, who looked exactly as Michael had described him. Tatomir was, Michael said, a most talented painter and photographer. But for work, he was a graphic designer, and for that, was paid handsomely.

Michael had met Tatomir in Sibiu at the Nae Ionescu Jazz Club and then again at the jazz festival. They had hit it off and soon discovered they had some mutual friends. Immediately following Ceaușescu's overthrow, Tatomir had opened up his own advertising company. He had been hired to decorate two of the most trendy night clubs in Sibiu. He also made signage for restaurants and stores and would run into Michael quite often, because both knew many of those bidding on the same projects. And both had frequented the Hard Rock Café, another popular place to meet friends and enjoy good music.

One year before us, he and his wife and young son had won the green card lottery. Upon hearing from Michael that we had too and were coming to America, Tatomir and his wife had invited us to stay with them until we found a place of our own.

"Michael, it's amazing, isn't it, that two years from the time you met Tatomir in Sibiu, we're staying at his home in America!"

"I know. He'll also be helpful on what to do and what not to do now that we're here."

"Really? You talked about that?"

"Of course."

"You didn't tell me that. What did he say?"

"To be sure to avoid the common mistakes new immigrants make."

"And what might those be?"

"Not to invest all the money you bring with you in a car; never apply for a job you've never heard of."

"That's it?"

"No, it's big long list, actually."

We left LAX, and Tatomir chose to drive the local streets so that Michael and I could admire the new city that would make or break us. The streets were clean and wide, and the traffic stretched as far as the eye could see. Sitting in the backseat, just taking it all in, I felt small and insignificant, an immigrant who had come to this huge metropolis to edge my way in, not at all confident that anyone would accept me. Though filled with optimism, I also felt an odd sense of intimidation: me, the immigrant. At least I was a legal immigrant.

The mega-dimensions of American cars made me feel Lilliputian. *Zummmm*, a car passed us. What's that? A Lexus? Never saw one before. Ford . . . Explorer? Oh, my God, who was driving such a monster? Even the models I recognized were bigger here than in Europe.

I'd enjoyed movies I'd assumed were filmed in LA, like *Pretty Woman*, and couldn't wait to see Hollywood Boulevard, the Chinese Theatre, the glamorous shops on Rodeo Drive, the Beverly Wilshire Hotel. I looked through the window of Tatomir's car at people loaded down with shopping bags. And street after street lined with palm trees. And that's when my confidence began to blossom. *Yes*, I belonged to this paradise, where the palm fronds curved and danced and nodded in the warm breeze, the sun brightening their colors, their crowns standing tall against the high-rises. I could feel the city's welcoming vibes. It was if I had lived here before. I belonged in the world of Julia Roberts, Michael Jackson, Elizabeth Taylor, Disney, and McDonalds. I moved into that altered state called "joie de vivre." *This was home.*

I rolled down my window to breath it all in. It was spring, the spring of my new life.

Tatomir stopped at a stop sign.

"What are we waiting for?" I asked Tatomir.

"This is called a four-way stop," he said. "The first car in the intersection is the first to go." *Hmmm.* We didn't have four-way stops in Romania. Knowing I'd need to master driving here, I decided to pay attention to more than my surroundings, though it was difficult with paradise unfolding itself in front of my eyes.

"Those trees with the clouds of lavender blossoms—do you know them, Tatomir?"

"Jacaranda. I've shot photos with their blossoms covering the ground like purple snow. Those huge white flowers are magnolias."

I looked higher and gasped. The Marlboro man smoked his cigarette on a billboard. We drove by the tall, white, nicely adorned Argyle Hotel on Sunset Strip. And here was Chateau Marmont Hotel, also catering to a celebrity clientele over its long history. More palm trees, and more palm trees.

A dazzling silver line appeared at the horizon. What could it be? A Fata Morgana? The nearer we came to it, the bigger it became, the more powerful its shine, as bright as the sun, almost blinding. Closer still, I watched it turn deep blue. Tatomir parked the car, and I beheld the immensity and splendor of the Pacific Ocean. I thought that with all the drama of the last forty-eight hours, my waterworks had dried up, but no. Teary-eyed, I removed my shoes, jumped out of the car and ran onto the beach, out into the waves, where I felt myself dissolving in simultaneous delirium and serenity. Conquistadores, immigrants, ordinary travelers—none of their hearts beat faster than mine did the first time I saw this blue Pacific and felt its cold waters lap at my ankles.

"America, America, America!" I screamed as I ran. "I love you!" I didn't care who heard me, nor if anyone thought I was a blooming idiot.

It finally seemed real to me, a Romanian-born young woman of twenty-six years who had won the green card lottery out of eight million applicants.

"This is Playa del Rey," Tatomir said calmly.

After crawling through traffic, we arrived at Tatomir's apartment on the corner of Sweetzer Avenue and Sunset Boulevard. We parked, retrieved our meager luggage, and went inside. Tatomir introduced us to his wife, a graceful Romanian woman with blue eyes and long blond hair—very beautiful. Corina hugged me as if she'd known me forever.

Tomorrow our new life would start. As I fell into bed, I tried to recall the names of all the streets Tatomir had pointed out on our drive. I thought of my parents, and, as ecstatic as I'd been that afternoon, I suddenly missed them dearly.

As though he could read my mind, Michael embraced me and said, "We'll give your parents a call first thing in the morning. Better get some sleep. Big days ahead! Life is going to be good now, from here on out."

As always, I took comfort in Michael's strength. He was right. The City of Angels would help us grow wings, and all our dreams would come true.

Meanwhile, love would keep us afloat.

27

The Reality of Paradise

Stu, 1bd, 2bd, 1 bath, 6m lease, no
pets, $675–800, pl sec dep . . .

IN THE *LOS ANGELES TIMES* CLASSIFIED ADS, THE HEADING SAID
"Apartments for Rent," but had I picked up the Chinese edition by
mistake? What could these numbers and letters mean?

The employment section read: Hostess, front desk agt, foreign
lang a plus, 401K, med benef, paid sick days.

Our future depended on our ability to decode such cryptic
messages. English, the same language I had learned in school,
became foreign once again. Of course, I had learned British English. LA English included slang, jargon, truncations, and region-
alisms, even Spanglish. What should I do with slang phrases like
"'t's up, dude?" The word "cool" could carry three different pitches.
"Hot" was a staccato drumbeat at the end of a sentence. It seemed
like everyone mumbled, linking their words together in a song of
blended notes without meaning. *Open up your musical ears, Aura,*
I said to myself. I turned up the volume of the Pitarius's radio and
TV, I eavesdropped on conversations I heard on the streets and in
stores.

I also practiced ordering meals. With Michael, Tatomir, and Corina waiting in the car, I entered a McDonald's in Malibu on PCH—this meant Pacific Coast Highway, but nobody called it that—and waited in line. At the counter, I said, "I would like a takeaway meal."

The young woman appeared to be about my age. "Ya mean a Happy Meal?"

I glanced around, thinking I certainly didn't want to order an unhappy meal. The place looked like a tsunami had recently hit it. The McDonald's restaurants I'd known in Bucharest and Brasov offered a salad bar, nice flower arrangements on every table, marble floors, and menus. University students competed to work there because the customers who could afford the place left nice tips. Here in the Malibu McDonald's, two homeless people lay on a table, snoring. I'd passed three others by the front door who were laughing and begging for money or food. Teenagers had bumped into me on my way inside.

"For kids?" the impatient order-taker asked.

"No . . . for adults. Takeaway." I guess my accent bothered her.

"Te-KAway? We don't have *that*." She blew her bangs out of her face.

"No takeaway meal? Do we have to eat it here?" I asked, bewildered.

"No. What numba?" She was getting annoyed.

"What . . . number?" I asked as politely as I could.

"The *numba*. What d'ya want?" Now she was pissed.

I looked at the line, trying to figure out if she meant the number of people in my party. "Four!" I said, hoping I was getting somewhere. "To take it with me." I made my voice as kind as I could, as if I were speaking to Buni.

"Numba four . . . *to go!*" She hit a key on her cash register and turned away to address a kitchen worker.

What had I just done?

The guy behind me explained the brightly lit menu on the wall behind the cashier—the one I'd thought was simply advertising—

and the selections with the different combinations, each having a number. I'd ordered a Big Mac combo instead of the Filet-O-Fish sandwich I'd wanted for myself and none of what the others wanted. At least it came with a huge serving of fries and a shake. Michael and Tatomir split the burger, and Corina and I split the rest.

Well, a good start, even if I did feel inept in doing something as simple as ordering fast food.

Wanting to share the excitement of the day, I called my parents that night at 10:30, 8:30 in the morning in Sibiu. My dad had just finished his exercise and shower routine, and Mom was making breakfast. I told them about the McDonald's incident, thinking to make them laugh. But Dad said, "Derelicts lying on a dining table? What kind of a place is it?" The week before he had asked, "What is so great about palm trees?" and "How is the Pacific any freer than the Black Sea?"

I'd bought an overseas phone card for fifty dollars and started calling my parents on Wednesdays and Saturdays or when I had something special to share. I learned never to tell them anything negative, only the positive side of my life, so they wouldn't worry.

Corina told me it took about three months for postal packages to reach Sibiu, so I had to find something to send Mom for her birthday right away. At fifty-six bucks, the shipping would cost more than what I budgeted for her gift, but Corina had introduced me to a chain store called Ross, where I found nice things at reduced prices.

After two weeks in LA, and not wanting to continue relying on Tatomir and Corina for rides, we purchased our first car: a white Hyundai for the huge price of $500. It proved to be in workable condition despite the worn gray upholstery still redolent of cigarette smoke and beer; it became our first American treasure.

Excited with our new "wheels," we called Sam and Leslee Mayo, the outgoing couple we had met at the airport in France, and they invited us to come for a visit. I stared at the classy card Sam had given me that included the title "Professor," along with his address and phone number.

"Do you know where this Mulholland Drive is?" I asked Tatomir.

His eyebrows shot up. "Mulholland Drive? It's a street in Bel-Air where the movie stars live. It's world-famous."

"I've heard of it in movies, but I didn't know people made such a big fuss over it."

"Uh, Michael," Tatomir said, "I don't think your Hyundai will make it up there. The road is twisted and hilly. I'd better take you."

We all climbed into Tatomir's car and eventually pulled onto a private road and parked in front of a mansion that overlooked the valley and hills: a one-eighty panorama. Michael and I thanked Tatomir and walked toward the entrance of the house.

I soon learned that the Mayos' many trips around the world had beautified their home: blue tile trim and a stunning hand-embroidered wall hanging from Portugal, huge Spanish vases full of flowers, a Mexican fountain, a German grandfather clock, French porcelain and antiques, Persian rugs, an Austrian crystal chandelier, a British phone booth. Interesting and beautiful pieces filled armoires and cabinets with beveled glass doors: an old casino slot machine, silver cutlery, fine china, antique porcelain statues, perfect miniature cars, and clocks of all kinds. Fireplaces conveyed warmth and welcome. A grand piano implied a love of music. Walls of bookcases stored hundreds, probably thousands, of books. Beauty, classicism, culture, and history all blended in harmony inside Sam and Leslee's mansion.

They greeted us with huge smiles and sparkling eyes in the coziness of their living room. An intellectual conversation sprang up almost instantly, jumping from James Joyce to Alexander Dumas, from Chopin to Strauss, from the city of lights to the city of music, all continued over dinner, and all in an atmosphere of camaraderie, amusement, and enthusiasm. I loved these people and their lifestyle. I now had a new vision of the joy and richness—

not just monetary—that life had to offer. But we, on the other hand, had to start small.

We finally found a place of our own: an unfurnished one-bedroom apartment for $575 a month, plus security deposit. Our palace. Dad's farewell money enabled us to get a five-month lease on a place on Hollywood Boulevard in a two-story building with four other units. The apartment was clean enough but looked more like a jail cell compared with my home in Romania, which was sumptuous in comparison to the empty white living room, run-down appliances, and worn, dingy carpet. Still, we took it, gladly. Gradually we acquired things. Corina gave us a mattress and bed frame, sheets, a blanket, two pots, and one pan. Eventually a neighbor gave us an old sofa. The silver cutlery I just couldn't leave behind in Sibiu added the only sparkle to an otherwise dreary place. Heirloom silver alongside paper plates.

But *our* paper plates. *Our* apartment. Everything was ours, and it gave us a good feeling of establishing ourselves. Old and tattered or not, it was shelter, and a place to come home to. It was a start. Our start. We laughed. And we loved. And talked about what we'd do when we got rich.

To ensure we kept a roof over our heads, we paid the whole five month's rent in a lump sum, leaving us a mere $400 to live on. We would have to live even more simply than before, and I had to get a job. Michael had found a college where he would get a certificate in computer programming, so whether we ate or not was up to me.

The race against time started, and I had to make ends meet, and thus began my job marathon. The phrase "you have no credit history" attached itself to us like a criminal record. It seemed to carry the message that we didn't quite exist. In Romania, I'd made the "Who's Who" list, but in LA, I was insignificant. After being a graduate student in a PhD program in Romania, a former journalist and assistant professor at the university, I was now applying for dozens of low-paying jobs and receiving dozens of rejections: I was overqualified. I didn't have American experience. I had no credit history.

What should I do?

Another sleepless night. I needed a job, and I needed it fast. The $400 left in our bank account was not enough, not even for a one-way plane ticket to Romania.

While waiting to be called in by HR—which I learned stood for Human Resources, but nobody called it that—for a hostess job interview at the Intercontinental Hotel for $8.25 an hour, I met a pale, red-haired woman with sparkling blue eyes whose name was Rita. She read me as if my situation were as obvious as a headline.

"Drop the sophisticated degrees," she said. "Just tell them you have two years of college, you speak five languages, and you worked for the hotel industry in Europe. Smile and be positive. That's it."

Baffled, I followed her advice in the interview and got the job so fast, I'd barely gotten comfortable in my chair.

I was employed in America! We could go grocery shopping at a supermarket. I wouldn't get paid for a month, but we were going to make it.

Tired to the bone at the end of my first shift, I found Michael waiting for me, with three yellow roses in a small vase.

We both cried, certain that better days lay ahead.

At the front desk, I learned to keep my radar tuned for the presence of the supervisor and his constant admonishments.

"Stand up straight, Aura."

"Aura! Don't lean against the front desk, no matter what!"

My back started to ache, and my feet were swollen each night. But then, my first paycheck arrived: *1,320 dollars,* printed in green on white paper. I bought two ultra-thin gold bracelets, one each for Mom and Olguta, some chocolate, and four blouses from Ross; I made a small package and shipped it to Romania.

I didn't tell my parents where I was working. I told them about buying a new dining set, but not that it was K-Mart's cheapest or that the new dishes we purchased came from Ralphs Grocery. "They look great with the silver," I said cheerfully. I'm sure they saw through my game, but we all pretended to accept the view through rose-tinted lenses.

I knew that this was just the beginning, and I accepted it gracefully. I also knew that one thing was sacred: my PhD track. It wouldn't happen as quickly as Dad wanted, but I worked on it every evening. Buried in books and papers covering the floor, I studied every night after work. Days turned into nights, dawn came far too soon, and I woke up with excruciating headaches. My parents sent me two packages filled with Romanian books to help me study for my exam and write my thesis, which had to be a minimum of two hundred and fifty pages. I wrote in Romanian, yet I had already started to think in English. An unfortunate new language came into being: Romglish. "Do you want to see a movie together?" came out as "Vrei sa see un movie?" and I said, "Eram tare busy la servici" instead of "I was very busy at work." The confusion was funny and frustrating at the same time.

By this time, Michael was going to school at the community college and drawing on his considerable variety of skills for contract work; the time he didn't spend going to school or working, he spent looking for more work. He had also made a new friend named Adrian—also from Romania—who taught high school math and who told me about the special credentials I'd need to teach in California schools. Apparently, I was going to have to take even more college courses in addition to my PhD work. I could have finished my PhD in the United States, but I wanted badly to continue studying at Lucian Blaga University with Dumitru Ciocoi-Pop, the professor I so admired.

It was our first summer in the United States. If we had time, we'd stroll on the beach, watching the tide come in and wash out back to sea or oohing and aahing over the gorgeous purple and red sunsets. We watched the crabs pick tiny prey from the oozing little holes that bubbled up in the sand when the water left the shore. Then came the sea gulls, to peck up the tiny crabs and gobble them down. Life—coming and going, all of us depending on one another, preying upon one another. But we were here. Even cloudy days in Southern California were better than the smoky gray ones in Romania. It was a calm summer, with no money but a lot of love and understanding. The only thing wrong was that in the back of my mind, I knew Mom and Dad were tortured without me, no doubt worrying about me every single day—maybe even plotting how to convince me to come back.

I worried about them, too. Every day I would feel their presence. Many times, I found myself talking out loud, asking them for their opinions on this or that: "Do you like this color, Mom?" "Dad, how much is reasonable to pay for two used tires?"

Fall came, but it didn't feel like it. Used to the dark gloomy days of covered grey skies, chilly temperatures, drizzle, and fog in Romania, I looked around, and the only clue that the seasons were changing was the date on my calendar. I loved this, too. Perpetual summer!

Come October, I would need to go back to Romania to pass the required exams to enter the PhD program. Nickel by nickel and dollar by dollar, I was saving for the round-trip plane ticket. Then the lease on our apartment ran out. Rent and the still-ongoing loan payments for the jazz festival would have to take priority now. Michael found an unfurnished studio apartment on Argyle Street for $485, a substantial monthly savings that allowed me to buy my plane ticket, but the carpets in the apartment alone could bring on clinical depression. We took it anyway.

The hotel gave me a week off without pay for my trip, and in mid-October, I returned to my native land. As the plane circled above Bucharest, I could sense my parents waiting below. I teared up immediately, but as the plane descended, I tried to compose myself, or we'd all be sobbing messes at the airport.

Our reunion was overwhelming. Mom cried, I cried, and even Dad showed tearful eyes. I could tell Mom had truly suffered in my absence, although she tried to hide it. I would later discover that she was on the brink of depression.

I'd brought Christmas presents with me to save on shipping cost, but forbade my parents or the Chioreans to open them yet. My parents had moved their bedroom into Buni's old room. I studied in my own room, enjoying the painting by Uncle Petre, the Persian rug, and the doll from Buni. I passed the exam I'd come for and was again offered the teaching position with my alma mater—a perpetually open door. The brief visit ended . . . but was my home in LA or Sibiu? The immigrant dilemma. Every transition was hard, but the six months in LA had claimed me, despite the difficulties with language, culture, and finding work. Nobody wanted to believe that I excluded every possibility of coming back. Yet I couldn't leave the door ajar, or the strings of the past might pull me back. At the airport, tears rolled once again; it was like reliving the ordeal of May, with the same prolonged hugs and sad emotions. Despite their feelings, my parents didn't ask me to come back this time. They refused to be the hurdle that stopped me from achieving my dreams. Thanking God for their stoicism and for their love, I boarded the plane.

It was during that visit that I realized with finality that Romania, and especially the government, even after the demise of the Communist regime, was impossibly stifling for someone like me. Despite the revolution, Romanian society was still rigid and monotone compared to America. I could never live in Romania again, not for any length of time. At least, this was my feeling at the time.

October nights in LA with thousands of sparkling lights, the freeways beaded with long lines of red and white car lights, yellow streetlamps, the colorful neon . . . the vibes—this city gave me goose bumps. I loved LA. I had no doubt this was home. At the airport, Michael hugged me as if he'd feared I wouldn't come back and told me how much he'd missed me.

"I missed you, too," I said. "And I'm home. I missed LA."

But when the holiday season started, I felt panicky inside. I had anxiety attacks, and I wasn't sure I'd made the right decision in leaving my parents behind. What was Christmas without your family?

Suddenly, everything bothered me. Big things, like no money. Little things, like no snow. Worst of all, no parents with whom to share the day. I grew sick thinking of the smiles I wouldn't see when our dear ones in Romania opened their gifts, sang, and ate traditional turta cake, Ness cake—featuring Nescafe—apple pie, sarmale, polenta and sour cream, and so much more.

Twenty red globes adorned our scrawny Christmas tree. Michael topped it with a red hat that didn't cheer me. I could hardly look at the tree sitting on the ragged carpet. The mismatched second-hand nightstands beside the bed illuminated a poverty-stricken existence like nothing else. Back in Romania, Mom would be preparing a lavish dinner to be served on a red tablecloth with candles, the gleam of crystal, the fresh scent of pine and holly.

The more I thought about the two worlds, the more tear-laden storm clouds gathered inside me. Night rolled in, and Michael made a dinner of expensive salmon with peanut sauce served with steamed vegetables that had butter and sour cream. He'd earned a little money repairing a computer for his friend Adrian. For dessert, *papanasi,* a Romanian dessert made out of boiled cheese dumplings rolled in breadcrumbs with brown sugar and layered with whipped cream. He managed to chase my blues away. Afterward, we shared coffee, hot kisses, and then love by candlelight. Love was my Christmas gift, and it was enough.

"Au-raah . . ." Michael was singing my name. "Au-raah . . ."

Dimly, I saw candles burning around the Christmas tree and on the table. I rubbed my eyes. Two or three hours had passed, but everything seemed to have changed. The apartment glowed in candlelight and fragrance filled the room. A plastic Santa started singing and dancing merrily. Michael smiled at me, and a flash blinded me. Laughter. There went another one. He was taking pictures of me.

"You look like a little girl!"

I didn't know how to take that comment.

"You look like a porcelain doll, my Bobo!"

I started laughing and crawled out of bed. In two steps, I reached the Christmas tree to find gifts underneath it. Puzzled, I looked at Michael.

"Honey, Santa came and brought you gifts."

"Who?"

"The American Santa Claus!"

"Michael, my love. . . . How did you do this?" I gawked at the nicely wrapped packages and opened the smallest one. Inside was a watch with a brown band and a matching belt.

"I just bought you some little somethings. I promise that the moment I make real money, I'll give you whatever you can dream of."

"You know you don't have to—"

"Open the next one."

Blinking back tears, I unwrapped a small bottle of Priscilla Presley's Moments perfume to replace the one I'd used up. I opened it and breathed in its flirty scent. Michael trailed the stopper along my neck and kissed me.

"Okay, now open up the big one!"

I untied the red bow, tore back the green and red wrapping and the soft tissue paper, exposing a stylish cream-colored suit.

"Bobo, this is for your future interviews when you become a teacher. You'll need something professional. I know it's not the unique look you used to have, but you'll be smashing in it."

Michael had thought ahead and nourished my dream. I gave him the lone bottle of Aramis I had bought him, and he pronounced it magnificent. I was the happiest, luckiest young woman in the world.

My new year's resolutions spurred me to seek a promotion, a transfer to the front desk agent position. I was often called on to translate, anyway, so I thought the promotion was a sure thing. I didn't know that my boss wanted to keep me in his low-paying department. When I found out, my anger led me on another job search.

But this time things were different. This time, I officially existed. I had job experience with a top hotel. Why not kick it up a notch? Hotel Bel-Air was paradise. Did an immigrant girl dare try her luck in the world of the rich and powerful? Could I really have a job at a place that featured beautiful architecture, twelve gorgeously landscaped acres of gardens, fountains, ponds, pools, swans . . . and celebrities?

The moment I stepped onto the brochure-perfect grounds of Hotel Bel-Air, my inner voice said, *This is it. You will work here.* The tall palms, the lacy ficus trees, the blooming perennials. A pristine swan preening its feathers. Sunlight sparkling on an oval-shaped pool. I belonged here.

I checked in with HR and waited on a white bench, soaking up the bliss.

"Hi, my name is Duncan," a tall, ultra-slim guy said in a British accent. He gave me an appraising once-over and studied my application. "So, you're from Transylvania. Hmmm. How about that!"

"Transylvania means 'beyond the forest' in medieval Latin," I said, and gestured toward the leafy patio just outside. "That's probably why I'm so in love with nature."

"Sprechen Sie Deutsch?" he asked.

"Ich spreche Deutsch, Französisch, und Rumanisch. Und ich verstehe Italienisch und Spanish."

He smiled. "When can you start?"

Life changed its colors again. New job description: *facilitate sojourns in paradise.* Edmond from reservations became my mentor, but Charles (the head concierge), Donna (another concierge), Tony (the bell captain), and others offered advice and support. My salary increased to eleven dollars per hour, which meant my monthly take-home pay increased by four hundred dollars. Michael and I bought our first TV set.

Hollywood celebrities and world dignitaries became a daily excitement, whether in person or when I passed the portraits of Grace Kelly, Jackie Gleason, Cary Grant, Marilyn Monroe, and so many others who evoked Hollywood's past glory.

I often crossed paths with my personal icons: Elizabeth Taylor, the amazing, eternal icon Elizabeth; Michael Jackson, my musical idol; Julia Roberts, the pretty woman; and George Clooney, my ideal of a handsome man. Celebrities asked me for assistance: the modest, down-to-earth Robin Williams, Sean Connery and his wife, Michelin; Nicole Kidman (with her then-husband Tom Cruise, the kids, and two nannies), Don Johnson, Donatella Versace, Prince Edward of England, Sean Penn, Uma Thurman. . . . The A-list went on and on. I couldn't help but think of the difference from our famous and talented "perfect 10" Nadia Comaneci—imprisoned and used by her government.

I had been in the US for fourteen months, and I already worked for those who were "more equal": celebrities. I wasn't permitted to take pictures of them, nor could I ask for autographs, but the thrill and the memories compensated.

But each night I returned to the studio apartment where we lived, finding each return more painful than the one before. Though we'd thrown a crimson rug over the awful carpet, nothing could be done to remove the trees that obstructed my view and choked back the sun's rays from penetrating the barred windows. The contrast stirred powerful longings. I told myself I wasn't exactly dissatisfied. How could I be? I'd always known I'd have to start "at the bottom." *Everything's fine,* I told myself—just as I told my parents, "We're doing very well." That wasn't untrue, exactly. Yet part of me harbored an imagined birthright from the proud Imbarus legacy of land, heirloom jewels, access to fine universities, esteemed careers, social prominence. If Communism hadn't stolen my family's property, I could be a guest at Hotel Bel-Air instead of an employee—instead of "the help." I felt like a Cinderella who had to smile as her stepsisters enjoyed the privileges that were rightfully hers. I know I'd said I would wash dishes just to be in America. But now that I was here, I wanted more from paradise. Wasn't that part of the American Dream, too?

28

The Hoop-Jumper

I DIDN'T ACTUALLY FEEL SORRY FOR MYSELF JUST BECAUSE I HAD TO walk up Stone Canyon Road to get to work. The late February day promised to be the sort that drew all the snowbirds to Southern California. I thought of the ice storm my parents were enduring in Romania as I passed sprinklers watering the Bel-Air landscape. Someone was swimming laps in a pool that emanated steam into the cool dawn air. I could hear a tick-tock, tick-tock of tennis balls being lobbed across a net somewhere in the neighborhood.

I drank it all in—so beautiful, almost like a picture. All around me, lush gardens, pagodas and lanterns, statues and topaz blue swimming pools, walled courtyards of rocks and sand gardens, arbors of wisteria and spreading junipers—all were so enchanting. The lavender blooms of wisteria added to the winter show along with camellias and azaleas in white and many shades of pink. There were ponds with water lilies and weeping willows, while lotus and iris decorated the front yards of mansions. Wood or brick adorned frontispieces hidden by arbors, arches, and pergolas. Pink cape chestnuts, lavender-blue jacarandas, and the mauve orchid trees were courting the twigs of the golden trumpet trees, densely covered with fine, matted, golden-brown hairs resembling flocking. Everything manicured to perfection. Bel-Air was sheer splendor.

Five-twenty in the morning, and I was walking to work.

Our small car had been overheating and because we couldn't afford a mechanic, Michael's skills were coming in handy. He could repair everything: computers, faxes, phones, cars, leaks, faucets, anything. The lack of income honed his skills, and in this way, he earned a little extra money. He had to do a complete overhaul on our Hyundai in three days. We both relied on that car, and being without one in sprawling LA, which lacked convenient public transportation, could endanger job security. I had to take the bus to the UCLA campus and walk the rest of the way to work from there. But the walks had allowed me to drink in my surroundings.

The morning-fresh breeze and the smell of roses while passing one Victorian-style house delighted my nostrils. I could just see myself coming downstairs in a huge mansion, where Michael had freshly squeezed orange juice awaiting me in the kitchen.

My daydreaming was interrupted by a baby-blue convertible zooming past me, sending my hair and a cloud of road grit into my eyes as I hobbled along in my heels. The car looked like something James Bond might drive, and staring at it, I had a life changing moment—I wanted that car so badly. Once again, I felt that gnawing sense of dissatisfaction—something needed to change.

When I reached the hotel, I saw the car—a BMW Z3—again, parked in the catering manager's space. A catering manager could own such an automobile? He was also "the help," albeit somewhat higher on the food chain than I. At that moment, I vowed that I would work however hard I had to in order to afford the car of my dreams: convertible Z3, in aubergine, like the hotel's well-tailored suit I changed into every day upon arrival. Why not? It was my fantasy. An aubergine Z3, my new goal in life, the embodiment— to me—of the American dream.

I gave it some thought. If I were to stay in the hotel business, the Bel-Air was certainly the best place to be, but was that what I really wanted?

I missed teaching, my first love.

I'd already visited UCLA to find out what requirements I would need to fulfill to teach in LA. Answer: it depended on how much of my Romanian education was accepted as equivalent. Oprah defines "luck" as "preparation meeting opportunity." Well, I had prepared hard in Romania to document my academic achievements there, and soon opportunity presented itself. In March, notification arrived announcing that *all* my degrees were recognized by the American educational system: BA, MA, Lifetime European Teaching Credential; even my PhD exams found their way into my equivalency report. I was credentialed to teach in the USA.

More or less.

On my day off, percolating with optimism, I spoke with one of the recruiters for LAUSD, the Los Angeles Unified School District. She told me that to teach English at the K–12 level, I first and foremost needed a single-subject teaching credential. Oh, and did I have my CLAD certificate?

Blink. "What's that?"

"Cross-cultural language academic development. It addresses the cultural barriers that teachers encounter in LA's diverse classrooms."

Okay . . .

Oh, and did I want to teach English as a second language? Then I'd need a TESOL certificate: Teaching English to Speakers of Other Languages.

Was that it?

No, I'd also need to enroll in a TEFL program: Teaching English as a Foreign Language.

Holy Mother and all the muses! Were these pieces of paper really worth my effort, time, and money? Seven intense years of higher education and counting, and it *still* wasn't enough?

"But!" the lady said, smiling. "Once you're enrolled in a course of study to obtain these credentials, you can start interviewing."

"Before I complete them?"

"Yes."

One bright spot. I thanked her and did some research. I didn't yet qualify as a resident of California, so UCLA's program would cost way too much. Instead, I applied to California State, Los Angeles, for the single-subject credential, which would require twelve classes. Then I'd need to take seven classes for the TESOL, six for TEFL, and five for the CLAD. Thirty more classes that I was determined to take at UCLA. Ninety units.

"In America, we have to apply for a TP certificate to qualify for using toilet paper," I told Michael bitterly that evening.

I was just blowing off steam, as they say. Buni had taught me the Hungarian version of "it's a jungle out there." Her caution that the hungriest wolves came out of the bleakest night also meant that every human being had to do whatever it takes to survive and thrive, even to the point of becoming the wolf. I could handle all these classes, but my poor nose: it would get grindstone syndrome.

In the umpteenth lap of my paper chase, I decided to work especially hard on my PhD thesis while waiting to enter Cal State in the fall. I was jumping through academic hoops at home and celebrity hoops at the hotel, Monday through Sunday, all to acquire a stack of certificates—pretty ironic for the proud little Romanian girl who had considered bureaucratic paperwork utterly meaningless at her marriage non-ceremony.

I started making regular visits to the LAUSD office in downtown LA, hoping for a full-time teaching position. In May of that year, 1998, Michael earned his own special piece of paper: his certificate in computer programming. He quickly found temporary work through an agency, which relieved some of our financial pressures. We had also finally paid off the jazz festival debt, but had agreed to simply roll the money set aside for those payments into helping our parents.

In the hope of earning a double income, and unable to endure the studio apartment a day longer, we moved again in June—our fourth move in a year. It was still in Hollywood, and this time the place offered a security fence and underground parking, although I didn't love the low ceilings, the narrow hallways, the small dark rooms, and the creepy surroundings: Our neighbors on one side were transvestites; on the other, poor Latinos; above us lived a large Armenian family.

As our schedules became more hectic, Michael and I divided the chores. I fixed breakfasts, cleaned, and did laundry. Michael went grocery shopping and made dinners.

"Hi, Mickey."

"Bye, Pushkin. Love you."

Kiss, kiss. Hurry, hurry.

Despite my daily visits to LAUSD and applying for numerous positions, I wasn't getting anywhere. I began to think I'd be stuck in the hotel business forever. . . . And I knew people who'd been at the Bel-Air for fifteen years and were only making fifteen dollars an hour. That was no way to get a BMW Z3. Worse, in two weeks I'd be returning to Romania to advance my PhD, and I had hoped to be able to tell my parents I'd landed a teaching job.

July 2, 1998—my second birthday in America. No time or money to celebrate. As usual, Michael dropped me off at Hotel Bel-Air, but as I was about to get out of the car, he handed me a small envelope. His shoulders drooped apologetically.

"Happy birthday, my love. I don't have more than a card to give you now . . . and my endless love for you."

"Oh, Michael . . ." I started to tear up, but I needed to hurry. At six-thirty every morning, a certain celebrity's wife called my extension with various complaints. She always added, "Do you realize who I am?" I didn't think people actually said that sort of thing, but I can testify that they do. Today the celebrity wife was probably going to complain—again—about a certain other celebrity who was having a screaming, wall-banging, marathon affair in the suite directly above hers.

I kissed Michael more quickly than I wanted to, grabbed the envelope, and headed for the employee entrance, tears rolling down my cheeks. In this hotel, guests paid one thousand dollars for one room for one night—almost my take-home pay for the month. I told myself I wasn't envious of them or depressed about being "the help"—just a bit emotional about my birthday and feeling lucky to be with my prince, poor or not.

I ignored the blinking light on the phone and opened my card. There was a red ribbon and . . . oh, my God! The trickle of tears became a fountain. Hanging on the ribbon was a golden ring with a row of small, glittering diamonds.

Michael must have used all his first paychecks to buy this. He'd hoarded the money, knowing I'd use it to pay the bills if he gave it to me. Tears smeared my mascara. I dashed to the restroom, composed myself, freshened up, and called Michael from the hotel's house phone.

"Michael, I love you, now and forever," I said.

"I love you, too, Bobo!" he whispered back.

I knew he was choked with emotion. As excruciating as our deprivation and fears of failure were, the harsh moments also brought us even closer together. This thin diamond band bound us more beautifully than any vow or paper license ever could.

I returned to deal with the annoying celeb wife and got an approval to upgrade her and her husband to the Grace Kelly room, which, though far more luxurious, proved to be the subject of yet another complaint. Her husband was a famous spy action hero and couldn't be expected to stay in a room decorated exclusively in pink. The fact that people often had to reserve this room a year in advance or that Michael Jackson loved this suite carried no weight with them whatsoever.

This episode sent me to LAUSD after work to check for any new job openings I could apply for, especially at Le Conte Junior High School. Its magnet program interested me as much as its proximity to our apartment. "Sorry," the lady said. Nothing at Le Conte. Or anywhere else.

I dragged myself home. Latino music blasted from the apartment next door. Armenian children romped like baby elephants through the rooms above. Michael handed me a glass of ice water. "Go over to Le Conte and apply in person," he said.

I sipped the water. "The District just told me nothing is available."

"Then you have nothing to lose."

I had the following day off, so I took Michael's advice and presented myself at Le Conte.

"We don't have any openings. Sorry," said the young, good-looking principal. "What are you qualified to teach?"

"English. But my BA is in foreign languages. I speak five."

"Hmmm, okay. We'll keep your résumé on file and let you know when we have an opening."

Five minutes later, I drooped into our apartment. Michael was there, temporarily between jobs.

"Same old story," I said.

"Le Conte just called. Maybe they've got something for you."

"But I just talked to them. They didn't have anything. It's probably just a routine question or something."

He grinned, practically vibrating with hope. "Call them!"

I did. I spoke to the principal for a few minutes and hung up. Michael was staring at me. I looked back at him, then couldn't stand it anymore. "Oh, my God. Oh, my God, Michael! They have something after all! They want me to go back for an interview in two hours!"

"Bobo, what did I tell you? You have the perfect thing to wear, you know."

I dressed in the cream suit he'd bought me for Christmas and appraised my reflection. I glided swan-like around Michael. "How do I look?"

"Cream," he said. I laughed. Whenever I had asked Dad for his opinion about one of my wild outfits, he'd always responded with the color—a response both safe and honest.

"Good luck." Michael kissed me three or four times. "You were great. That's why they called you back. Go and prove to them you're the one they need."

The interview lasted an hour and twenty minutes. At the end, I was hired to teach introduction to foreign languages, concentrating on four different languages for two months each. I would create my own curriculum and order the necessary books, videotapes, and notebooks.

Michael and I celebrated by going out to dinner, and the next day, I quit my job at Hotel Bel-Air. A week after that, I flew to Romania again, leaving a dejected Michael at the airport. Another temporary job had ended for him, so he would be unemployed while I was gone. He called every day on our international calling card, so I didn't worry too much about him.

Although in hindsight, I should have.

In Sibiu, I focused completely on my academic mission at the university. I had gotten so good at jumping through hoops that I wanted more of them, and I wanted them held higher. It was intoxicating. Here I was, an internationally accredited teacher, jetting off from my home in LA to work on a PhD in Europe.

With my attention focused squarely on navigating my hectic daily schedule, I didn't see what lay right in front of me. I didn't notice the changes in my mother.

29
Teaching in a War Zone

MY PARENTS HAD ASSEMBLED A STACK OF BOOKS I'D NEED FOR THE next phase of my PhD program. I pored over them for the next three weeks, enjoyed meals with Mom and Dad, and visited a few relatives—but mostly I stayed in my room, studying. I didn't notice that there weren't as many summer flowers in the yard that year, or that Dad was the one tending the garden. I didn't think too much about Mom's softening figure or the way she gazed into the distance between momentary flashes of her bright smile. She used to put on her makeup and arrange her hair just so, even to bring in the mail. Now she wore no makeup, and though her hair was combed, it wasn't styled. Even if I had noticed, I was too busy to think about what it might mean.

I was also too preoccupied to see what was shaping my ideas about "success." There were powerful forces at work—like the images beckoning me each time I passed through Schiphol Airport in Holland on my way to see my parents. Here, in every terminal, were stores with expensive labels, such as Armani, Dolce and Gabbana, Chanel, and LV. Meticulous storefronts showcased gorgeous rail-thin mannequins wearing finely tailored silk blouses, artful designer scarves, chic berets, snow white angora sweaters, gorgeous gems and glittering Swarovski crystals. All items were to be desired—and taken home by the perfect buyer. But I was not one of them.

I could not afford these items—but obviously Americans could. Or at least they must strive for such things. Or so I thought. And I did love color, style, and high fashion. I myself had made so many of my own clothes growing up in the dull gray-plaid world of zombie-land, where such fine things were forbidden.

Thus I should set my standard at acquiring these things, too. I would need to double my efforts if I was ever to afford them. So be it that the American Dream was very material—big cars, big houses, expensive clothing.

It was in the same damn terminal, waiting for my flight back to LA, when I finally took the time to more accurately assess my mother's health: her blank stares and her looking for something without any idea of what it was she was actually looking for. She would open the refrigerator and then look surprised that she'd opened it. Her spark was gone. Nothing held her interest . . . not even her beloved garden. She was obviously in a state of deep depression, and she needed me. It was so difficult to head home to LA, but even if I had stayed, what would I do for her? How could I help her regain her health? How could I reverse whatever ailed her? Would my presence alone help?

Just then my cell phone buzzed in my pocket. "Honey, it's me. I just got hired—on a temporary basis—by Paramount Pictures!"

He would start work after Labor Day. I felt a twinge of remorse that I wasn't there in the flesh for his exciting moment, especially since he was always there for mine. I told him how much I missed him and that I couldn't wait to get back.

"Oh, guess what else?" he said. "I saw a BMW Z3 in a used car lot. An aubergine Z3. It's way more than we can afford, but I thought you'd like to know it's there waiting for you."

Poor him! He loved me so much. I loved him, too. If only he knew how conflicted I felt straddling the line between two homes, equally loving the family in each. But I needed to be strong and encouraging for him, too. So I said only, "I can't wait to be home so we can celebrate your victory, honey!"

Once again, time flapped its wings, and I was landing at LAX. I ran into Michael's arms.

"I *hate* it when you're gone so long," he said. "I spent the best part of the summer *alone*." We shared one nice weekend at the beach before school started. Then we both dove into our new jobs, and I began attending Cal State as well. Back on the round-the-clock track, where I continued being a robot striving to get everything on my daily to-do list accomplished.

Each day after school ended at Le Conte International, at 3:00 PM, I walked to the metro station in Hollywood and took the Red Line to Cal State LA for my English methodology classes.

Michael loved his work at Paramount and often put in long hours, so he didn't seem too upset that we saw each other so rarely: late at night and early in the morning, with an occasional Sunday outing. He also made a point of picking me up either at Cal State or the metro station at night. This was for protection as well as courtesy. Tensions had grown between two of the major ethnic groups in the area, Latinos and Armenians. Derelicts, drug addicts, and hookers hung out on the street corners. We rarely had working streetlights because gangs shot out the light bulbs. Every other week there was a beating, a rape, or a stabbing in the neighborhood. Drive-by shootings occurred more and more often, and closer and closer to my school and our apartment. Michael and I decided to have our cell phones at all times; it was an essential expense. In many ways, I'd felt safer in the streets of Romania during the revolution. But there was one big difference: the revolution had been everywhere. This war zone was one we could escape if we worked hard enough.

On one particular Wednesday night in September, when I got out of school, Michael was fixing the Hyundai at a friend's house, so he was unable to pick me up as he usually did. Armed with a can of pepper spray, I strode purposefully down the street toward my apartment.

Everything was fine at first, but as I passed a small park, I glimpsed a shadow sliding behind the trunk of a tree. A large shadow. A moment later, I heard footsteps behind me. Getting closer. I walked faster. So did the footsteps. Without looking back, I broke into a jog with the pepper spray clutched in one hand. My apartment building came into view down a corridor of irregular light and darkness from the lack of working streetlights. Would I have time to stop and unlock the door at the main entrance before my pursuer reached me? No. Nor could I possibly operate the code-operated gate for the parking garage in time.

It was a terrible dilemma. I didn't want to trust the pepper spray; in my fear I could barely tell which way to point the nozzle. So I ran instead, accelerating toward the chain link fence, hitting it hard, somehow clawing my way up without stopping to judge its height—eight feet, as I later discovered. At the top, I turned to drop down inside the grounds and saw a dark-skinned man, breathing heavily, standing a mere five feet from the fence.

The moment Michael returned home, I crashed into his arms. It took a while before I calmed down enough to tell him what had happened. Then, sitting in his lap, I said, "Michael, I want to move."

He stroked my hair. "Of course. I don't want anything to happen to you, my love. I'm so sorry for not being able to pick you up. I'm going to ask some people I work with to recommend school districts with a more stable population."

We found another apartment on Argyle Street, near the famous Capital Records tower in Hollywood. I applied to work at the Torrance Unified School District, even though I feared it would be difficult to be hired at such a plum location. Teachers didn't leave Torrance; they retired from it. Still, I mailed in my résumé and other qualifying paperwork.

Five days later, they called me in for an interview. I had to stop myself from gasping when I heard the date: August 25, five years to the day since Buni died. Standing on the little balcony of the Argyle apartment, our new Hollywood-based apartment, the sixth one, I shivered in the summer heat.

"Aura, I will pray for you even in my grave. I will pray for you to be healthy, happy, and lucky."

My dear Buni, my beloved Cretii. I could see her curly hair, smell her lavender shampoo, feel her presence in a way I hadn't in many overly busy months. I reflected on how she had seemed to help me get into this country through a sea of eight million applicants—and now, on the anniversary of her death, I was about to try to buck the odds again.

On the morning of the interview, I dressed in my lucky cream suit. Michael took time off from his new job at Fox and drove me down to Torrance. He waited outside for me, car windows rolled down in the intense August sun. He kissed me for good luck.

As I walked toward a cluster of Spanish-style buildings set among leafy, well-tended grounds, I sensed a pressure on my shoulder, as if one of my grandmother's strong hands had given me a squeeze. A cool breeze fanned my cheek; a ray of sunlight filtered through a sycamore onto my face. I thought I saw Buni's smile in that light. Once again, I felt no barrier of time or flesh; Buni was close to me, reassuring me that I had what it took to ace this interview. An overpowering sense of love for my grandmother filled me—and then, even though I walked into the sudden cool of an air-conditioned reception area, I felt surrounded by warmth.

In a small room lined with framed awards and plaques, I faced a panel for forty-five minutes as they drilled me on how I would respond to real-life situations. They asked me to write a short essay on a given topic. I finished the required two pages and turned them in to the secretary.

"Honey," she said, "they gave you the maximum score on your interview. I haven't seen this in twenty years. They want to offer you a contract on the spot."

Just like that? I was stunned. Trying not to bubble over, I followed her to HR to sign the paperwork. As I did so, I felt a soft dust-settling sensation on the top of my head. Once again my guardian angel had been watching over me.

Michael was so excited, we went out together that evening and bought a used champagne-colored Chrysler Sebring convertible. I was elated. Having a car was more important than clothing, as a form of expression—it was a second skin. Also, since I was so seldom at home, if I had to choose between spending money on a car and a home, I would choose the wheels. For three years we'd gotten by with an old clunker; this convertible marked a return to dignity.

Before pulling out of the lot, Michael turned to me and said, "Pretty soon we'll get you your Z3. I promise."

I had already made a decision that would hasten that day, but when I told Michael about it, he thought I was crazy.

Teaching for me was not a job; it was a calling. TUSD had assigned me to teach philosophy and world humanities, but that still wasn't enough for me. I also got a job teaching a class at Los Angeles Harbor College.

"So," Michael said coldly, "a full load of classes at UCLA, a full-time teaching job, and your damn PhD thesis aren't enough for you? Do you expect me to make appointments when I want to see you?"

"Come on, Michael. You know how hard we've worked to get where we are, and we've got so much further to go . . ."

"You're burning your candle at both ends. We work, work, work, but where is the time to enjoy all we're working for?"

"Oh, Michael . . ." I kissed him and toyed with his ears. "We have Sundays to go on little trips in our new convertible . . ."

By this time I was blinded by the opportunities I perceived, by the obstacles I faced, by the options that multiplied daily before me. I didn't realize I wasn't just losing myself, I was losing Michael, too.

The hourglass was constantly empty, and I was running on fumes. Time was money, and money bought dreams. As an immigrant wanting to get ahead, it all seemed so logical to me. But I didn't realize the price I was paying—what was slipping away.

With so many commitments, I had to become a manager of minutes, allotting fixed amounts of time for everything. My devotion to work and study sometimes interfered with Michael's need to relax and get away from it all. I didn't have *any* extra time, but I was beginning to bring home more pay. In fact, my combined paychecks now crept toward a six-figure annual income. Ah! The American Dream of abundance was within my reach!

We moved yet again, this time to a new one-bedroom apartment five minutes from West High, and the place brought us close together again. The bright spacious room allowed in the light, and we enjoyed the oval pool and a sizable terrace overlooking Palos Verdes. This was more like what I had visualized our life in Los Angeles would be, and I could tell he felt the same way, too.

We also purchased two time-shares: one in Carlsbad, on the beach, and one in Sedona, Arizona—a place so many of my friends had said was a must-see. Michael took a week of his vacation time, and together we rebuilt our loving connection in the serenity of the red rocks, the leafy shade along Oak Creek, the spectacular sunsets.

And things continued to get better. Palm Springs, Las Vegas, Santa Barbara, San Francisco, Hawaii, Spain, France, Sweden, Monaco—all these places we experienced. My aubergine BMW Z3 became a reality. Another move to a two-story townhouse in Miraleste Canyon, a private, guarded community with three large pools. The panoramic view of LA Harbor, Long Beach Harbor, and the ocean beyond made the place seem like our own resort.

Summer was here, and we felt glorious; money was not an issue anymore. We traveled and bought designer clothes; another BMW—a Z4—and a Hummer, and later an RV. My American Dream was materializing. I bought a US flag and proudly put it up. No more dark nights in bleak and unheated spaces, no more lukewarm water and rationed food. No more nightmares about a government listening to my conversations and opening up my mail. I was now truly an American citizen!

I thought and worked like an American; I planned things months ahead of time, like an American. I started to understand how it is to park in a driveway and drive in a parkway, things that hadn't made sense in the beginning. I ordered "to go" meals and ate popcorn at movies. I had a standing weekly manicure-and-pedicure appointment. I acquired one credit card, and another and another, from silver to gold to platinum. I learned to "shop till you drop." I got the best microwave, the fastest wi-fi in the world, and every time a new cell phone design came out, I "traded up." I was, in fact, quite pleased with being "Americanized."

My vocabulary was now sprinkled with words like "cool" and "hot" and "awesome," and I was using them to mean what Americans mean when they use these words—which was grossly different from their use in other cultures! And I was fast changing my values: I'd ask, "How ya doing?" but learned to not be all that interested in how they were really "doing." I got used to the expression, "I'll call you back, ASAP," and learned that no one expected that you would, because ASAP can wait too.

I learned that the majority of folks in Hollywood were actresses, models, or movie producers—even if they hadn't actually done anything yet.

Everyone bragged about "multitasking," even if to my way of thinking, it just meant you were doing a whole lot of jobs and probably were more stressed than was good for you. But maybe it was good: I'd been multitasking since I arrived in America, and already I'd purchased a huge TV—and then a flat screen, and then an even bigger flat screen—even though I never really had time to watch anything because I was working morning until night. I taped my favorite TV shows and never watched them; I took my leftovers home from restaurants and never ate them.

Multitasking R-Us. Life was good. No complaints.

Although I needed only one more trip to Sibiu to finish my PhD, I decided to bring my parents to LA instead of flying to Romania. After months of wrangling, they finally agreed to come—then Dad said he was needed at work and couldn't get away, and Mom refused to travel alone.

I had to threaten not to come back to Romania ever again if she didn't take a turn coming to see us. She arrived in a black Nike jogging outfit, sitting like a plump, well-behaved baby in a wheelchair, her face all smiles, although her eyes filled with tears when she saw me.

I fussed over her, driving her around on tours of LA, explaining the sights, taking her to restaurants, theaters, shops, parks, Palm Springs.

"My darling girl," she said to me as we sat in the condo one day, gazing out over the dazzling water in the harbor. "I see why your life is here. You belong here."

I hugged her and felt a big sense of relief.

A trip to Kona, on the big island of Hawaii, was her birthday gift. A two-bedroom apartment with shell pink tiles and a huge lanai overlooking the Pacific became our home for ten days. We visited fresh-food markets and clothing boutiques, while Michael prepared wonderful meals: oriental salad, mahi mahi, salmon, chicken with peanut sauce, pineapple chicken, baked bread with papaya and banana. Heaven couldn't have been any more wonderful, yet Mom still went in and out of focus from time to time, as if she had temporarily checked into another dimension.

When we returned to LA, I finally discovered why. As we were unpacking, I found a package of antidepressants. She confessed that she'd been taking them ever since I'd left Romania, growing increasingly incapacitated and heavy.

I threw them all in the trash.

"Aura, I can't sleep without these pills!" she cried.

"Oh, I think you can."

I enrolled her in my gym and worked out beside her on the elliptical machine until she begged to get off. I threw all the high-carbohydrate foods in the trash, and all three of us went on the Atkins diet for a month. We walked everywhere, and Mom fell exhausted into bed at night.

"I didn't say I wanted to compete for Miss America, so why are we doing this?" she moaned. But I could tell she loved all the attention—and she lost two dress sizes.

One night I came home early from a night class I was teaching and discovered Michael and Mom talking and laughing, drinking coffee . . . and eating doughnuts. I wagged my finger.

"Lighten up, Aura," Michael said as he chomped on a doughnut. He smiled—yet on some level, I knew he meant it.

I not only ignored this small protest, but after Mom returned to Romania, I took a photo of him with his stomach relaxed. He'd gained a few pounds. I framed the picture and put it on the refrigerator.

"You live in the land of the beautiful," I told him. "No pouches allowed. Besides, it's not healthy." He accepted the challenge, spent more time in the gym, and cooked lighter foods. He acted as if this didn't bother him at all, so I assumed he was pleased with his return to fitness and, therefore, was happy with my prodding.

"You're so edgy," he said. "Relax. Chill out."

Chill?

It was an interesting remark. I thought about it. I always thought of myself as serene. It struck me that in Sibiu, I had known how to chill: the benefits of those long walks on sunny days in shady summers, or fall afternoons among trees blazing with color, or ankle deep in crackling leaves, or winter evenings with snowflakes bussing my cheeks, or freezing, ice-limned mornings with the sun's rays dazzling the world into crystalline glory, or through the rebirth of tender green in springtime—every step left me feeling serene, "chilled," and, better yet, had put me in touch with my intuitive side. The long days I'd spent in Tante Tilli's garden had been meditative, walking among the chestnut trees. I had been open and receptive; I had dreamt of the future instead of only working toward it. I had felt the feathery caress of Buni's angel wing.

Now, I thought of freedom as something outside me. I was a determined woman on a mission. I meditated from 6:15 to 6:30 every morning. I exercised in the gym, hurrying to fit it in between teaching and taking classes. I worked. And worked. I earned salaries that were unimaginable in Romania. I organized life so that I could cram in as many weekend excursions to as many locales as possible. In seventy-three-degree winter weather, I zoomed my BMW into the parking lot of a wonderful school and jetted away in the afternoons. My students thought I was pretty cool. *I* thought I was pretty cool.

It did not occur to me that I no longer dreamt of future events or experienced twinges of *déjà vu*. In all my movement and activity, it did not occur to me that I no longer felt Buni's caress. Or my husband's growing resentment toward me.

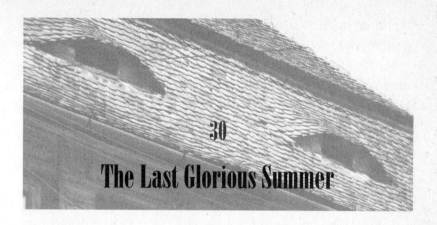

30
The Last Glorious Summer

IN THE SPIRIT OF HIGH COMPETITION, TORRANCE UNIFIED SCHOOL District pursued awards of excellence. Flyers constantly circulated, requesting nominations and announcing competitive events, honors, and distinctions. In the spring of 2003, my students nominated me for an Outstanding Young Educator certificate—and so did the Junior Chamber of Commerce of Torrance. The Torrance City Council, the County of Los Angeles, California State Senate, and California State Assembly all awarded me certificates of recognition and presented them at an awards ceremony. Michael held my hand underneath the table.

As always, he honored my freedom to be who I was and do what I wanted, and loved me for myself. Once again, he let me shine in the spotlight, never pointing out the sacrifices he had made along the way.

I left him again for almost the entire summer so I could go to Romania and finish my PhD. This was it. The moment I had worked toward for so long and so hard. But when I successfully defended my thesis and called Michael to beg him to come for the dissertation, he refused. I was stunned. This was the first really important moment in our married life that Michael was not going to share with me.

My father, on the other hand, was thrilled, as was Mom. I nearly came unhinged with pride, relief, and excitement at joining the august parade of robed scholars receiving their honors.

Lucian Blaga University awarded me my PhD, cum laude, closing another chapter of hard work in my life. The degree was duly transferred to and recognized by the American educational system. Best of all, I got an additional stipend from TUSD for my newly received degree.

I think Dad's pride in me compelled him to finally agree to come to LA with Mom the following year. By then Michael had been promoted to client-services manager at Fox, and with both of us earning more money, we were able to pay off the time-shares and use the extra income to fix up the condo before my parents arrived. We added new appliances, granite kitchen counters, and curtains; painted the walls in harmonizing shades of gold and honey—and, as a finishing touch, potted colorful flowers around a new fountain that spouted water from the top and from the four sides of a column that stood in a Moorish pool out on our terrace.

We picked up my parents at LAX in Michael's brand-new Sebring convertible. When we entered the condo, Mom said, "Aura, you two have changed so many things since I was here. It looks wonderful!"

Dad wandered from room to room, commenting on the house, the décor, our cars, the guarded community, the amazing harbor view, the lush landscape, and especially our fountain. He loved the private guest bath in their room. Seeing him like this was a moment of intense validation for me, and we couldn't stop hugging each other—all of us, including Michael. Tears filled my eyes, of course. Mom's, too.

Then we revealed our travel plans for the summer: Palm Springs, the Grand Canyon, Vegas, San Diego.

"It's too much," Dad said. "You shouldn't spend so much money."

"And Hawaii . . ." Michael said.

"Way too much!" Mom protested, but I could tell she was secretly delighted.

As for me, I was thrilled to give my parents the kind of life they might have enjoyed if it hadn't been for Eastern Europe's ghastly experiment with Communism.

"There's also a surprise for this first weekend," Michael said.

I had told him one of my favorite stories about my dad. For one of my teenage birthdays, Mom had cooked for days to provide food, drinks, and music for a party. The whole house was nicely decorated, the furniture pushed aside so we could dance all night, Romanian style. Food in the kitchen, drinks in the ice-filled bathtub, a hundred people coming and going with friends and friends of friends. The chandelier in the living room swayed while crazy dancers thundered on the wood floors, the girls in high heels and miniskirts.

At around 10:00 PM, though, I had noticed a strange shortage of guys. Were they going home? I went outside and discovered the missing males competing against each other and my father, jumping and hurling themselves about in frenzied competition, oblivious to the girls, booze, and music. Dad taunted them with his humor, drawing volleys of male laughter as he bested them. Soon the girls, tired of dancing by themselves, crowded into the already packed space in the yard. My Mom hauled the food outside. Even Buni was there, cheering Dad on. He gave my friends hilarious consolation speeches that prodded them to do better in the future.

Michael also knew that while Dad had attended technical college in Timisoara, he kayaked professionally on the Bega River. He loved kayaking above all sports. If his family hadn't required more income from him, he would have become a gym teacher. He lived by the Latin proverb, *mens sana in corpore sano* (a healthy mind in a healthy body), which is why he worked out every morning of his life.

These stories were what inspired Michael's surprise. We dressed for a day at the beach, piled into the convertible, put the top down, and drove to the Naples canals in Long Beach. We drove along

Ocean Boulevard, past its restaurants and shops, found a parking spot, and walked for a few minutes to a recreational center on the Alamitos Bay side of the strand.

On such a gorgeous summer day, all manner of watercraft navigated the calm waters: sailboats, motorboats, pedal-boats, jet-skis, Venetian-style gondolas with jaunty boatmen in blue and white striped shirts and red neckerchiefs . . . and kayaks.

"Kayaks?" Dad sounded like a kid again. "We're going kayaking?"

"We are," Michael said.

"Oh, no. No," Mom said. "I'll watch. I'm not a swimmer. No, I can't come."

"Mom," I said, "you'll be with me. Nothing bad will happen to you. Trust me."

"But what if the boat rolls over, and I fall in water?"

"You'll float with your life vest, even if you don't want to," I said.

"No, I'll just stay here and take care of our stuff."

"No, Mom. You're coming with us, and you'll have a great time."

"Ahhh, fine, fine . . ."

It was Dad's turn to tear up. "This is the biggest and most beautiful surprise you could ever make for me. Thank you, Michael. Thank you, Aura. I thought I'd never see a kayak again. I haven't touched one in forty-three years."

We paddled around the Rivo Alto Canal, gawking at the gorgeous beach homes. Michael and Dad would race off and then rejoin us, their taunting laughter preceding them. We circled the little Treasure Island and continued toward the marinas, admiring, enjoying, and then returning, drenched but with no capsizes. We ate lunch at a little beach café.

"Aura," Dad said, setting down his half-eaten burger. "What you have accomplished here in seven years, people cannot duplicate in a lifetime in Romania." He turned toward Michael. "Now I truly understand why you don't want to come back. I understand both of you. I would have made the same decision at your age. This is your life, and this is your home."

Mom said, "I told him the same thing when I went back to Romania in 2002. Wherever you are, your happiness is our happiness."

"Looks like I earned some points on that," Michael whispered to me and then asked, "How did you like kayaking, Rica?"

"No words to describe it. I'm just speechless."

The summer with my parents had just begun. We jetted over to Hawaii and then Maui. Michael took Dad on a snorkeling excursion to swim with turtles and dolphins inside a crescent bay formed by the half crater of the Molokini volcano.

While they were gone, Mom and I spent money in Whalers' Village on Kaanapali Beach. We took our shopping seriously, filling the trunk of our rental car with gifts for Mom's relatives and my neighbors and friends.

That evening, Mom and I feasted at a luau at the Marriott Hotel. She had no idea what to expect. Tiki torches blazed around low tables offering poi, *kalua* pig, *ahi poke*—sort of a sushi salad with sweet Maui onions, *lomi* salmon, rice, yams, and tropical fruits. We asked what *opihi* was, and the wise man next to us said, "Things they pull off their fishing boats." They looked like gelatinous little scallops, but tasted not bad. For dessert, something called *haupia* was served in little white bricks.

"Ooh, this is like a coconut blancmange," Mom said.

The hula, the *mele* chanting, the drums, and *Jawaiian*—Hawaiian reggae—carried us away on a festival tide, a mood that mellowed as Mom and I later walked in the balmy blackness of the night. Laden with ancient whispers and distant calls of the conch shell, a seductive breeze beckoned me deeper into paradise. I felt as if I strolled along the edge of a cliff, and freedom was something I could just stretch my arms and glide into, weightless as a moonbeam.

We got home around midnight. Michael and Dad were waiting for us, tanned and animated, spouting a flow of vivid descriptions: hot sun and clear deep water, red coral, manta rays, neon-colored fish, a curious green sea turtle.

As the warm days passed, we walked on the beaches and took long drives, heard birds calling in the mornings and evenings, spotted dolphins just beyond the surf, deepened our tans on the beach or around the pool, ate mangoes and pineapples. In a warm rain, we bought orchids and yellow hibiscus for Mom's birthday. We lit candles and enjoyed the very air.

It was the last time we would to be together like this.

Our last glorious summer.

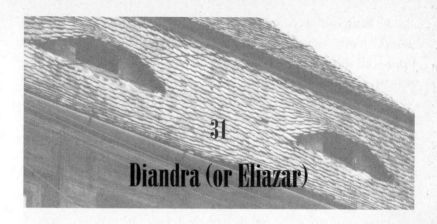

31
Diandra (or Eliazar)

SOON AFTER MY PARENTS RETURNED TO ROMANIA, I WAS BACK IN THE grind of another school term. That profound glimpse of a soul-deep freedom I'd experienced after the Maui luau—had that been real or some kind of magic that happened only in the tropics? I couldn't seem to reconnect with the serene woman who had been liberated by the island darkness and its ancient spirits. I tried to write poetically of the experience, but found myself describing waves smashing themselves endlessly against the land, fighting to regain their lost territories.

I put my poetry aside. I put my sense of unease aside. Why was I even thinking about such things? The Hawaii vacation had been nice, but it was over. Time to move on. Time to put aside strange, formless musings and mystical mumbo-jumbo. Life was something to be measured, weighed, and consumed, bite by bite.

Michael, I texted from the parking lot at El Camino College at 8:45 PM, *Rly wnt NEW BMWZ4!!!*

So, the following Saturday, we went and bought one out of the showroom. Not aubergine this time but dark blue, with tinted windows, fully loaded. Top speed: 155 miles per hour. Now *that* was freedom. It could go from 0 to 62 in 5.7 seconds. Kind of like me, accelerating from zero money to a new leased car, time-shares paid in full, an upscale condo with a gorgeous view, trips to exotic locations—all in seven years. My new Z4 was my metaphorical doppelganger.

A year later, on the morning of July 1, 2005, as I was cruising along, I turned thirty-four years old. The digital clock in my Z4 didn't tick, yet the passing time inexorably registered. I checked my destiny's agenda, and there it was: *Have child by age thirty-five.* Of course, my biological clock didn't know that I could barely accommodate my husband in my schedule, let alone an infant. Never mind. . . . "Baby" was now on my list.

Perhaps the urgency I felt was brought on by the mentoring relationship I had developed with Emily. She had been one of the brightest stars in one of the first high school classes I had taught. Though born and raised in Los Angeles, her dad was originally from Singapore and her mother from Malaysia. Awareness of cultural differences was something we had in common. Over the years, she came to me for advice on many things, and we spent more and more time engaged in conversation, sometimes about her friends or talking about family and cultural issues. Imagine my surprise when she came to me in her junior year and asked me to be her godmother. "What?" I had asked, not really knowing what she was getting at.

"Oh," she said, with tears in her eyes, "My godmother passed away three months ago. You resemble her so much. I already told my parents about you, and they would love to meet you, because I told them I want you to be a part of our family."

"A part of your family?" I asked.

"Yes. I love my mother, but it's all right for some people to have two mothers. And think of it this way: You don't have children of your own. So now you do."

Michael had been promoted to senior technical analyst at Fox—now making a six-figure annual income himself—where he now worked almost as late as I did. He hardly had a chance to take two weeks off for vacation, and his high-powered clients transferred their own intense pressure into demands on Michael. He started losing his temper with me over small, insignificant things. I would turn away from his anger, and the more I turned away, the more he isolated himself. We went to bed at different times and rushed away from one another in the mornings. I couldn't remember the last time he had tucked a note under my pillow or bought me flowers—or the last time I had rubbed his shoulders or kissed his neck. We never had time for romantic dinners anymore.

Well, tonight would be different; the calendar said it was my birthday. We would have dinner at Café Roma in Beverly Hills. Romance, candlelight, the best tiramisu in town. What better opportunity to rekindle romance and talk about a family?

I put on a crimson red "look-at-me" dress designed by Shoji Tadashi—the designer for the Miss Universe Organization. I slipped into Louis Vuitton stilettos, traced my neck with a little Emporium Armani perfume, and tucked the bottle into my matching LV purse. Surely I was irresistible.

Our salads that evening were garden-fresh works of art, our gourmet entrees beautifully presented, our conversation pleasant. Everything was going exactly as I'd planned.

"Michael, I want a child. Her name will be Diandra."

He smiled. "What if it's a boy?"

He thought I was joking. He wasn't taking me seriously. "Eliazar," I said. "Eliazar Brian."

"Why such a complicated name?" He polished off his seafood risotto.

"Eliazar, in memory of my Aunt Bettie—Elizabeth—who left me the house in Sibiu."

He looked around for a waiter. "Do you still want the tiramisu, or are you too full?"

"On my birthday? Of course, I want some. And a cappuccino . . ." I produced my most seductive smile, ". . . and I want to make a baby tonight."

He stopped trying to get the waiter's attention and stared at me. A vertical line formed between his brows. "Aura, this is ridiculous. For starters, when would you have time to take care of a child? You're never home. You have no clue how demanding parenthood is. You wouldn't have time for yourself anymore."

At least he's taking me seriously, I thought. "Well, I don't have much time for myself anyway, so I wouldn't be losing anything." I realized I didn't have the option my own parents had relied on— turning their child over to the care of their parents—and I didn't want Diandra or Eliazar to be raised by some nanny, because then what would be the point of having a child at all? I didn't have the answer, but I expected Michael to come up with one. And it had better be a positive one.

He said nothing.

I frowned. "I was hoping you'd feel happy about this, Michael. Can't you just see our beautiful baby smiling? Our child in innocent play—?"

"Aura, stop it. Innocent play? You'd set him straight about that right off! If our child didn't rise to your expectations, you'd crush him with your personality!"

I stared at him, then glanced around to see if others were watching. A woman across from me turned away.

I had to admit that Michael's words, while harsh, were not entirely untrue. "I know I can be a perfectionist, and if I can't do something exactly right, I prefer not to do it at all. But your mellowness would balance that out. Michael, my biological clock is ticking, and I want a baby!"

"Aura, you always want, want, want . . . but can you give anything? From where? You don't have time for me, let alone a baby." He took his napkin off his lap and draped it on the table. "I stood next to you over all the years you crammed in your education, but I thought that once that was over, you'd have time for me." He shook his head, looked at the ceiling, then back at me. "I want more from you, Aura. I want *you!* I don't want your endless studying; I don't want your endless working; I don't want your 'I-can-fit-you-in-on-Sunday." I don't want your trips to Romania for six weeks and more."

"Michael, you knew when you married me that I'd be going back to finish my PhD. It wasn't like I was fooling around while I was there. It was work and work and more work. Yes, I enjoyed it, but how do I know what you were doing while I was gone? How do I know you weren't fooling around with someone?"

"My God. . . . You haven't heard a thing I've said . . ."

I burst into tears at the look of cold disgust on his face. He stood and walked out of the restaurant without another word, without a gesture to let me know he was going. I was in shock, stunned by the embarrassing situation—and stunned again when a pain, sharp and asthmatic, a pain such as I hadn't felt in years, gripped my chest. I started wheezing. An invisible vise crushed my head. I swayed in my seat, then realized someone was standing beside me, speaking. I looked up to see the waiter.

He cleared his throat. "Will the order of tiramisu be for one or two?"

What was he asking? Tiramisu? Oh, right, I'd announced gleefully that we'd be having tiramisu and cappuccino for dessert since it was my birthday. I shook my head. "No tiramisu."

"A cappuccino?"

"Just the check. Please."

The restaurant blurred through fresh tears. I tried to control the sobs gathering in my throat, tried to get a steady breath. I checked the tab. Not meeting the waiter's eyes, I threw down too much money and, in my red designer dress, tried to avoid the curious eyes of strangers as I walked out into the parking lot.

Michael was waiting beside my Z4, arms crossed. I had the keys.

"Let's go!" he said.

And then I issued the slamming words, "Do *not* raise your voice to me."

I got into the car and unlocked the passenger door for him. We drove off in silence. The dashed lines on Santa Monica Boulevard almost disappeared through my tears. As we passed the LA Country Club golf course, I had to hit the break hard to keep from rear-ending the car in front of us.

"Pay attention to your driving, Aura!"

My knees shook. "I can't control my reflexes."

"Then you should not *be driving!*"

"Stop yelling."

"Stop the car right now."

I jerked the car to a halt across from the Century City shopping center. Michael got out and slammed the door, and I sped away, tears streaming down my cheeks.

I was driving almost blind. I needed to pull over again, but could barely see the road, far less a safe place to stop. Finally, I managed to park in front of a closed-down sushi restaurant. I switched on the emergency lights and sat there sobbing. The glow of passing headlights revealed tear stains all over my red dress. Although I could barely breathe, I somehow managed to both hyperventilate and fog up the windows. Then numbness, like a thousand sharp needles, spread along my arms, converging on my chest. My God, was I having a heart attack?

Mom, Dad, I need you. . . .

I couldn't think of what to do.

Happy birthday, Aura! It was not my buni's voice, or my grandfather's, or even Michael's. It was my own.

How was it possible that Michael and I had lost the warmth and affection we had spent so long developing? Well, surely the answer was clear enough: in refusing to give me a baby, Michael had rejected me in the most profound way. Oh, he might claim that I had rejected him, too—for work, education, possessions—but that was not the same. Not at all. He just didn't understand. The Michael I had fallen in love with all those years ago, the Michael I had married and brought with me to America, that Michael would have understood. But not this new, blaming, shouting Michael.

I was the same Aura I had always been; he'd said so himself. He was the one who had changed.

Someone knocked on the cloudy glass of the passenger-side door. No doubt an angry driver wanting me to move my car. But when I looked up, I saw Michael peering through the fog.

Looking at his curly hair, I felt an immense sadness. I loved him, yet I knew our relationship was over.

I unlocked the door. He got in and buckled his seat belt. I started the car and drove toward the freeway, sadder but calmer. We didn't speak.

I could smell his cologne. His collection now included Cartier, Dolce and Gabbana, Polo, Gucci, Chanel. All of them were great, but they didn't say "Michael" the way Aramis still did. I was glad *this* Michael wasn't wearing it.

Diandra or Eliazar would never exist. Even their imaginary existence had been too much, tearing a tiny crack between Michael and me into an unbridgeable chasm. It lay there between us as I drove home.

Michael stayed in the guest bedroom that night, but sleeping on our issues didn't erase them. It hardened them into concrete. And it hurt so much.

We went through the motions of reconciliation. We flew to the French Riviera, where we shouted at each other over every little thing. We couldn't even agree on restaurants. I expected Michael to soften his decision against giving me a child. He thought I might soften about keeping all my jobs. These shared fictions carried us through the next year and even enabled us to attain something like companionability, so long as none of the forbidden subjects came up: children, my working hours, whether it was sunny or not.

All our parents planned to come for a four-month visit that summer of 2006. Michael and I agreed to at least fake a marriage until after they'd left, even if that meant sharing the same bed.

My parents arrived first, and again we took them on a whirl-wind tour: Hawaii again, Lake Isabella, the Grand Canyon,

Sedona, Palm Springs. All nice trips. While we were in LA, Mom and Dad stayed in our extra bedroom, and Michael and I slept as far as possible from one another on our huge bed.

One day, while Michael was at work, I told my parents about my wanting a child and Michael refusing. They told me it was completely my choice, and that they supported me no matter what. Then they left. They loved me, but this was not their home.

Soon Michael's parents arrived. His father had heart problems, so we cringed over the rigors of his traveling and risked only a single trip to Las Vegas. I said nothing about children and clearly Michael didn't, either.

When we were alone again, I sat down with Michael on the terrace without bothering to turn on the fountain.

"I'm so unhappy, Michael. I'm sorry. I need to go in a different direction for a while."

"I understand." He reached out and caressed my hands, his face miserable. "We've always been friends. That's how our relationship started . . ."

"Yes, I'd love to chat with you from time to time," I said. "I still love you, Michael, but now it's a love that hurts."

"For me, too."

With that, the arguments stopped. We agreed to file for divorce in Sibiu by phone, fax, and e-mail, using the same lawyer to represent us both. We would share the condo until I could buy something for myself. I told Michael he could keep everything. He told me I could take the furniture, and he'd help me when it was time to move.

I thought I was becoming free again, free of a love that now mostly hurt. Instead, I was slowly losing connection to everything that mattered. And I was losing my connection to myself.

I had been feeling so alone. Now I was alone.

32

A Year in the Navel of the Universe

THAT MICHAEL AND I WERE ESTRANGED LEFT ME DEVASTATED. LIFE was so complicated.

My girlfriends pitched in to help distract me from my loneliness. I started going to concerts, movies, restaurants, and nightclubs. I played volleyball on Friday nights at Playa de Rey. I started buying new things to wear—I could no longer stand to wear things that reminded of my time with Michael.

I also took charge of a group of professionals of European origin and organized special events: a book signing, a night of Italian music, a Halloween ball, a New Year's party. Or we met at different venues in Beverly Hills: Café Roma, the Beverly Hills Country Club, Aqua, Camden House, Via Alloro. Then we tried Hollywood sites: Falcon and the Sofitel Hotel.

I started going to the monthly meetings that the Romanian-American Professional Network (RAPN) held at places like the Nirvana Restaurant in Beverly Hills, the Dakota Lounge, the Bungalow Club. We danced, talked, ate, made friends, and I got to know and be known in the Romanian community—something I hadn't bothered doing before. In fact, my attitude had been quite the opposite: feeling like I wanted to leave Romania behind, I'd actually distanced myself from my countrymen as much as I could. But now, being with them was a comforting solace.

Although Michael and I still lived under the same roof, I started dating. This marked a real departure from life as I knew it. Michael's life underwent big change, too. He quit his job at Fox, withdrew half our joint savings, and started a cabinet-making business, further proving to me that we were no longer on the same path. He said he wanted a job he actually enjoyed, whether it brought in much money or not. I said I wanted a man with enough money to allow me to cut back on my work hours and still afford to raise a child.

Nice men took me to nice places in Beverly Hills: Mastro's, Mr. Chow, News Café, Spago. I met guys. Lots of guys, all good looking and many who had established careers. We'd exchange phone numbers. They'd call; we'd go out. They drove Porsches, Aston Martins, Maseratis, Lamborghinis. They paid for dinner. Their conversations were interesting . . . some of them, anyway. But at the end of each night—the many, many nights—I still missed Michael.

"Are you still seeing the judge?" my new girlfriend Gianna asked me.

"Yes," I said. Even to myself I sounded as if I were responding to a question about visiting the dentist. "We usually see each other at the end of the week."

"And?"

"And nothing. He has two nice homes, money, cars, a great job, but still . . . nothing. Or, at least, nothing for me."

"Are you crazy, girl? Move in with him! Get him to marry you! You could have an amazing life!"

"Could I? That's what I want to know, too," I said.

Months passed. I dined at Katsuya, the Ivy, the Magic Castle, saw more shows, met more handsome guys.

"Hey, what happened to that movie producer you were dating?" Jill, another new friend, asked.

"We're done."

"Oh, my God! I cannot believe this! Why?"

"He was nice, really nice. . . . But not for me."

I started going to polo games in Del Mar and Brentwood. I attended fashion shows in Beverly Hills. I was invited to a private party at Les Deux and another at the Edison nightclub. I met an attractive attorney, then a pharmacist. *Life is good,* I told myself. *I'm moving in the right social circles.*

Another new friend, Lesley, asked me about my weekend.

"I sailed on a forty-foot yacht with some friends to Catalina. Great food, great music, interesting people. I'm going again next weekend. Want to come?"

"Are you nuts? Of course! Oh, my God! You must be so happy, girl! You have all these interesting people in your life!"

Happy? The fast pace was stimulating, and mastering the dating scene lifted my self-esteem. Party on Monday? *I'm in.* Another on Wednesday? *How could I miss it?* Three parties on Friday? *I'll make all of them.*

Adrenaline kicked in. *I want more,* I thought, and blindly stumbled forward.

I signed up with dating agencies and started online dating. I became addicted to the computer and the phone, chained to technology, eager to see who had e-mailed, texted, or called. I started a Facebook account, and one on Twitter, and MySpace. I bought an iPhone, an iPod.

I became an AI—and it didn't stand for Aura Imbarus. It stood for Artificial Intelligence, Artifice Image, the Appearance of Invincibility, Alienated Identity. Addict. Insanity. All of the above. My addiction to things, which had been growing unnoticed for years, became overwhelming. I had to have the latest cell phone, the latest slick accessory. Had to eat at the finest restaurants. Credit cards supplied me with endless diversion. New jewelry to replace the old. New clothes to hide the same old girl. I needed piles of new things to feel welcome in my hated home and worthy of being acknowledged by others.

I, I, I . . .

I was the navel of the universe, a confirmed solipsist.

And then I met another navel. Mark was a doctor. He was smart and good looking. He owned a fabulous house in Beverly Hills. Our dates possessed the right romantic ambiance; he seemed sincere. But he talked incessantly about himself: I have so many cars, and I race them. I travel a lot to foreign countries. I'm constantly called by women, but I'm not very interested in them. I want to find the love of my life . . . I have, I do, I am, I want . . .

I, I, I . . .

Oh, dear God. He sounded just like me.

It was after that date that I finally looked at myself: You're just chasing your tail. Get a grip, my friend. Find yourself. Slow down. Come back.

I'd totally forgotten Ralph Waldo Emerson's words, the words that used to be so dear to me: "It is easy in the world to live after the world's opinion; it is easy in solitude to live after our own; but the great man is he who in the midst of the crowd keeps with perfect sweetness the independence of solitude."

Clearly I needed to get back to things that brought me joy, peace, and purpose, but introspection seemed so painful. If I did slow down and take a long look inside myself, would I still like what I saw? Was I still the same person who had aspired to those dreams of freedom that we all felt during the days of the revolution? Or had I become an empty vessel, with superficial ambitions that meant nothing? I soon found that my time spent with the members of RAPN was the time that soothed me most. Aside from my growing friendship with the founder of the organization, Ilie Ardelean, and others, being a member of the board helped me to channel my own need to lead, to organize, and to be in charge. Perhaps not surprisingly, as I reconnected with my own culture, these experiences made me actually grow to miss my beautiful Transylvania, with its hundreds of castles and fortresses and fortified churches and its gorgeous mountains where I used to go hiking.

My renewed interest in Romania coincided perfectly with Romania's rebirth. In the summer of 2007, I returned to Romania for the first time in three years. Sibiu had been selected as one of that year's two cultural capitals of Europe, and my parents were eager for me to see what they called the "new city."

To my delight, those who revamped the new city understood the old one. Touring the city with my parents, I saw it: beyond plaster and fresh paint, the renovation glorified Sibiu's unique blend of history. Soaring Gothic arcades imposed their dignity over voluptuous Renaissance curves; exuberant Baroque combined with quaintly sleek Art Nouveau in a communion of new and old. And yet up above, the dormer windows of the buildings still stared at me, their expression an eerie reminder of my past. At least now they could cast their eyes upon Sibiu as a city of art and culture, knowing Romanians had persevered after all. They had rebuilt their museums, reerected monuments, sponsored and hosted artistic and cultural events aimed at restoring the history and culture of a proud people.

I wept knowing how "they" had hurt my city and its people. And how so many, I among them, had left their beloved homeland as a result.

My parents and I strolled up and down the main street, Corso. The sort of Romanian cuisine products that had never been available to Romanians under Communism, or affordable under Iliescu, were now on display in many stores, alongside Romanian wines— a burgeoning new industry. The rhythm of jazz heated up and cooled down the lofts and cellars of the old buildings. I felt like I was in a big European capital like Prague.

"This is amazing!" I said to my parents.

I spent mornings with my family and Dia, my new "sister." She had dated Michael's brother for many years, and she got along so well with my mom that often when I called from LA, I was told the two of them were gossiping together over coffee and pie.

Dia and I went to many concerts in the Piata Mare. The performers used the same portable stage Michael had created for the 1995 International Jazz Festival. *How he would love to see this . . .* Tears rolled down my cheeks. Dia pretended to think they were tears of joy for my reborn city.

I had quiet summer breakfasts in the garden, surrounded by Mom's roses, daisies, and petunias. I didn't even realize how much I had missed being with my family, here in the old routine, staying long enough to notice the scents of cinnamon and vanilla lingering on my clothes after Mom washed them. Perching on a wooden bench in the garden, listening to the chirping of the birds or the crickets' songs at night. The yellow light of the *pitici*—the dwarfs, as Mom named the yard lights I had sent—reminded me of how I used to sit next to Michael and across from my parents, and we used to chuckle while the wind spread our happiness over the night.

As I gazed through the deep green leaves of the chestnut trees, I saw Sibiu through a new set of eyes. Or maybe the eyes of Sibiu, so old and experienced, so lofty in their perspective, had changed me.

33

The Family Jewels

WHEN I RETURNED TO LA, I FOUND THAT MICHAEL HAD LANDED several big cabinetry contracts for his new business, bread-and-butter jobs. I didn't want to be involved with his business; I didn't want to be involved with *him*. We were still roommates, but probably not for long. A buyer had expressed interest in the condo. School was about to start. Our divorce would be final in a month.

In Sibiu, I had missed Michael and thought of him often. But that was a memory—Michael, a romantic fiction. Here, in real life, rekindling our relationship was just not going to happen.

On September 27, 2007, while in a lengthy meeting in Beverly Hills to arrange a networking party for RAPN, I took a quick bathroom break and checked my phone for messages. Five from Michael, all close together.

My heart pounded as I pushed the *play* option.

"Aura, the house was broken into! Please get back here ASAP!"

My heart pounded harder.

"Aura, I called the police. Aura . . . honey . . . your jewelry is gone."

My fingers gripped the phone. The same weird tingling I'd experienced the night of my big fight with Michael spread from my fingertips to my shoulders. I shivered so hard I lost my balance and almost fell against the bathroom sink.

The messages continued, but I couldn't understand what Michael was saying. I wanted him to tell me the thief had been caught and the jewels recovered. But that didn't seem to be what he was saying at all.

Half in daze, I drove home. My legs and arms felt numb. Michael called every twenty minutes to see where I was. "Please take care of yourself," he said. "Please concentrate on driving. Keep your eyes on the road, please, Bobo, please. Watch your speed . . ."

I couldn't stop the tears. I had no insurance on my heirlooms, no pictures of the diamond rings, diamond bracelets, the strings of huge pearls I got as a wedding gift from Olguta, the ones she got from *her* mother. Things worth so much more than money.

The police simply *had* to do their job, no matter what. They had to find the jewels, recover them, and send the thief to jail.

I reached the gate of the condo tract, secured twenty-four hours a day. As always, my ID was checked. How had a thief gotten past the guards?

When I parked, the doorway to the condo gaped open at me. I had trouble getting out of the car. My legs didn't want to carry me forward.

Michael met me at the door and hugged me. "Don't touch anything. The police haven't come yet."

"I can't imagine what's taking them so long." I drifted past him into the chaos of a tsunami: shelves pulled out, doors wide open, random objects flung everywhere. I shuddered. Someone had gone through my things, touched my valuables, fingered my intimate belongings. Some parasite who thought of me as a carcass to be picked.

Michael put his arm around me. "I don't know how this could have happened. I'm so sorry, Aura."

I calmed down a bit. "Michael, look at all these open drawers. It doesn't look like anything was taken from them. Nothing seems to be moved."

"You think someone just pretended to be looking for other stuff?"

"Yes. I think the thief knew exactly where to look and what to look for."

I turned toward the main door. One small window above a stack of Michael's boxes was broken. "There's no way a person could squeeze through there."

Michael walked over and inspected the boxes below the window. "If someone had stepped on this, he'd have dented it. Nobody came in through this window. And they couldn't have stuck their arm in far enough to reach the lock." He looked closely at the lock and jamb. "No sign of forced entry."

"When did you call the police?"

His face darkened. "Two hours ago. I came home around seven thirty, and had a panic attack when I saw everything. Not only is your beautiful jewelry gone, they took my laptop and my watch."

"The Rolex?"

He nodded dismally. In the bedroom, I took several deep breaths to quiet my racing pulse. The drawer from the armoire that had held the jewelry lay empty and smashed—the only ransacked drawer in the room. I saw that the tiny, golden box that had held three lockets of hair belonging to my beloved buni, mom, and dad was also gone. Right now the box was in someone else's hands, probably empty, Buni's curly locket of hair lying in some ditch.

Out of the bleakest winter night come the hungriest wolves. You have to fight for what you want. Whatever it takes.

I had forgotten. I'd forgotten to look for wolves, forgotten to be a wolf in defense of my own. I had thought that in this country the wolves were not so hungry. I had thought I'd purchased security. Yet a wolf in America had accomplished what the Communists in Romania could not. The last of the Imbarus heirlooms, entrusted to me to keep here in this safe country, were gone. How could I face my parents again? Or Olguta?

A foghorn out of San Pedro lowed out its first warning of the coming evening. Outside, the lights of LA Harbor flickered on like the diamonds of my great-grandmother's necklace, shining under a darkening crimson sky. Dock workers chained the mighty ships against the ocean's pull for the night, then rushed home, a receding tide of honest labor.

Inside my world, I was about to leave the bedroom when I noticed something lying coiled on my bedstand: my amber necklace. Somehow the thieves had missed this single piece, not part of the heirloom collection, but still worth over a thousand dollars. Michael had chosen it for me.

I snatched it up, marveling that it was here, that it was real. What did you see? Who did this? And why didn't he take you, too?

I closed my eyes and thought back to the last time I'd worn the amber necklace: last Friday. Victoria, my new cleaning lady, was working in the upstairs bathroom. She had come with good referrals, so after two months I'd entrusted her with a house key so she could let herself in on Thursdays. At some point she'd started bringing along a young man she introduced as her nephew. He kept himself busy, but I caught him watching me all the time. He was around twenty years old, with a street smartness about him— the kind of young guy you looked at and thought, *Here comes trouble.* I'd seen that look plenty of times at Le Conte.

I had been in my bedroom, deciding what pieces of jewelry I would wear to a party that night. I was trying on the amber necklace, an astounding piece of jewelry with its three long strings of stones increasing in size, their color shifting from shades of yellow to gold, chestnut, light brown, chocolate brown, and finally to something close to mahogany.

I heard footsteps in the bathroom as I placed the amber strands around my neck, admiring the effect in the mirror. In the reflection, I saw that the bathroom door had opened a crack. Two eyes were watching me. The envy in Victoria's eyes haunts me still, a blend of spite and hatred. I observed it, and I sensed it. And I ignored it.

Victoria did this. She came in while everybody was at work,

probably flirting with the guard as she drove in. I was such an idiot. I could have prevented it in so many ways.

At 11:00 PM, a cop finally arrived and noted everything we told him. Two days later a detective called me, asked more questions, and advised me to start checking all the pawnshops in the area. Apparently, I'd have to take a month off from teaching to do my own detective work. "What about Victoria?" I asked. She claimed she'd been in Las Vegas at the time, attending a conference on how to expand her business.

Which business? Selling stolen jewelry for fun and profit?

It seemed to me that the police were never very interested in solving the case. Maybe if my name were "Hilton," they would have moved very quickly. Police dismissed my case very easily, for there were no security cameras in my house, but the property I lived on was in a gated community with security cameras all over and security guards patrolling the area. The back entrance was used by people who wanted to avoid registration at the main gate.

Michael had worked until seven that evening. His business partner confirmed that they were together the whole day seeing clients. The police never questioned me, Michael, the neighbors, anybody, but instead were telling *me* to check with all the pawnshops in the area for the next three months or so. Their job became my job.

I never received any mail from the police, nothing in writing to say they were taking care of the burglary. The only time we communicated was when I went down to the police station. They had sent a detective after a week, who took fingerprints. The detective told me he "might invite the maid for a questioning," but if the maid denied everything, there was nothing they could do.

I left a message in Spanish for Victoria, begging her to at least leave me the golden box with my three lockets of hair. No reply.

Ultimately, the detective called one more time. I hoped for a second that he'd caught Victoria and found the jewels, but he got right to the point.

"Ms. Imbarus"—he pronounced it *embarrass*—"did you stage this *robbery* yourself?"

Now I was a character in Kafka's *The Trial,* accused instead of defended, the thief instead of the victim.

This can't be happening. These things don't really happen.

"Ms. Imbarus?"

"I don't have insurance on my jewelry, if that is what you're trying to imply."

"Well, some people do that sort of thing, you know?"

That was the last time I heard from the good detective. Nothing was solved, and nothing was found. Nobody went to jail.

Freedom?

Was this what happened to people in the land of the free?

I couldn't wait to get out of that house—forever.

34

Losses on Paper

A MONTH AFTER THE ROBBERY, MY DIVORCE FROM MICHAEL BECAME final.

Divorced. I stared at the piece of paper that ended it all. Just a piece of paper, replacing that other piece of paper we had signed with such optimism on September 2, 1996. Another bureaucratic procedure. I'd glibly dismissed the first one, but, strangely, this one struck me like a blow from a blunt object.

Although my parents were terribly upset about the jewels, they told me not to feel too bad. Mom had held onto a few pieces. But I couldn't let go. These treasured heirlooms had been given to me for safekeeping, and they were stolen on my watch. I was mortified I hadn't better protected them by putting them in a vault or someplace safer.

And now this piece of paper: loss upon loss.

I discovered a three-bedroom townhouse in Rancho Palos Verdes, a place where I could go to escape this condo and its reminders of the past. I called J, a family friend who managed my and Michael's investments, and told him about the townhouse. "I want to pull $150,000 from my account for a down payment."

"Aura, hold on. This is not the time to pull money out of the stock market. This is the time to make more money by leaving your funds sitting there for a while. Don't worry. By the end of 2008, real estate prices will be even lower, plus you'll have more investment capital available. That's the time to purchase a place."

"But J, I love this house. I need a place of my own, and I don't think I should let it slip through my fingers."

"I understand, but listen to me. I've owned real estate companies for more than thirty years, but I also have plenty of experience with day trading and aggressive stock investments with margin— and I advise you, as both your investment guru and a family friend—not to pull your money out of the market right now. It would be a huge mistake."

"Fine, okay, you win. I'll just live in a place I hate until December of 2008, and then I'll pull my money out. Happy?"

"Waiting one more year is a smart decision."

It was one of the worst decisions I'd ever made in my life. I stayed in the condo, but I couldn't live peacefully there. I couldn't stand to sit around inhaling the salty breeze. I'd even lost Buni's presence. She never visited me anymore, and no wonder: I'd allowed what she had so fiercely guarded to be stolen. The silhouettes of palm trees formed black gashes against a horizon that reddened like a hemorrhage at every sunset. The ocean pounded furiously on the cliffs. *Give them a break,* I thought. *Stop roaring.* Even the dolphins seemed jumpy, hounding the fishing boats. Empty seashells scattered on the beach only made me think about how their vital insides had died.

Again and again, I returned to help RAPN expand its mission, and when I was asked to become the president of the Los Angeles chapter, I said yes to this, too. RAPN was beginning to be central to my activities. When the board asked if I would join the Beverly Hills mayor for a meet and greet with Prince Radu of Romania— who had come to the US on a "friendship tour" designed to promote Romania's major interests in the US—of course I said yes.

Dressed in a smart white suit, I joined other RAPN members in the mayor's office, where we talked about programs and activities that RAPN could spearhead to strengthen bilateral relations between the US and Romania.

From this meeting, it was decided to turn RAPN into a non-profit, offering a support program to the incoming Romanian immigrants, and plan activities such as creating a database for Romanians coming to America to help them learn things such as where and how to get a social security card, best ways to interview, how and where to find employment, and, yes, not to spend all their money on a car nor to interview for a job they didn't first learn something about.

When Stefania, a good friend of Ilie Ardelean, asked me to mentor a Romanian student at a university in Iasi through the Blue Heron Foundation, I said yes. I discovered that Nadia Comaneci was on the board of a charity to help orphaned and abandoned Romanian children. The two organizations began cross promoting themselves in the activities they did.

Our new and improved organization promoted career advancement of the Romanian-American professionals while keeping them informed on Romanian-related issues, encouraging activities with a positive impact on the Romanian community.

Without even realizing it, my desire to run away from my loneliness was turning into a purposeful way of giving back, and I was beginning to feel that I was part of a real community. What I realized was that if my life was to make sense, if I was to have a semblance of happiness, peace, and order, I needed to accept who I had become. Not a Romanian but not an American. I was a Romanian-American.

My cell phone rang. It was Michael.

"Hi, Michael," I said. "What's up?"

"Aura." His tone was dark. It was always dark these days, or so it seemed. "We need to call J. In the past two days we lost a quarter of the money in our accounts."

"What?" I asked, disbelieving what I was hearing.

"We have to tell him to pull our money out of the market. Now."

"OK, I'll send him an e-mail tonight."

"Aura, call him and send him an e-mail . . . right now. He's going to tell you not to panic. He'll say you should wait because the market will go up again. But I disagree. We need to get out of the market now."

I e-mailed J from my iPhone and followed up with a call, but he didn't pick up. I left him a message.

Twenty-four hours passed, the market sliding, sliding. In that time we lost another quarter of the money we had invested. No answer from J. No e-mail. No phone call.

The next day before work, Michael followed me into the kitchen. "Aura, call J now! Now!" His face grew red. "All our savings, our endless hours of work in the last eleven years—down the drain! Right before our eyes!" Even if Michael had already taken his share of our savings to put toward his business, there was still a feeling of "ours."

I dialed while standing in front of Michael. No answer. I left another message. "Hi, J. This is Aura. Please pull out of the market. This is imperative. Take action now. Pull out of the market. Whatever we have left, pull it out."

Two more days had passed until J finally responded. "Aura, my dear Aura, stop panicking. Everything will be fine. The market will bounce back at the start of 2008."

Two thousand and eight? And what about until then? But soon, this would be the last thing on my mind.

On March 15, 2008, my roommate, Michael, prepared us a nice breakfast. We chatted in a civil way, and then I placed my daily phone call to Romania. My mom answered, and we started our usual gossiping. I told her whom I'd met and what was said, what I wore, and the perfume I had chosen, the food I had eaten. No detail was too trivial to include.

"Aura," she said, "I've been losing weight since February."

"Oh, Mom, you started your diet earlier this year! Are you getting ready for our trip to Ibiza?"

She explained that it was more about her stomach pains.

"I thought that was from the gallstones. But they removed your gall bladder last year, right?"

"Yes, but . . . now the doctors tell me I have cirrhosis."

I finally let what she was saying sink in. I could hear her breathing, hear her feet scuffling. Despite the distance between us, our emotions were palpable over the phone line.

"Cirrhosis?" I asked her, while asking God at the same time. It made no sense. Alcoholism, hepatitis, and fatty liver disease were the most common causes of cirrhosis. Mom had never had any of these problems. So how had she ended up with this diagnosis?

I peered at Mom's tiny image on my telephone screen. She'd dyed her hair at my "orders," but her dark, blackberry eyes had faded to brown and looked watery.

"Aura, Aura, Aura," Mom said, her voice suddenly lightening. "Honey, you don't have to worry. Everything will be fine. I'm fine. I only lost weight in the first place so you won't have a reason to fuss."

"Mom, I love you, and I believe everything will be just fine. We'll all be fine."

I ended the call and thought about my mother. She'd had so many health issues over the past few years, from kidney surgery to melanoma. Her sudden, unplanned weight loss frightened me.

Michael saw the expression on my face and took me in his arms. I clung to him. "How long will God keep burdening my mother?" I asked.

35

Three to Six Months

THE PHONE RANG AT 8:00 AM; IT WAS DAD. WITHOUT MUCH PREAMBLE, he asked me to look up the results of a clinical trial for him. "Dr. Maria wants your mom to be part of this American-funded research program. It's free, and apparently it's had very positive results. It is also being done here in Sibiu, so we won't have to go to Cluj anymore."

"Of course, I'll check into it. How's Mom? Where is she?"

"She's great. Out visiting friends, gossiping in the neighborhood. The usual."

"Can she eat?"

"She ate very well today. We have high hopes for this program." Click.

"Bye, Dad," I said, talking to myself.

I rushed upstairs, looking for a pen and a pad to write things down. I got on the computer and typed in the name of the clinical trial, opened the link and began to read. A few sentences in, all the strength flowed out of my body. I read the sentences again. They said the same thing as before. The treatment Dad was asking about was intended for patients suffering from metastatic liver cancer "whose life expectancy is between three to six months."

Liver cancer? Three to six months? The room disappeared. My brain stalled, unable to formulate any thought except two words: liver cancer.

This had to be a mistake. Mom had cirrhosis, not cancer. I'd obviously entered the words and names incorrectly. I looked back at my search terms. The words were correct. Well then, Mom's doctor had misdiagnosed her. Mom was just fine, or soon would be.

I couldn't breathe right. I couldn't get enough air. Needles of pain prickled all over my body. I started crying. Three to six months.

I heard Michael clambering up the stairs. He rushed to my side and caressed my hair, kissing my wet cheeks. I'd gone limp, but he held me tightly, not allowing me to slip. He asked no questions. My mind raced back to 1995 when my buni died. Michael had been there then, too, holding me, cherishing me.

I felt as if an army tank had rolled over me. Taking deep breaths, I told Michael about the study and its target population. He caressed my shoulders. "She'll probably need to do chemo, and then she'll recuperate."

Chemo. The thought of having to kill off your own cancerous cells was ghastly in itself, and didn't take into consideration the hair loss, the nausea, the weight loss.

I thought about the child I had wanted so much—the main reason Michael and I had divorced. If something happened to my mom, I would not want that new human life anymore. I wouldn't raise a child without Mom to be there as a grandmother. I would want that child to know Mom's attention, love, care, smooches, and bear hugs—just as I had.

Three to six months.

I sleepwalked through the rest of the semester, driving to school and back, barely able to remember my students' names. I graded papers mechanically.

There went another dawn and dusk, another Monday, another Sunday, as if nothing in the universe had changed. Students still crowded the schools, working for their diplomas and SAT scores. They still broke into raucous laughter and squealing giggles. The garbage man still said hello in the morning with a big smile on his face. The baristas at the Coffee Bean still served my tall latte with the outrageous oatmeal cookie. Nothing changed, except me. I had trouble thinking of a single thing worth caring about. I prayed for miracles.

My mother waited for me to come to Sibiu in June before she started her chemo.

I left LAX with my baggage loaded down with remedies like Essiac herb and Iscador—a mistletoe derivative—and pills to alkalinize the water Mom drank. I had also found out about a new drug that apparently helped create apoptosis—programmed cell death in cancer cells. I wanted to make sure her doctors knew about all these things. If they couldn't cure her, I was determined to do so.

Dia picked me up at the airport. Her father had died of liver cancer, so she understood the situation as no one else did. I sobbed on her shoulder.

"You must never lose hope," she said. "Never."

Lose hope? Hope was all I had.

So, this would be my biggest challenge ever: to trust my own façade. I had never lied to my mother. Not ever. But how could I level with her now? How could I tell her she was running out of time? She was dying. Soon.

My entire body ached.

Dia stopped the car, so I could calm down and reapply my makeup. Then she drove me to the street where my chestnut trees wore their summer green. My house was painted a shade of orange, bright against the others that still appeared gray or brown, darkened by the heavy shawl of Communism their residents had yet to shake off. Dad waited for me in front of the house, waving energetically. He'd lost a little weight, too, but his vigorous hug told me how much he'd missed me.

I ran inside to see Mom. With tears flooding her eyes, she ran into my arms like a child.

"Mom, you will be okay, I promise." The words came out of my mouth with no difficulty. I would tell her whatever I had to to make her happy. To give her hope. To not be fearful.

On July 8, Mom's chemotherapy began. At the hospital, we walked down a hallway where people who'd lost their hair wore bandanas; others pushed their IV stands from one room to another with needles and cords hanging from different parts of their bodies. We stepped into a large room with beds separated from one another by sliding white curtains. Moans came from all directions. The nurse covered the bag of yellow liquid—which probably cost several hundred dollars—with a white cloth to protect it from the light. Lying in bed, Mom received a steady IV drip of toxic chemicals, to be guzzled by cells laboring under cancer's slave-driving metabolic rates. These malfunctioning cells would, hopefully, die off before the toxins killed the slower-working normal cells. I stared at the yellow liquid, willing Mom's cancer cells to become thoroughly intoxicated.

Though fighting for her life, Mom smiled the whole time, happy just to be with me.

I sat at her bedside and held her left hand. She tried to return my squeeze, but her grip lacked strength. I kissed her cheeks and fussed with her hair, praying that my strength would somehow be infused into her. We whispered and told stories.

When the drip was almost finished, I hurried out to the flower lady in the hall and grabbed some roses. I came back hiding them behind my back and then, voila! "Mom, you passed the first day of chemo! You surprised me how well you behaved in this saloon! Congratulations!"

She smiled. "Where is Fanel?"

"Just outside."

I went into the hallway, leaned out the open window that faced the street, and waved at Dad. He jumped up from the bench he was sitting on and came to meet us at the entrance.

"Well, how was it? Did it hurt, Rica?" he asked.

She shook her head, still smiling.

During one of mom's sessions, I spoke with Dr. Maria, Mom's oncologist. I showed her all the extra remedies I'd brought, but she wouldn't allow them. I thought that in these crucial moments, people should try everything possible. "Will she throw up?" I asked Dr. Maria. "Will she be nauseated? High fever maybe? Will she lose her hair?"

Yes. Yes. Yes. Yes.

Mom's birthday was in four days. I wanted to cheer her, to give her a really special evening before the nausea set in.

I noticed that at home, whenever she arranged flowers in her bedroom—freshly painted that spring in her favorite shade of blue—she always looked at the empty wall above the chest. I knew a local artist whose work would go well on that wall above the brilliant floral hues.

I also checked about the best restaurants in town, chose one, and made reservations for four; Dia would be included.

"Fellini's!" I announced on the afternoon of her birthday.

"But I heard it's expensive," Mom said.

"You're not the one paying," I said, smiling. "But you are the one eating all you can. Deal?"

"I guess you're the boss, honey."

We gorged on pasta. Even Mom managed to eat a good-sized meal.

Later, when she opened her wrapped painting, her eyes filled with tears and she said, "You've always known what I want for my birthday. Did you read my mind?"

"Of course," I said, winking at Dad. "My grandmother was a Hungarian fortune-teller."

She rested well that night, but the next morning we had to go back to the hospital. The same zone of destruction unfolded before us. Wherever we looked there were saline pumps, syringes, blood containers, urine containers, and IV poles of different heights, matched like dancing partners to each patient. It looked like a battlefield, where the doctors and nurses formed determined platoons to defend their patients lying in the trenches, at the mercy of God. Frail people waiting for miracles.

A month passed, and needle marks and bruises in various stages and colorations marred Mom's arms. Terrible indigestion left her stomach bloated, and she was constantly thirsty. Dad nursed her round the clock, feeding her the pure protein shakes and multivitamins I provided. We monitored her food intake. We hovered.

"Mom, did you take your vitamins?"

"Rica, eat all your food?"

"Mom, did you drink two liters of water today?"

She started throwing up and lost another five pounds.

Construction workers crowded the hospital's narrow hallways, further crowding the bed space for chemo patients. Food aromas mixed with the stench of urine, blood, and sweat, worsening Mom's nausea. Patients stood in line, waiting for the doctors to come in, while the understaffed wards buzzed with nurses, technicians, and orderlies trying to make their rounds. Moans and cries sounded above the ordinary hum, giving the place a disintegrating aspect, as if neglect would lead to rot in short order. The patients who had been there longest knew who had passed away recently and who had only a few more days to live.

We didn't stay on the ward one second longer than necessary.

At 4:00 AM on most mornings, some inner alarm woke both Mom and me. I was sleeping in my old bedroom. Dad was staying in the second house while I was around. Half asleep, I would sneak into Mom's bed, where we cuddled and gossiped and laughed until the summer sunrise brightened the room. Sometimes I massaged her arms, legs, and feet, swollen with retained water. I thought about being five years old, unable to breathe because of my asthma attacks, and Mom lying down beside me for extra warmth, placing sacks of warmed salt on my chest. So many memories. So much love. After all we'd been through, I couldn't imagine my life without my mother in it.

August 29 was the last day of my stay; I'd be leaving early the next morning. I looked at Mom's bedroom walls, so blue, so hopeful, so calming. I lit a lilac-scented candle, and its flickering light revealed the two paintings I'd bought her. Gray dawn light filtered in through the shutters, giving the room an ethereal, dreamlike mood.

"Aura," Mom said. "I am happy, now. I was depressed when you first left because you have always been my daughter and my best friend, my confidante, my sunshine . . ."

I started to say something, but she stopped me.

"Since you came into to this world, you have given me only pink days, only reasons to smile. You have been an amazing daughter. I am so proud to be your mother. . . ."

Now I couldn't speak even if I wanted to. Then I realized what she was doing. "Oh, no you don't. You are not telling me goodbye forever. I'll see you in couple of months, I promise. Before Christmas, I will be back with you."

"Aura, I will not see you again." Her chest quaked as she fought back sobs.

My mind filled with memories of us together: shopping for my school uniforms; how she listened to all my stories of boys and the never-ending dramas; carrying my diplomas after graduations; carefully drying the red rose crown when I'd been class valedictorian; and waiting up for me to return home and rehash the fun evenings I'd had. How she always called me her "little Nadia" after that perfect 10 performance. My loving mother, who had been there for me night and day, cooking, tending to me, sacrificing her whole life, it seemed, for me and her family. Anything for her "little Nadia."

I sat straight up. "Yes, you will. I promise. And you know I always keep my promises. Mom you are a fighter. You are my Nadia, and you will get the perfect score. You will beat this, and everything will be the way it was: perfect."

"Yes," she said. "I will try to be here waiting for you."

I boarded the plane knowing I might not see my mother again.

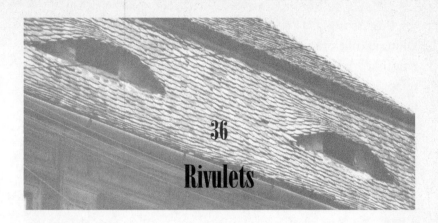

36
Rivulets

MICHAEL PICKED ME UP AT LAX, LOOKING ALMOST AS BEREFT AS I felt. We drove in silence to the townhouse where I still lived with him. I wanted to be alone so I could weep in peace. I didn't want him to feel as if he had to take care of me. I didn't want him to see me break down. But most of all, I wanted to be alone with thoughts of my very sick mother.

My solution was to rent a guesthouse in Palos Verdes on the canyon side, sharing the territory with butterflies, chirping birds, squirrels, rabbits, opossums, and lizards. I named it Hummingbird House. It had an unfurnished living room on the first floor and a sunny little kitchen. My bedroom would be a room on the second floor with a spacious balcony on two sides from which I could glimpse the harbor and ocean. A second bedroom occupied the third floor. Its balcony overlooked an Eden of yellow and white roses, gardenias, bougainvillea, poinsettias, succulents, and lemon trees.

Day after day, I sat at the windows or on one of the balconies and stared. Despite my gentle new environment, everything around me seemed to be falling apart. I lost a good friend from West High School, my workout buddy, Jill Crine. My Rotary mentor, Professor Mary Borell, died of cancer. I learned that my friend Diana Skidmore's mother had passed away because of cancer. Another friend, Jeanne Morgen, a powerful attorney, suffered a relapse of her cancer. All these catastrophes happened within a few months' time.

After each chat with my mom on the phone, or with Dia, I told myself that Mom was regaining her health, but my instincts told me something different.

I bought a few pieces of furniture to fill the empty rooms, but my own emptiness left thoughts echoing in my heart and mind. I told God constantly how merciless he was, all the while begging Him to comfort and heal my mother.

One day in late September, my cell phone chimed the tune I'd programmed for Michael.

"Hi, Michael. Now what?"

"Aura!" he fumed, not even greeting me. "My God! Ameritrade shows sixteen thousand in one of our accounts and only two thousand in another! And both numbers are in brackets! What's going on? Please tell me you pulled that eighteen thousand out of our accounts!"

"No. Dear God, no!" My pulse hammered in my ears. "I'll call you right back."

I clicked off and jumped over to my laptop. I soon saw exactly what Michael was seeing. Where had our money gone?

I called J, but he didn't answer. I sent him two e-mails. Nothing. I left another message. "J, pull out of the market. Now. And I hope you took out the money I already insisted you do. Call me. It's urgent."

Another day passed. The accounts stayed the same. What was going on? Driving to my second job of the day, I called J again. He picked up.

"J! Oh, thank God you answered. What's going on with our money? I left a couple of messages for you. Where were you?"

Silence.

"J?"

"Yes, I am here. . . ."

"What's going on? Where is our money, J? That was all the money we had. All my savings. Everything!"

Silence.

"J?"

"Aura, I am so sorry. I lost all your money. Your account is in the red. You owe Ameritrade eighteen thousand. I'm sorry. I'm really sorry. I lost my own money, too. I lost everybody's money. I lost millions. I have no words to express myself."

It was my turn to remain silent. Then, "J, you're saying you lost a quarter of a million of our dollars? I was going to buy a house in Palos Verdes and bring my parents there while my mom recovers from cancer. And now I'm broke? Now I have nothing? *Nothing?*"

I tossed the phone on the passenger seat and pulled my car to the side of the road and sobbed.

Why was everything a struggle? I'd fought for my virginity on the brink of losing it; I fought for my dreams in a Communist country; I stood up for what I believed in. I left my Transylvania to come to the Promised Land and chase the American Dream. My whole life was a struggle, and all my accomplishments were the result of my hard work. Despite all of it, where was I now? My marriage had crumbled. I had worked two and three jobs, and now had nothing to show for it. My mind went back to the endless hours of study by candlelight to save energy, in rooms where the temperature was similar to what it was outside. I would never forget those days. Never!

Now more than ever, I needed to channel my warrior's spirit. I lived in the City of Angels, where dreams can come true . . .

In early November, the rains arrived. A rivulet formed alongside the guesthouse driveway. I followed it out to the canyon and watched it tumble and fall as it joined another to form a wider stream. Watching it from under my umbrella, the rain so gentle it made no sound, I thought of a rainy fall day with Buni scraping the mud off her garden boots. I stood there watching the ephemeral little brook, imagining my grandmother beside me. Imagining her, but not *feeling* her.

I've tried so hard, Buni. How could I have lost so much?

The tiny freshet babbled. I'm sure I wasn't the first to hear its reminders that life flows constantly, its streams diverted, blocked by pebbles and boulders, curves, drastic falls. And sometimes, it whispered, sometimes it becomes deeper when joined by another—a stronger stream, rushing, meandering, and flowing toward the infinity of the blue ocean.

I walked back to the driveway in time to see Michael's Hummer approach. We'd bought it when we thought we had a hefty savings account. It wasn't completely paid for, and I didn't know how long he could continue making payments on it.

He climbed out, smiling, bearing containers of chicken with peanut sauce and rice, like we'd loved in Hawaii. This wasn't the first time he'd brought me a meal. He did it several times a week, usually when I was gone; food would just appear in my refrigerator as if by magic. I knew he worried that otherwise I'd eat nothing but yogurt and cookies.

He hugged me, and I invited him to join me for the dinner he'd cooked. After we'd eaten, he asked about Mom.

"She's still losing weight and her voice is growing weaker every day," I said. "Dia says she can't walk anymore, so a nurse comes to help out."

"And your dad?"

"I'm sure he's exhausted. He tends to her round the clock. He feeds her and tries to cheer her up. I'm scraping the money together to fly there for Thanksgiving."

He nodded. "I'll take you to the airport."

I kissed him on the cheek.

Armed with more protein powder, as well as dried fruits, alkaline drops, and powdered vegetables, I flew to Romania. Dad looked thin and exhausted. Mom was now living and sleeping in my room, its rose-colored walls unchanged since the day I left in 1997.

Like a small child, all bundled up in red pajamas, Mom raised her eyes and looked at me. She couldn't lift herself from the bed, so I helped her sit on the edge. Only then did I realize how much weight she'd lost. I let her head rest on my shoulder and tried not to weep.

I could only stay a few days, and she spent much of the time asleep. At least I gave Dad a break, letting him get some rest as well. I fed Mom and helped the nurse bathe her. I told her stories and showed her photos, but she could barely keep her eyes open. Dia spent several long evenings with us. She helped me hide my tears from Mom and Dad and spill them with her instead—until the day came for me to leave Sibiu. Then, nothing could stop them.

On January 1, 2009, the call came to my little rented house.

"Aura, your mother is gone. She passed easily and softly, the way a candle is blown out by the wind." Dad sounded very composed. I'm sure he planned what to say long before he called. "Her suffering has ended. She is free."

I instantly made flight plans.

It was snowing in Transylvania, a peaceful white blanket folding down on the cold earth. I wanted to feel that this peace extended to my mom, that the snow's purity was an apt tribute to her, so I wore white to her funeral. Dad wore a somber black suit, blending in with the mass of other mourners. He requested a dignified service without tears, so I held mine in check, though many friends and relatives were crying. Dad and I had decided to have a closed coffin. I stood next to him, my hand gripping his arm.

The snow continued to fall, broken only by an occasional sunbeam. I could feel Mom in every glittering snowflake, my snow angel.

37

Out of the Transylvania Night

I HAD REACHED ROCK BOTTOM. MY MOTHER'S DEATH WAS THE ULTIMATE
and final torment of that terrible year.

Throughout January, I meditated on my family's role in my life,
on how blessed I had been to have them as an example to admire,
and as a source of unwavering support. Despite all the losses we
had endured, my family had found a way to survive. Our land,
money, and jewelry confiscated, we still maintained a heritage that
could never be forgotten. I was an Imbarus. My proud family history was the unshakeable rock upon which I could stand. There
was nothing I needed to prove.

On a mild evening in May, I sat on the west-facing balcony,
where I could watch a quarter moon head for the ocean's dark
horizon. A dog barked in the distance. I looked out over the quiet
harbor, the foghorn one of the few sounds in the sleeping neighborhood. The stars were diamonds sewn into the black gown of
the night. A shooting star flitted across the sky. Below the balcony where I sat, the gardenias were in bloom, and their tropical
scent wafted upward. I thought of that trip to Hawaii when Rica,
Fanel, Michael, and I were all so happy, breathing in a sense of
personal freedom, yet connected by ties of marriage and family.

A time when I was still connected to myself, to my history, to my own soul.

I stood up, looked at the harbor, and turned to go back inside.

I had grown up a prisoner in Romania. We were all prisoners, every man, woman, and child living under Ceauşescu's Communist regime. Even after the revolution, little changed. I had to escape and I did. Yet I quickly found myself in a prison of my own making. Walled off by responsibilities and wealth and material things, I had lost track of myself and my connections to my husband, my family, my community, my history. I had lost that hereditary strength on which the Imbarus family prided itself. By that night in May, I had had nearly five months to process all I'd been through and all I'd become, and determine what I wanted from life once I emerged from my self-imposed exile and began to reconnect. Perhaps my visions would be restored, and I would once again have a sense of myself and my place, both in my past and my future.

As I came in from the balcony, I felt more optimistic than I had in quite some time. In the white living room, I lit candles—white ones that reminded me of the pure, unconditional love that Mom always wrapped around me—and I started gathering my thought and energies.

The phone rang.

"Hi," said the sparkling voice of my friend Vanessa Florez. "How are you doing? I know you are going through a tough time right now . . . but I sure could use your help. I know Nadia Comaneci has been your idol since you were a kid, so I wanted to see if you are interested in a fundraising red-carpet event for one of her charities. She would be delighted to have you aboard. Say you will!"

"Oh, sure! I'd love to!" I told her. This, too, had been a new part of my life and reconnection with the land of my birth. Nadia Comaneci frequently held fundraisers for her children's clinic in Bucharest, which provided low-cost and free medical and social support to Romanian children, and RAPN had been one of the organizations that aided her. If someone had told me, when I stood outside her fence and watched her practice, that one day I'd be helping her fulfill her dream of assisting the children of our shared homeland—well, who would have believed it?

The candle flames flickered in the fresh salty breeze that ruffled the leaves of my indoor plants, my begonias, and my white button mums. The cinnamon smell of the melting wax took me back to Mom's kitchen, where cookies and chocolate cakes appeared before my eyes to reward me after my own Olympic games were coming to an end in the yard, where my childhood friends, Monika, Ildiko, Lulu, Vicentiu, Adi, Daniela, were competing against each other. Back then, I was my mom's "little Nadia." Now, I would be organizing a red carpet charity event for that famous Nadia who had been my namesake.

I left the living room and looked at myself in the bathroom mirror. I was surprised by the change. Instead of that unrecognizable face I'd seen a few months earlier, the face of a ghost with dark circles under her eyes and swollen eyelids, I saw a tall, slender woman with long, wavy blond hair and green-honey eyes. My smile was still there. Restoration had begun.

Feeling renewed, I went to my bedroom. A picture of Mom and me in Tangier reminded me that time was the most precious thing, and it should not be wasted. One more picture taken with Mom at Fellini Restaurant in the summer of 2008, when she was in chemo. She still looked great then: happy, even healthy. I stopped before an arrangement of photos in a big divided frame. Here I was at five months old, delighted to see my beautiful mother with her long ebony hair and dark eyes, bringing me a rose. There was Benny, my dog, a Saint Bernard, horselike in stature, sitting well behaved next to Mom. Over here, me celebrating my second birthday, the one when Mom baked a wonderful German chocolate cake. And there was Emily—my stand-in child.

I thought of the children I didn't have. Thank God for Emily, who had truly become like a daughter to me. A bright, charming, and funny young girl—someone who now has blossomed into a talented piano player and professional golfer. I realized that in some ways, in Emily, I have my Diandra. Certainly, Emily is everyting I would want in a daughter: thoughtful, sweet, sensitive, intelligent, caring.

I was coming back to myself and my family, slowly but surely. It was to Buni, to Mom, to Dad, to the Imbarus family, to myself, and to Michael to make the most of the gifts life had bestowed on me, gifts I was only now beginning to truly appreciate.

The glow of two lit candles were reflected in the glass of a mirror, its frame adorned with still more pictures of family. A huge bouquet of yellow roses, brought by Michael, lent some color to the whiteness around me: white walls, white furniture, my own pale skin.

I found myself gazing at the digital photo frame on the bedside table. Another gift from Michael, it shuffled steadily through hundreds of images. Places and smiles: Hawaii, Spain, Africa, America—all of them shared with Michael. Pictures. Images. Memories. They were everywhere.

Michael, and another picture of Michael.

The photos, the digital frame, this rented house, the properties and possessions I had acquired with such pride . . . they had all been heady symbols of success and status. Symbols to which I had become enslaved. Cars, travel, excitement, wealth—the cost had been so great. But what was the point of having all these *things* if there was precious little time to enjoy them—and worse, nobody to share them with?

Michael had seen what was happening. Michael had known all along. He'd tried to tell me in so many ways, but had at last given up his efforts to warn me. I hadn't wanted to listen, or hear. I hadn't wanted to face up to another immigrant's pitfall, one to which I was already susceptible because of how I was raised, because I was an Imbarus. Building a life and getting ahead in a new country requires hard work. But hard work may also become destructive—an addiction—a hard worker may become a workaholic. Michael had seen work take over my life, muscling everything else aside—him included. If I wanted to recover the connections to community, to the important things in life, and to the love of my life, I had to make room for them.

A strange sensation distracted my thoughts. Nothing moved, but one candle flickered like a strobe. I smelled cinnamon and Mom's perfume—not a fragrance I owned. The candle kept flickering while the other went out and unreeled a ribbon of smoke.

It seemed to me a sign that could not have been clearer. I sensed my mother looking at me, watching me. And then it sank in. Of course she would be with me. She was within me everywhere and for always: in every candle that flickered, in every soft breeze, in the budding flower. I'd made a big space for her within my heart, and there she would be. Always.

"Oh, Mom, I longed for this. I'm better now. I feel strong again," I cried. And in that unearthly moment, the knot of loss untangled in my heart.

I picked up the phone and speed-dialed Michael's cell number. It was time to come back to my husband.

"Aura . . . Aura? Where are you?" Michael's voice, soft and concerned, brought a smile to my face. He had come.

"I'm here, Michael. In the bedroom."

His footsteps approached, and I lay back on the bed as yet another huge bouquet of flowers appeared around the doorframe: red roses, daisies, hyacinths, yellow roses—the color spectrum displayed in all its glory. Their fresh aroma engulfed my senses and raised my spirits. A moment later a hand, and then a head: Michael, dressed in white and navy blue, his hair freshly cut, looked more handsome than ever.

"For a woman who is loved," he said, handing me the flowers. "You *do* know how many people love you, don't you?" he asked. "Me, Monika, Dia, Emily, Mark, Diana, Fashi, Yafa . . . your family, your dad and mom . . . and Buni. You're blessed to have so many souls who care for you."

I noticed that Michael had placed himself at the head of the list.

He loved me. Of course, he loved me. The person I thought I had divorced through a court procedure, cut out of my heart for good—that man was still here. He had always been here, right here beside me. I had thought of myself as the tenacious one, the over-achiever, the one who clawed relentlessly after goals. But it was Michael who had never walked away for long, who had never given up, who had never quit. Not on me.

And I wouldn't give up on him. I would make room for him, cut back on work.

I stood and put my arms around him and kissed him. Then I spoke without hesitation, the words clear and strong. "Michael, why don't you move in with me?"

For a moment he looked stunned. He studied my face. "Are you sure that's what you want?" Tears clung in his eyes.

"Yes." There it was, the one word that can make or break a person's life. "Yes, Michael, yes. I want us to be together. Please come back. I love you!"

There was a silence. I thought of all we had been through together, and I was certain that our love had never died.

"I never lost hope in you coming back to us," Michael said, and pulled me toward him. His embrace was warm, kind. It felt right. It felt the way it used to feel when we first fell in love. Basking in it, I silently gave thanks to the signs that had finally led me back to the path I was always meant to follow—the path that included my soul mate.

We celebrated that evening at a little intimate restaurant, where we could focus on one another and not be distracted by crowds and noise. I was so excited to fill Michael in on the positive things I had done over the past year.

"Do you remember RAPN? The Romanian-American Professionals Network? The group Ilie Ardelean started a few years ago?"

"Of course. That's when we finally started to meet more Romanians here in the States."

"Remember how, even though we were thrilled to come to the

United States, we really had no idea what life would be like here? Well, Raoul, Jacob, and I decided RAPN could help Romanian immigrants like us adjust to life in the United States without them feeling that they have to give up their identity. We grant scholarships, offer mentoring, and are even creating a yearly Romanian festival, with art, dance, and music. We think showing pride in our culture helps newer immigrants feel secure—and proud."

"This is fantastic. Truly," Michael said.

"And you won't believe what else! Through RAPN, I've been asked to help Nadia Comenici raise funds for her children's clinic in Bucharest. Do you believe it!"

"You're having a lot of fun, aren't you?" Michael asked.

"So much . . ." I replied. "I've finally found true meaning again. I'm not the 'have and get' Aura any longer. I really think I'm the 'being and becoming' Aura now. I'm just so sorry it took me so long to understand it all and so thankful that you never stopped believing in me. It all feels so right."

"So are you happy, Aura?"

"Yes, absolutely! I thought for a moment. "I think I had to rediscover where I came from. I had been so set on blocking out our past and conquering the American Dream—and I didn't even know what it really was. I feel like Transylvania feeds my roots, but I define myself as an American of Romanian descent—that's who I am.

I paused again to collect my thoughts. "If we had to do it again, I wouldn't do anything differently. It may have taken me a while to learn my lessons, but there are no regrets, no remorse. America is everything I dreamt of and more. And yet, I need to stay in touch with my community. Our community."

Michael started laughing. "Hmm, that's the Aura I know. You are a fearless trailblazer. I just love that about you."

"I'm so thankful you didn't give up on me, Michael. I know you think I have too many irons in the fire, but I can't live any differently. I just can't. And I especially don't want to live without you in my life. You are my love. You are my life."

"I know that," he said. "I love you just the way you are. I just wanted you to be happy, to stop chasing your dreams for the sake of chasing them. To able to sit back and truly enjoy them."

I promised him I would.

"We've been through so much," he said softly. "We survived a revolution, came here with only a couple pieces of luggage, willing to start over, to make something of our lives in a place we knew so little about." Reaching across the table to hold my hand, he looked at me with such tenderness and added, "But we made it. We are indomitable human spirits, you and I."

Epilogue
Los Angeles—Summer 2010

IT HAS BEEN ABOUT A YEAR SINCE MICHAEL AND I REUNITED, AND OUR bond has never been stronger. Though our schedules are still hectic, they are not crazy, and we are gradually paying off the debt that J left us in. Most importantly, though, I've found that life is so much richer with Michael at the top of my priority list.

This past year has been one of learning to apply the lessons that freedom has taught me. I am acutely aware that the things that drive me today have little to do with the material comforts I once pursued so slavishly. No possession can ever have the lasting power to satiate the deeper hunger and longing within me: no, that requires the people in our lives who love us and root for us and make us better human beings than we would have been without them.

I myself aspire to be such a person through my work with RAPN: I am grateful for the opportunity to share my hard-earned wisdom with others who have journeyed to the land of the free (which is also, most certainly, the home of the brave!).

I am, afer all, well acquainted with the dues we must pay, the mindfields we must navigate, once we attain our freedom—and I also know that to succeed at both, it helps to have a little warrior in your blood.

Author's Note: In July 2010, international headlines read: "Ex-Romanian Dictator Ceauşescu and Wife Exhumed." For me, it felt as if my life had come full circle, still haunted by the mysteries of the past. Like so many Romanians, I too believed for years that the Ceauşescus's deaths may have been staged, because he was known to have at least five others who stood in for him, and we the people were supposed to pretend we could be fooled by these stand-ins. And, like many Romanians, I too, wondered if the Ceauşescu's really did die on that day, were they really buried in the Ghencea military cemetery in Bucharest. The investigation is long overdue.

As of this writing, officials say it will take a number of months to determine the true identity of the remains. Nevertheless, the news of the exhumation is welcomed. Perhaps now the time has come when the ghosts of the past can finally be laid to rest.

Book Group Discussion Questions

- In many ways, Aura is one of those driven, unsinkable characters. What forged this trait in her? What role did Grandpa, Buni, Fanel, and Rica each play in nurturing this trait? What evidence supports the idea that indomitability is innate in Aura? What were the vulnerable chinks in her unstoppable nature? How are you like or unlike Aura?

- Did Aura make the "right" decision to leave Romania? Would you have made that decision in her situation? To what extent should we live for our families? To what extent for ourselves?

- *Out of the Transylvania Night* unfolds on many levels, exposing the Romanian political, economic, cultural, and social strata as seen through the eyes of a young woman. How did you respond to the author's depiction of growing up under Communism? What kind of images did you find effective in conveying these strands?

- How did Aura pit herself against the system? How did her stance help her? How did it hinder her?

- Think about the haunting "eyes" of Sibiu: Did they represent only Communist tyranny? How did their gaze affect Aura as a teenager? To what extent did they keep "watching" her in later years? Have you ever had a similar experience?

- In the very first chapters of the book, Aura fantasizes about a "someone" to whom she felt attracted, and it sustained her in some ways. Was this early fascination with Michael merely a crush?

- How did Michael feel about this character trait when he wanted her help with the jazz festival? When she "proposed"? Later on?

- Aura seemed attuned to extrasensory perceptions while in Transylvania, but in America the trait didn't manifest in the dramatic ways of her youth. What do you think accounts for this shift?

- What was the nature of Aura's hunger? What did Aura really want? What did she need?

- Discuss the irony of Aura's "pieces of paper": marriage certificate, immigration papers, certificates/credentials, divorce decree.

- In what ways did adaptation to a new environment and acculturation strengthen Aura's and Michael's bond? In what ways did it pull them apart? How do you think their relationship would have evolved if they'd stayed in Romania?

- Aura's ability to reinvent herself under duress certainly seems formidable. How did she reinvent herself after the shock of losing Buni? Following her split with Michael? After the "eternal night" that followed the loss of her mother?

- How did the heirloom jewels contribute to Aura's journey?

- What inner qualities allowed Aura and Michael to rediscover their love for each other?

- What expectations of freedom proved to be a hindrance in Aura's life? What moments brought Aura her greatest freedom? How do you imagine you would have behaved in a similar situation?

- How do love, belonging, and responsibility fit into Aura's sense of freedom? What kind of "freedom" did Aura gain at the end of her journey?

- How do you define the American Dream? In what ways has your definition of it changed over the years?

About the Author

AURA IMBARUS, PHD is a former popular journalist in Europe, university professor, speaker, and award-winning educator. She is a co-founder and ambassador of the Romanian-American Professional Network (RAPN) and the president of its Los Angeles chapter. She is also president of EuroCircle's Los Angeles chapter.

To contact:

www.AuraImbarus.com
www.TransylvaniaNight.com